At the Center of the Circle

At the Center of the Circle

Harriet de Boinville (1773–1847)
and the Writers She Influenced During
Europe's Revolutionary Era

Barbara de Boinville

Washington, DC

Copyright © 2022 by Barbara de Boinville

New Academia Publishing, 2023

All rights reserved. No part of this book may be reproduced or transmitted in any form or by any means, electronic or mechanical, including photocopying, recording, or by any information storage and retrieval system.

Printed in the United States of America

Library of Congress Control Number: 2023901156
ISBN 979-8-9852214-9-7 paperback (alk. paper)
ISBN 979-8-9875893-2-8 ebook

New Academia Publishing, 4401-A Connecticut Ave. NW, #236,
Washington, DC 20008
info@newacademia.com - www.newacademia.com

To Bryan

For walking every step of the way with me

A loving Soul bears about within itself a living spring of affection which keeps it fresh in spite of blights from evil things & evil Men and suffers no good feeling to wither & to die.

Harriet de Boinville
Letter to Thomas Jefferson Hogg
March 11, 1814

Contents

List of Illustrations	ix
Note on Harriet's Name	x
Note on Harriet's Family	xi
Preface	xiii
Acknowledgments	xvii

PART I Early Life

1. Birth and Life in the Dangerous Tropics, 1773-1788	3
2. "Une Enfant de la Révolution," 1789-1792	11
3. A Disobedient Daughter Marries for Love, 1793	17
4. From Domesticity to Dangers at Sea, 1793-1796	25
5. A Young Mother in a War-torn Colony, 1797	29
6. A Bold Traveler Between Nations at War, 1797-1800	35
7. An Empathetic Friend to Frances Burney d'Arblay, 1800-1808	41

PART II Life in London

8. With the Proponent of Political Justice, William Godwin, 1809-1811	51
9. Harriet's Husband Rescues Madam d'Arblay, 1810-1812	61
10. Aaron Burr and the London Wedding of Godwin's Protégé, 1812-1813	69
11. Percy Bysshe Shelley Meets "Miamuna," Spring 1813	79
12. Vegetarians and Egalitarians "Return to Nature," Summer 1813	89
13. Shelley Retreats to Harriet's Home at Bracknell," February and March 1814	97
14. Broken Hearts and a Mourning Widow, Spring and Summer 1814	105

15. More than a Beauty: Cornelia Collins Newton, 1815-1816 ... 115
16. The Deaths of Fanny Godwin and Harriet Shelley, Fall and Winter 1816 ... 123
17. Mary's *Frankenstein*, Byron's "Love" Child, and Harriet's Son, 1817-1818 ... 135
18. "Tell them, especially Mrs. Boinville, I have not forgotten them," 1819-1826 ... 145

PART III Life in Paris
19. Leaving London and Reconciling with Mary Shelley, 1827-1829 ... 155
20. Godwin's Death and Significance, "The Extinction of a Mastermind," 1830-1836 ... 165
21. Harriet Rescues Shelley's *Queen Mab* for Posterity, 1837-1841 ... 175
22. "A Noble Nature and a Loyal, Loving Heart," 1842 ... 183
23. Claire Clairmont Joins Harriet's Circle in Paris, 1842-1845 ... 189
24. Welcoming Refugees in Her Final Years, 1845-1846 ... 197
25. Harriet Dies and Giovanni Ruffini Comforts Her Family, 1847-1848 ... 201
26. Cornelia Turner and Vernon Lee Continue the Literary Life, 1848-1874 ... 207

AFTERWORD: Mark Twain and the Boinville Circle ... 217
Appendix Letters ... 225
Notes ... 251
Bibliography ... 275
Index ... 293

List of Illustrations

Figure 1.1. St. Kitts where Harriet Collins was born in 1773	4
Figure 1.2. John Collins's 1803 manual on the management and medical treatment of slaves	6
Figure 2.1. Portrait of John Baptiste Chastel de Boinville	12
Figure 2.2. Map showing Boinville in Lorraine in the eighteenth century	15
Figure 3.1. The old blacksmith's shop in Gretna Green	20
Figure 3.2. Portrait of Frances Burney d'Arblay by her cousin Edward Francis Burney	21
Figure 5.1. Carib (Kalina or Galibi) Indian family after a painting by John Gabriel Stedman	30
Figure 5.2. Map of St. Vincent by Bryan Edwards in 1794	32
Figure 8.1. A page of William Godwin's 1809 diary	55
Figure 8.2. Mary Wollstonecraft's *A Vindication of the Rights of Woman* (1792)	56
Figure 9.1. Portrait of Francis Burney by Charles Turner after Edward Francis Burney, published 16 May 1840 by Paul and Dominic Colnaghi & Co.	64
Figure 11.1 Mrs. Boinville's letter to Mary Shelley about *Queen Mab*	87
Figure 18.1. Percy Bysshe Shelley by Alfred Clint, 1819	146
Figure 19.1. Harriet de Boinville's letter to Mary Shelley about *Queen Mab*, October 16, 1829	159
Figure 20.1. The revolutionary invention of a threshing machine	167
Figure 21.1. Portrait of Mary Shelley by Richard Rothwell, 1840	181
Figure 25.1. Harriet de Boinville in old age	203
Figure 26.1. Tombstone memorializing Harriet and her daughter, Cemetery Montmartre	214
Figure A-1. Handwritten letter from Harriet de Boinville to Mary Shelley, October 1829	239

A Note on Harriet's Name

Harriet's last name has long vexed scholars. She is cited in indexes under B, or D, or C. This confusion has a basis in history. Harriet signed her name in different ways and was referred to in different ways. "What is in a name?" Shakespeare asked in *Romeo and Juliet.* "That which we call a rose by any other name would smell as sweet." Mindful of this adage, I have not imposed a consistency that was lacking in the historical record.

In his will John Collins referred to Henriette Chastel de Boinville, his daughter's legal name and the one inscribed on her tombstone. She signed her name "H. Boinville" in letters to Frances Burney d'Arblay (March 7, 1814) and Thomas Jefferson Hogg (March 11th and 18th, 1814). She signed "H. de Boinville" in letters to Mary Shelley (October 16, 1829; June 11, 1836; December 18, 1837; and January 26, 1839).

Percy Bysshe Shelley called Harriet his friend "Mrs. Boinville" or "Mrs. B." In a letter to Thomas Love Peacock (August 24, 1819), he referred to her as Mrs. Boinville *and* Mrs. de Boinville. "H Boinville" appears in William Godwin's diary; Mrs. Boinville is how Godwin referred to her in a July 2, 1826, letter to Mary Jane Godwin. The 1880 memoir by Harriet's grandson refers to Charles Chastel de Boinville.

In 1793 Harriet Collins married Jean Baptiste Chastel de Boinville, the second son of Jean Baptiste Ignace Chastel de Villemont and Francoise Pauline Lucie Dupaquier de Dommartin. Villemont signified where the family owned property north and west of Strasburg and close to France's current borders with Germany, Luxembourg, and Belgium. Jean Baptiste was my husband's great, great, great, great grandfather. Today the village where Jean Baptiste once owned property is called Boinville-en-Woëvre.

A Note on Harriet's Family

Jean Baptiste Ignace Chastel de Villemont (b. 1712; d. 1774) married Francoise Pauline Lucie Dupaquier de Dommartin. Their second son was Harriet's husband Jean Baptiste. He had a son Eugene by his first wife, who died after childbirth. Eugene had no children.

Jean Baptiste Chastel de Boinville (b. July 15, 1756, Metz; d. February 7, 1813, Wilna, Poland)

Henriette Chastel de Boinville, née Collins (b. St. Kitts, 1773; d. Paris, March 1, 1847). They were married in 1793 (in Scotland and the next day in England) and had two children.

Cornelia Pauline Eugenia Chastel de Boinville (b. February 23, 1795, Willesden, England; d. October 25, 1874, Paris) and John Alfred Chastel de Boinville (b. 1797, St. Vincent; d. ?)

Cornelia married Thomas Turner on January 24, 1812. They had three children: Oswald Turner (b. 1814, Bracknell; d. Ivry, France, 1876); Alfred Turner (b. 1817; d. 1893); and Pauline Turner (b. 1825; d. January 6, 1842). Harriet's other grandchildren were the offspring of her son John Alfred and Harriet Lambe, who wed in London in 1818: Charles, Alexander, William, Frank, and Cornelia. Harriet's sister (as well as her daughter and a granddaughter) were all named Cornelia.

Cornelia Collins (b. 17??; d. September 2, 1816)
Harriet's younger sister Cornelia and her husband John Frank Newton had five children: Octavia, Camilla, Augustus, Chick, and Coraly.

Alfred Collins (b 17??; d. 18??).
Harriet's younger brother is referred to in his father's will as "my unfortunate son" because of his mental illness.

Preface

I married Bryan Chastel de Boinville in 1979 and began to hear stories, true stories, about his illustrious great, great, great, great grandfather, the Frenchman Jean Baptiste, General Lafayette's trusted aide who escorted Queen Marie Antoinette's carriage from Versailles. I became interested in Jean Baptiste's brave English wife Harriet in 2015, when I was a graduate student at George Mason University taking English Research Studies 701, a class that culminated in a research project based on primary sources. In the first class my professor, Kristin Samuelian, assigned a novel by William Godwin, *Things as They Are, or The Adventures of Caleb Williams* (1794), and my own adventure in literary history began.

Harriet de Boinville was a close friend of William Godwin, I learned from a memoir by Harriet's grandson. Published in 1880, the memoir recounted Harriet's birth in St. Kitts in 1773, her marriage in 1793, and her daring attempts to cross the Channel during the French Revolutionary and Napoleonic Wars. In Godwin's digitized diary, and in the rows of books about Shelley in George Mason's Fenwick Library, I discovered Harriet's main "calling card" to literary fame: Percy Bysshe Shelley, who idolized her in his writings. For example, "I could not help considering Mrs. B., when I knew her, as the most admirable specimen of human being I had ever seen," he wrote. "Nothing earthly ever appeared to be more perfect than her character & manners." Shelley became friends with her in 1813 and wrote about her until he died in 1822. This is the first biography of Harriet de Boinville's life, published on the two hundredth anniversary of his death.

Many Percy Bysshe Shelley scholars, as I discovered roaming

the Fenwick stacks, mention Harriet's beauty in 1813, at the age of forty, and her daughter Cornelia's beauty that year, at the age of eighteen. They mention the months Shelley spent living in her home outside London when he confided in Mrs. B, as he always called her, and fell in love with her daughter, an infatuation that nearly terminated their friendship.

Working on the research project, I discovered that Harriet de Boinville was far more interesting than the skimpy portrait presented in P. B. Shelley scholarship. She influenced Frances Burney, the author of the bestselling novel *Evelina, or the History of a Young Lady's Entrance into the World* (1778), and Mary Shelley, the author of the Gothic classic *Frankenstein, or the Modern Prometheus* (1818) and six other novels. Journals and letters reveal the contours of her close relationship with these pioneering women writers and the ways in which they counted on her.

A revolutionary woman in revolutionary times, Harriet de Boinville is fascinating not only because of the writers she befriended. She survived sea battles sailing 5,000 miles from Liverpool to St. Vincent in the Caribbean. She escaped detention at Dunkirk after being falsely arrested as a British spy. She weathered personal tragedy when her brother, her son, and her grandson were locked up in a madhouse in France.

As a player in the great drama that was Percy Bysshe Shelley's life, she appears not only in his lively and lengthy letters, but also in the letters of Claire Clairmont. Thanks to Claire—Mary's half sister, Lord Byron's lover, and Mrs. de Boinville's neighbor in Paris—I was able to write in detail about the last twenty years of Harriet's life. My hope is that readers of this biography will be inspired, as I was inspired, by her intelligence, kindness, and almost unbelievable courage in the face of adversity. Widowed young, when Jean Baptiste died during Napoleon's retreat from Moscow, she persevered, raised a family, and welcomed in her homes in London and Paris, not only writers, but also artists, musicians, and Italian exiles. She was immensely popular as a host, a tribute to her appealing personality and freedom from class-based prejudices.

Sixteen when the French Revolution began, Harriet de Boinville became an ardent believer in the republican ideals of liberty, equality, and fraternity. Her progressive views were one reason why P. B.

Shelley admired her so much. In Italy, three years before his death at the age of twenty-nine, he wrote about her to a friend:

> It is improbable that I shall ever meet again this person whom I once so much esteemed & still admire. I wish however you would tell her that I have not forgotten her, or any of the amiable circle once assembled round her.

An amazing and unconventional woman, Harriet de Boinville attracted to her side a wide-array of fascinating and famous people in the eighteenth and nineteenth centuries. I hope this twenty-first century biography will help move her from the fringes of literary history to the center stage where she belongs. She really was "at the center of the circle."

–*Barbara de Boinville*

Acknowledgments

I thank my beloved husband of forty-three years, Bryan Charles Michael Chastel de Boinville, for his steady encouragement and wisdom. Two Princeton classmates with extensive publishing experience were immensely helpful: Rob Low, my editor, and Juliet Packer, a writer who taught me how "less" really can be "more." I could never have written this book without Rob's organizational genius and moral support. Juliet repeatedly transformed a confusing mishmash of information into lean and coherent prose.

My longtime writing group in Bethesda, Maryland, critiqued draft after draft and patiently pointed out my bad habits as a writer. I believe I have deleted every "as we will see." As the manuscript approached completion, writing group member Peter Gorman carefully reviewed each chapter.

I thank Emma Davidson, Librarian II, The Henry W. and Albert A. Berg Collection of English and American Literature, The New York Public Library, for deciphering Harriet de Boinville's penmanship in letters to Frances Burney d'Arblay. Amy de Boinville, a talented graphic artist, provided design and formatting expertise. My good friend and former colleague at Congressional Quarterly Press, Carolyn McGovern, supplied the excellent index.

I mourn the passing of Allan Conrad Christensen, Professor Emeritus of English Literature at John Cabot University in Rome. Years of emails from Allan spurred on my research, and one of his many publications, *A European Version of Victorian Fiction: The Novels of Giovanni Ruffini*, opened my eyes to the literary importance of Harriet de Boinville's daughter, the novelist Cornelia Turner. I gratefully acknowledge Allan's meticulous scholarship and unfailing generosity to me, an inexperienced author. His wise words, "it will take the time it takes," helped me persevere with this biography.

The Preface explains the huge role played by my graduate advisor at George Mason University, Kristin Flieger Samuelian. How lucky I was to have experienced authors guide me on my literary way. Myrna Sislen introduced me to Anna Lawton, the head of New Academia Publishing. Thank you, Anna, for introducing Harriet de Boinville.

PART I
Early Life

Chapter 1

Birth and Life in the Dangerous Tropics 1773–1788

Blow, winds, and crack your cheeks! rage! blow!
You cataracts and hurricanoes [sic], spout
Till you have drenched our steeples, drown'd the cocks!
You sulphurous and thought-executing fires,
Vaunt-couriers to oak-cleaving thunderbolts
—Shakespeare, King Lear, Act 3, Scene 2

A hurricane destroyed St. Christopher, the Caribbean island where Henrietta Collins was born. It was a fitting start to a life characterized by adventure, tumult, and danger. Many times she crossed the Channel between England and France, wartime enemies. She also crisscrossed the Atlantic with her young children, spending weeks at sea at the mercy of winds and waves. Harriet would face adversity with determination and resilience.

The year of her birth, 1773, was the same year British statesman George Macartney described Great Britain as a "vast empire on which the sun never sets."[1] Three centuries earlier, Christopher Columbus discovered St. Christopher and named it after his patron saint, but there was nothing saintly or safe about this wild place, which became Britain's first colony in the Caribbean. The English who braved the journey from Portsmouth or Liverpool faced six weeks of treacherous sailing. These hardy risk-takers traveled 5,000 miles to reach the Leeward Islands, then called "the Caribbees," but once on shore the exhausted sailors were not out of danger. They had good reason to fear both man and nature.

For control of the Caribbean islands, British and the French colonists killed each other and the native people, the Caribs. Countless

African slaves died as well. Trade in sugar, "white gold," connected three continents: Africa, Europe, and North America. In the eighteenth century, one fourth of African slaves shipped to Caribbean plantations died within the first three or four years.²

Today St. Kitts, the tiny island where Harriet was born, brings to mind blue water, sandy beaches, and peaceful resorts, but then it was a scene of contention and catastrophe. The island is shaped like a club; nearby Nevis, like a ball—specks in the expanse of water where the Atlantic Ocean meets the Caribbean Sea. Hurricanes, volcanoes, diseases, and human cruelty killed men, women, and children, but newborn Harriet survived.

Harriet's Mother and Father

Like the waves washing back and forth over the volcanic beaches, time has washed away the name of Harriet's mother as well as the month and day in 1773 when the infant was born. Detailed information about Harriet's father and future husband is included in a

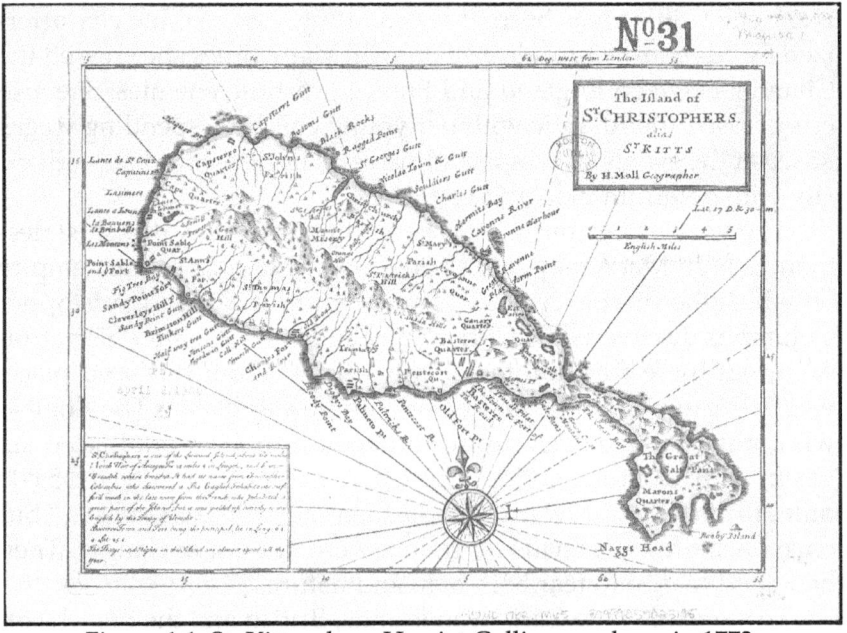

Figure 1.1. St. Kitts where Harriet Collins was born in 1773.

family memoir, but no mention is made of the woman who labored in the tropical heat to give her life.

This silence may simply reflect the way women were treated in the British colonies at that time. More likely is the possibility that she was considered lower class or biracial and therefore unworthy of official documentation. Harriet's mother may have been part "Creole," a term variously defined as anyone born in the Caribbean or to a mixed-race descendent of European settlers and African slaves. The memoir, published in 1880, was based on the journals and letters of Harriet's British grandson Charles. Perhaps the omission of any mention of Harriet's maternal ancestry reflected the greater importance given to men in Britain's patriarchal society. Sadly, Harriet's mother remains a mystery, whatever the reason.[3]

Harriet's father, John Collins, was an Englishman who married her mother and had two more children with her: Cornelia and Alfred. From the rising middle class in Britain, he was a member of the new meritocracy, not the aristocracy. He sailed out to the Caribbean to seek his fortune and succeeded.

Practical Rules

Collins was a medical doctor and an author, as well as a planter. He wrote a book entitled *Practical Rules for the Management and Medical Treatment of Negro Slaves in the Sugar Colonies by a Professional Planter*. William Wilberforce, a member of the British Parliament and a leading abolitionist, wrote, "I have often thought it might do much good if Collin's [sic] excellent work on the management of negroes were generally circulated."[4]

Collins wanted his book to be "extensively useful" and to lead to reform of the practices of "bad masters" in Britain's island colonies. The "practical rules" explained how planters could improve the management and medical treatment of their slaves. Collins also wrote about philosophy and morality. Profit, he argued,

> is not independent of the moral obligation which every man ought to feel, to treat his fellow creatures with kindness and humanity, for such they are, however debased and degraded. There are few men so very much lost to principle, as not,

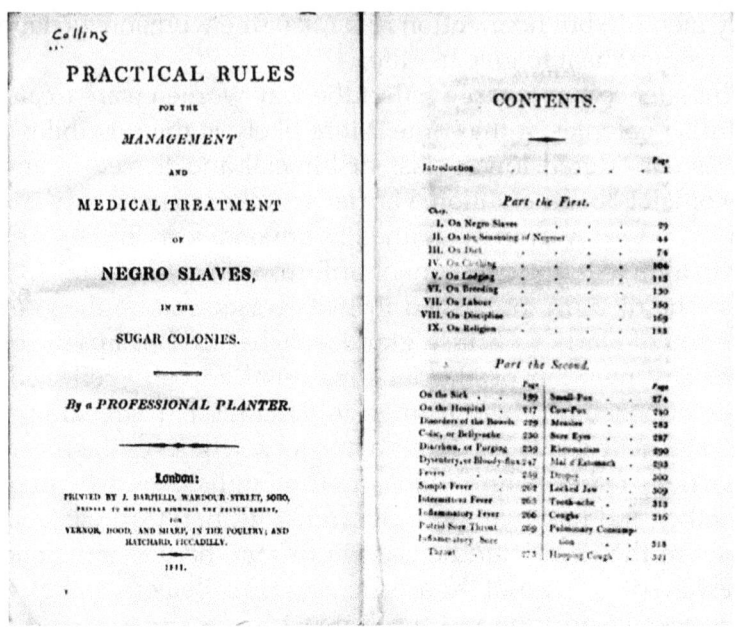

Figure 1.2. A manual by Harriet's British father, John Collins, on the management and medical treatment of slaves. Source: Public domain.

occasionally, to recognize the force of that duty. To have slaves (certainly in violation of natural right), to render them miserable, and to shorten their lives by vexations and cruelties of any kind, are crimes for which we must expect to be arraigned at that dread tribunal, to which we must all ultimately repair.[5]

The Society for the Mitigation and Gradual Abolition of Slavery Throughout the British Dominions, founded in 1823, praised *Practical Rules* as "a work of high authority."[6]

Harriet's Cold Start in a British Colony

Practical Rules contained explicit instructions about the medical treatment of infants. Over time Collins had developed these life-saving "best practices" as the result of close observation of mothers and babies on his plantation:

> The first thing that ought to be done ... to infants, after they come into the world, is, to plunge them over head and ears into a tub of cold water, with the side downwards, and, when withdrawn from the tub, let their limbs be examined to see if they have suffered any injury during the labour, that it may be addressed if they have. When dressed, and the mother has been properly taken care of, let the child be put to the breast... to withhold them from it is contrary to the indication of nature, and injurious both to mother and the child. Where the cold bathing has been neglected, infants are sometimes attacked, within nine or ten days after their birth, with the locked jaw, or jaw fall. I never knew it to be otherwise than fatal.[7]

Under her father's watchful eye, Harriet survived her cold start in life and her first months on an island ravaged by the hurricane of October 31, 1772.

The hurricane provides an interesting link between Harriet and Alexander Hamilton, born on Nevis around 1755. At the age of seventeen or eighteen, Hamilton wrote about the hurricane from the vantage point of St. Croix, to the west of St. Christopher and Nevis. "It seemed as if a total dissolution of nature was taking place. The roaring of the sea and wind, fiery meteors flying about, the prodigious glare of almost perpetual lightning, the crash of the falling houses and the ear-piercing shrieks of the distressed, were sufficient to strike astonishment into angels." Fortunately, a local paper published the teenager's description of the storm, publicity that led to an offer to go to North America to pursue his education.[8]

While Harriet was growing up on St. Christopher, Hamilton was in New York, studying at what became Columbia University. Three decades later, when Harriet was living in London, she would meet the American statesman who killed Hamilton in a duel, Aaron Burr.

Another eyewitness record, *An Account of the Late Dreadful Hurricane*, describes the losses in the harbor of St. Christopher—and in the homes of the white colonial class.[9] The ports of St. Christopher and Nevis became graveyards of shattered wood. The wreckage included thirteen sloops, twenty schooners, five brigs, and two ships from home ports as far away as London, Cork, Glasgow, and South Carolina. Sir Ralph Payne, the hero of the hour, averted widespread famine by writing colonial governors in North America for help, and Richard Penn of Philadelphia launched a flotilla of ships with provisions.

The dedication to Sir Ralph Payne provides a taste of the "British flavor" of Harriet's birthplace: "To his Excellency Sir Ralph Payne, Knight Companion of the Most Honourable Order of the Bath, Captain General and Governor in Chief in and over all his Majesty's Leeward Charibbee Islands in America, Chancellor, Vice Admiral and Ordinary of the Same, etc., etc."

An Account of the Late Dreadful Hurricane also presents a picture of the damaged homes of British colonists in St. Christopher. For example, the Reverend Mr. Thomas lost a marble slab that had been covered with silver plate; "the same gust of wind flying round the hall, penetrated behind a large mahogany beaufet [sic], full of valuable China." At Palmetto Point, one colonist's "single-horse chair... was whirled up in the air, and carried about two hundred yards into the sea."[10] No mention is made of the dreadful losses of slaves and Caribs.

After the Storm

Sunshine, heat, and rain soon transformed Harriet's birthplace into what looked like a lush and green paradise. Wild parrots and monkeys filled the trees; dolphins and porpoises swam in the blue waters; hummingbirds flitted from flower to flower. Fruits and vegetables abounded: bananas, mangoes, pomegranates, pineapples, avocados, yams, plantains, and pumpkin. Red meat and poultry were relatively scarce, but the colonists could eat hens, pigeons, rabbits, and turtles, a culinary delicacy.

Harriet enjoyed a childhood with all the advantages afforded white inhabitants at the top of the island's highly stratified society. She probably lived in a two-story wooden house with windows to welcome the breeze and furnishings that were surprisingly elegant. The colonists tried hard to replicate what they had left behind in England. Nevertheless, the foreign far exceeded the familiar in their transplanted lives. Harriet became a transplant herself at the age of twelve when she moved to St. Vincent, a British colony three hundred miles south of St. Christopher. Her father, with a partner, bought a half share in a sugar estate there. St. Vincent is shaped like an eye, with the Grenadines (more than thirty tiny islands) falling below like tears, an apt image in a region populated by slaves.

The sugar trade was a force as powerful and as lethal as a devastating storm. Africans who survived the voyage to the tropics were branded on shore with a mark identifying their owner. Plantation overseers then assigned each slave a name, which was sometimes related to the slave's tribe or personal characteristics. The names are a poignant reminder of the system that deprived men, women, and children even of their own names. According to deeds of sale for 1785 and 1800, Collins and his partner owned Cudjoe Cubinah, Peter Quashy, little Cumba, Yellow Boy, Richmond Scipeo, Bob Daniel Quasly, Big Boatswain, Dublin Montjoy, Hood Bath, Little Tom, Molly, Betty, and Old Fanny, and other slaves.[11]

The work of field slaves on a sugar plantation changed with the seasons. In November they hoed the terraced soil. In December, they dug square holes in meticulously precise rows. From January to June they cut the sugar cane, the most backbreaking work. One slave on a sugar estate not far from the Collins's plantation described his experiences.[12]

Harriet participated in the annual harvest celebrations (called "crop-overs") that were held in the home of the plantation manager. Colonists and slaves were invited to enjoy the music and the feast. One European, the Scottish magistrate John Anderson, disapproved of the notable familiarity existing between slaves and planters. Slaves "speak to their superiors on St. Vincent with a freedom [that] would astonish an Englishman, and they fondle and address children before their parents as familiarly as if they were their own"—and sometimes they were.[13]

Sometimes Harriet's father welcomed in his home visitors from London who dared to make the long sea voyage. One such visitor was James Marshall. He and his close friend William Godwin were young ambitious writers in London, and they were broke. Marshall sailed out to St. Vincent in 1784 to try and convince Collins, the wealthy planter, to fund their writings. Collins refused Marshall's request, but this rejection did not break the ties between his family and Godwin's family for decades to come.[14]

Thoughts on the Education of Daughters

William Godwin married the writer Mary Wollstonecraft. Nearly a decade before they married, she had written *Thoughts on the Education of Daughters, with Reflections on Female Conduct in the More Important Duties of Life*. In the eighteenth century, the usual education of daughters of the gentry included music, sewing, drawing, and a little geography—nothing very rigorous. Wollstonecraft criticized the gender disparities then prevailing in education. She believed the acquisition of knowledge was the way for girls to improve their lives. She emphasized the importance of reading and of teaching girls to think for themselves.

In St. Vincent Mrs. Carmichael, a longtime resident, wrote about education: "There are few children who remain in the island after ten or at most twelve years of age, for there is no possibility of procuring either public or private teachers, beyond merely reading and writing and those of very ordinary attainments." Options were few, she explained, "excepting that of sending children to Europe or leaving them to grow up totally ignorant." With regard to the education of boys, "there is no possibility of educating them in the West Indies."[15]

Exactly where and how Harriet was educated is not known, but the letters she and her younger sister Cornelia wrote as adults make clear that they became erudite persons. Both daughters far exceeded the ordinary attainments disparaged by Mrs. Carmichael. Their father wanted them to become well-read, well-informed, and well-traveled. Like most British colonial planters in the Caribbean at that time, he and his family periodically returned to England. He had a home in London, and there Harriet's education continued. Her experiences in St. Vincent had taught her a great deal, if not in a classroom. What she observed as a girl growing up on a plantation deeply impressed her and shaped her egalitarian principles, just as Hamilton's experiences in the Caribbean helped to make him a staunch abolitionist.

When we next meet Harriet, she will have left the tropics. She is sixteen, living in London, where she will meet a fascinating Frenchman who expands her knowledge of the French Revolution—and introduces her to romance.

Chapter 2

"Une Enfant de la Révolution" 1789–1792

> It looks to me as if I were in a great crisis, not of the affairs of France alone, but of all Europe, perhaps of more than Europe. All circumstances taken together, the French Revolution is the most astonishing that has hitherto happened in the world.
> —Edmund Burke, Member of British Parliament,
> *Reflections on the Revolution in France,* November 1790

With all the passion of a teenager with convictions, Harriet supported the French Revolution. Its beginning has been linked to July 14, 1789, when Parisians wearing red cockades (ribbons) in their caps stormed the medieval prison called the Bastille. In London, at her home, 44 Berners Street, Harriet would don a red sash as a sign of solidarity. "Round her slight figure she wore the badge of republicanism, a wide red band," her grandson later wrote, "and I have often heard her call herself une enfant de la Révolution."[1]

Today the French Revolution conjures up images of the guillotine, but then the ideals of republicanism—liberté, egalité, and fraternité—inspired many. William Wordsworth expressed the hopefulness of the age: "'twas a time when Europe was rejoiced, France standing at the top of golden hours, and human nature seeming born again." Percy Bysshe Shelley praised the French for daring to break "fetters of law."[2]

Harriet's interest in France was influenced by her father. John Collins had visited France as a young man and studied its history. He sympathized with French exiles in London. Many French "Constitutionalists," liberals favoring changes in the monarchy, came to his home. The Collins family lived north of the Thames River in East Marylebone, a residential district developed in the eighteenth century that was popular with writers and artists. At one time painters John Opie and Henry Fuseli lived there, as did Samuel Taylor Coleridge and relatives of Charles Dickens. North of Berners Street toward Somers Town stood an important landmark in literary history: St. Pancras Church. Writer Mary Wollstonecraft would be was buried in that quiet churchyard in 1797, and her daughter Mary would become Harriet's friend.[3]

Among the Constitutionalists who gathered on Berners Street was Jean Baptiste de Boinville, "a favourite guest." Harriet noticed him, and "it happened naturally enough that in frequent intercourse [how language has changed], an attachment arose between M. de Boinville and the eldest daughter of the family, who was at that time not only an ardent admirer of all that savored of liberty—which she remained to the last—but an exceedingly pretty girl, full of generous feeling, and with a mind of unusual power."[4]

Harriet fell in love. If the memoir's effusive portrait of her beau is to be believed, how could she resist? "His temper was remarkably sweet; his spirits even and cheerful; his mind was cultivated and intelligent; his taste exquisitely refined. In person he was tall and handsome; in manners and appearance, he was singularly agreeable."[5]

Figure 2.1. Portrait of the young Jean Baptiste Chastel de Boinville. Source: Courtesy of the family.

Jean Baptiste at Versailles

Everything related to the French Revolution interested Harriet. She listened attentively to Jean Baptiste's true stories about his experiences in the service of General Lafayette. By 1789 Lafayette had become the head of the Paris National Guard and Jean Baptiste had become his trusted aide-de-campe.

On October 5, 1789, word came of a plot against the royal family. The National Guard galloped off to Versailles, twelve miles away. Angry and starving Parisians, many of them women, had begun to fill the streets around the palace. By one in the morning all was quiet. Lafayette went to bed. Jean Baptiste retired to a room nearby in the palace. Screams awakened him. He dashed out to the hall, strewn with beheaded bodies. The mob had broken down the door of the queen's quarters; "the rooms were full of ruffians, so bent on finding Marie Antoinette that they even stabbed the mattresses of her bed with their swords and knives, thinking she might be hidden under them."[6]

Lafayette averted further bloodshed by persuading the King Louis XVI to accompany him to the balcony of the royal apartment. The insurgents shouted and waved their torches below. Playing to the crowd and using exaggerated gestures, Lafayette put his tricolored cap on the king's head and the king's white cap on his own head. This pantomime quieted the people long enough for Lafayette to be able to negotiate for the safe transport of the royal family back to Paris.

The general ordered Jean Baptiste to escort the queen's carriage, a dangerous mission because the people particularly despised the Austrian-born queen known for her extravagance. Spotting Jean Baptiste on his horse, next to her carriage window, Marie Antoinette turned to one of her attendants and said: "Je ne puis pas souffrir de voir M. de Boinville" (I cannot stand to look at Monsieur de Boinville.) Why she said this has long been debated by Jean Baptiste's descendants, but the explanation is probably a simple one. She wanted to remain at the palace and he made her leave.

Jean Baptiste in London

The reason Jean Baptiste left Paris and went to London was to fulfill an important assignment for Lafayette: spying on the activities of Louis-Philippe Joseph, Duc d'Orléans. Although the duke was a member of the royal family (the king's cousin), he called himself Citoyen Egalité. Lafayette feared what the duke might say or do in London. Walking a tightrope between the radicals and the moderates, Lafayette relied on Jean Baptiste to keep him informed. Referring to the duke, he wrote, "There is a lot of important information to be drawn from that source. Monsieur Boinville will make it his unique occupation to obtain it. I do not doubt at all that he will give me useful opinions."[7]

While in London Jean Baptiste was approached by the American statesman Gouverneur Morris, who had his own ideas about international diplomacy. Knowing Jean Baptiste was in Lafayette's confidence, Morris asked him to persuade Lafayette that France should declare war on England. Jean Baptiste conveyed the message to his general. Lafayette refused to consider the radical idea, and there the matter was left.[8]

While Harriet was becoming better acquainted with the handsome French soldier in the comfort of her London home, events in France careened in violent directions. In April 1792 France declared war on Austria. In August 1792 a mob broke into the chateau in the Tuileries and took the royal family. The king was manhandled and forced to put on a red cap. A month later Lafayette was forced to flee his country with the Army of the North. He was captured in Austria and thrown into prison. In January 1793, 1,200 guards marched the thirty-eight-year-old king to the guillotine. Among those who had voted in favor of his execution was none other than "Phillipe Egalité." His pretense of being a man of the people did not save the duke's neck, which was severed a month after Marie Antoinette's.

Although commoners had gained a voice in the representative assembly, this reform did not appease those in power, determined to obliterate anything related to the clergy and the nobility (the privileged groups in the ancien régime). Street signs were changed. Rue de Condé became rue de l'Egalité. Notre Dame became the Temple of Reason. Even playing cards had to be ideologically correct. Kings became Génie (genius), and Queens, Liberté. Gouverneur Morris wrote to a friend, 'The voracity of the court, the haughtiness of the nobles, the sensuality of the church, have met their punishment in the road of their transgressions. The oppressor has been squeezed by the hands of the oppressed."[9]

An Unfortunate Son

France declared war on Britain in February 1793. Harriet did not reveal to her father that she had fallen in love with his friend Jean Baptiste. Her beau came from one of the noblest, richest, and oldest families in northeastern France."[10] Born on July 15, 1756, he was the second son of Jean Baptiste Ignace Chastel de Villemont and Francoise Pauline Lucie Dupaquier de Dommartin. Chastel was a family name; Villemont signified where his father owned property. According to the custom of the time, Jean Baptiste took the name and title of *de Boinville*, from an estate and village of that name near Etain, about ten miles to the east of Verdun and to the west of Metz. Today this small village is called Boinville-en-Woëvre.[11]

Figure 2.2. Map showing Boinville (lower left) in Lorraine in the eighteenth century. Source: Public record.

Because Jean Baptiste's name was written on the list of émigrés, he lost his property. The Jacobins hanged seventeen members of his family, and they guillotined his friend Andre Chenier, a poet who wrote satirical verse offensive to Robespierre.[12] Fortunately, Jean Baptiste had obeyed Lafayette's order to go to London. He escaped The Terror with his life—but little else. Jean Baptiste's status as a penniless refugee from an enemy nation did not matter to Harriet, but it did to her father, who forbid her to see him again.

Chapter 3

A Disobedient Daughter Marries for Love, 1793

> *In each other's arms, as in a temple, with its summit lost in the clouds, the world is to be shut out, and every thought and wish that do not nurture pure affection and permanent virtue.*
> —Mary Wollstonecraft, *A Vindication of the Rights of Woman: With Strictures on Political and Moral Subjects* (1792)

Jean Baptiste wrote John Collins asking for his daughter's hand in marriage and received a written reply. Often welcomed on Berners Street, he was surprised at the rejection. Collins told Jean Baptiste that he had no objection to him personally, but "avec lui sa fille manquerait le pain," which is to say, he thought the impoverished exile would be a poor bread winner. Money was the problem, not Jean Baptiste's character. Harriet's father was sure that if his daughter married him, her future would be marked by financial difficulties and real hardship. And in many respects, he was right.[1]

Jean Baptiste received a good education, and when he was twenty-one, he became fermiér-général.[2] This profligate youth bore little resemblance to the Jean Baptiste Harriet loved. He was thirty-seven in 1793, a widower, with a grown son still in France. His first wife had died shortly after giving birth. Death, war, and misfortune had changed him.

Harriet was not dissuaded by her father's opposition. She promised Jean Baptiste she would marry him on one condition: he had to leave the French army. He complied with her demand and wrote Lafayette asking for permission to leave his service. From his prison cell in Austria, Lafayette wrote back a friendly letter. He gave his blessing and the epaulettes came off at once. Lafayette urged Jean

Baptiste to marry in London if he could.[3] Twenty-year-old Harriet was eager to marry him. The war between France and England did not stop her. Neither did her father.

The Norm of Obedience

Harriet's defiance of her father broke a well-established societal norm of behavior. "Conduct books," a popular literary genre, instructed young women in the importance of deference to their fathers. In fact, submission to all male relatives was expected, a father, a husband, or a brother. Under English law, women were completely without legal or financial rights in their own name.

In *A Father's Legacy to his Daughter*, John Gregory criticized the disturbing trend in "female manners" and defended the gender disparities of the day. He was upset that some women "seem to expect that they shall regain their ascendancy over us, by the fullest display of their personal charms, by being always in our eye at public places, by conversing with us with the same unreserved freedom as we do with one another; in short, by resembling us as nearly as they possibly can."[4] Harriet, however, was not swayed by this particular conduct book or any other. She was little interested in conformity with prevailing views of womanhood.

Two contemporaries of Harriet's (Jane Austen, born in 1775, and Dorothy Wordsworth, born in 1771) contended with the same absence of legal rights. They were more constrained than Harriet by financial circumstances. Money was in short supply in both households. The daughter of a country parson, Jane was one of eight children, and Dorothy, who lost both parents at a young age, had three brothers. As Austen scholar Lucy Worsley correctly notes, "the business of daughters in a large family was obedience and compliance and domestic duty."[5]

Harriet, however, had some financial autonomy, and she had a fiercely independent streak. The memoir describes her response when her father prohibited her from seeing Jean Baptiste again:

> At this she was indignant. Her father had large estates in St. Vincent's; the marriage-portion she had a right to expect was amply sufficient to sustain a family. She had 200

pounds a year of her own, left to her by her grandmother, and on this she determined to marry.[6]

A family that aspired to gentility needed at least 500 pounds a year.[7] Harriet had only one aspiration, to wed Jean Baptiste, and 200 pounds would suffice. She bided her time. She watched and waited. One day when her father was away from home, she seized her chance. Cornelia and Alfred helped her. The three siblings procured a carriage and four horses. Then Harriet and Jean Baptiste galloped off, taking the main route out of London in the direction of Scotland.

Harriet Elopes to Gretna Green

Harriet could not marry in England because she was only twenty and did not have her father's consent, but in Scotland boys as young as fourteen and girls as young as twelve could marry. The only requirement was that the couple be married in front of witnesses. In Scotland, blacksmiths were required to be citizens, and so these "anvil priests," as they were known, often officiated. For lovers in a hurry, the local forge was usually easy to find. A toll road to Graitney made Gretna Green the quickest village to reach across the English border. Harriet and Jean Baptiste were married in 1793 in either the Old Blacksmith's Shop, built around 1712, or the Gretna Hall Blacksmith Shop, built in 1710.

Gretna Green appears in Austen's novel *Pride and Prejudice*. The foolish Lydia Bennet, the heroine's sister, eloped there. "You will laugh when you know where I am gone," she wrote her family,

> and I cannot help laughing myself at your surprise to-morrow morning, as soon as I am missed. I am going to Gretna Green, and if you cannot guess with who, I shall think you a simpleton, for there is but one man in the world I love, and he is an angel. I should never be happy without him, so think it no harm to be off. You need not send them word at Longbourn of my going, if you do not like it, for it will make the surprise the greater, when I write to them and sign my name 'Lydia Wickham.' What a good joke it will be!

Figure 3.1. The old blacksmith's shop in Gretna Green. Source: "Old Blacksmiths Shop Gretna Green" by amandabhslater is licensed under CC BY-SA 2.0.

Frances Burney: A Literary Celebrity

Like Harriet, Frances Burney defied her father to marry a French exile in London in 1793. His name was Alexandre Piochard d'Arblay, a good friend of Jean Baptiste's. He had served as an adjutant-general under Lafayette in the Army of the North's campaign against Austria. Following Lafayette's capture, d'Arblay managed to make his way via Holland and Harwich to London. It was through Jean Baptiste that Harriet became acquainted with Frances Burney, the most famous female novelist in Britain.

Frances Burney's mother died when she was young. She revered her father and helped him as his amanuensis, copying his manuscripts. Dr. Charles Burney was at work on the second volume of a history of music at the same time Fanny was secretly writing *Evelina, or the History of a Young Lady's Entrance into the World*, published anonymously in 1778. A timid, first-time author, she did not want her identity discovered by her father or anyone else. Before she submitted the manuscript of the novel, she copied every page in a feigned hand, lest the Fleet Street printers recognize her handwriting. As her father's scribe, they had seen it before.

Despite this arduous effort at subterfuge, her identity was discovered. Frances Burney became the talk of London. Her second novel, another social satire, added to her fame: *Cecilia; or Memoirs of an Heiress* (1782). By 1793, the year Miss Collins and Miss Burney both married, she was the most celebrated woman writer in Britain.[9]

Figure 3.2. Portrait of Frances Burney (Madame d'Arblay) by her cousin Edward Francis Burney. Source: Public domain.

Another Disobedient Daughter

Miss Burney met Monsieur d'Arblay in Surrey at Juniper Hall, where he lived with a lively and colorful group of French exiles, including Louis de Narbonne (the ex-minister of war), Anne-Louise-Germaine de Staël, Princesse d'Hénin, and Charles Maurice de Talleyrand-Périgord, the future diplomat. Narbonne's friend, Monsieur d'Arblay, was the one who impressed Frances most strongly. He is "one of the most singularly interesting Characters that can ever have been formed," she wrote her sister Susan. "He has a sincerity, a frankness, an ingenuous openness of nature that I had been injust [sic] enough to think could not belong to a French Man."[10]

Like her conservative father, Frances Burney was a royalist. Her politics at the beginning of the French Revolution differed from Harriet's. When British Prime Minister William Pitt wrote *Reflections on the Revolution in France* in 1790, Burney agreed with Pitt's anti-revolutionary sentiments. Later she told him in person how much she admired his reasoned argument in favor of preserving the virtues of monarchic rule.[11] These opinions, however, began to change after she met Alexandre d'Arblay, a Constitutionalist in favor of reform, like his buddy Jean Baptiste.

In May 1793, Dr. Burney discovered his daughter's interest in Monsieur d'Arblay, and it made him "extremely uneasy." Do not, he warned in a long letter, become entangled in a "wild and romantic attachment." It will bring you nothing but poverty and unhappiness.[12] Like Harriet's father, he was concerned about his daughter's financial future if she married a French exile with no money and no prospect of making any.

"If the Queen should be displeased and withdraw her allowance, what would you do?" he plaintively asked. From 1786 to 1791, Frances Burney had been employed at Windsor Palace as "Keeper of the Robes," a ceremonial position at Court she disliked, but it had an income of 200 pounds a year. When Fanny left after five years of service, Queen Charlotte (an admirer of her character and her novels) awarded her an annual allowance of 100 pounds, money that was needed by the large Burney family.

The letter noted that Fanny's friends in England came from "the highest and most desirable class," a matter of importance to her father, who was the son of a portrait painter and dancing master of no fixed address, as Kate Chisholm explains in her essay on the Burney family. He rose above his station in life, and assiduously cultivated friendships with the 'ton', those with inherited wealth and genteel status.[13] Some have considered him a member of the pseudo-gentry, gentlemen without land or title but with artistic or intellectual credentials. After praising her desirable friends,

Dr. Burney said she should not "quit them, in order to make new friendships in a strange land." Dr. Burney, unlike John Collins, had little sympathy for the French, and he certainly had nothing good to say about France in 1793: "the generality of its inhabitants seem incapable of such virtues as friendship is built upon." He beseeched his daughter not to make the "wild and visionary" decision to marry the Frenchman.

Frances Burney considered her beloved father's objections, but in the end she disobeyed his wishes. She was determined to spend her life with her "chevalier" and "friend of my inmost heart." The English novelist and French exile married not once by twice. The first time on July 28, 1793, in a Protestant ceremony, and two days later in a Catholic church.

The following month the new bride wrote to her friend Marianne Waddington:

> You may be amazed not to see the name of my dear Father upon this solemn occasion: but his apprehension from the smallness of our income have made him cold and averse--& though he granted his consent, I could not even solicit his presence;—I feel satisfied, however, that Time will convince him that I have not been so imprudent as he now thinks me. Happiness is the great end of all our worldly views & proceedings; & no one can judge for another in what will produce it.[14]

Were Frances and Harriet happy with the men they chose? Frances Burney d'Arblay wrote a great deal about her feelings for her husband. Their happiness together is described in numerous letters and journals preserved in the Henry W. and Albert A. Berg Collection of English and American Literature in the New York Public Library. Included in that collection is a letter Jean Baptiste wrote Alexandre d'Arblay on September 24, 1793:

> I sincerely congratulate you on your happy marriage. I no longer doubt your future happiness, it is established on the amiableness and qualities of a charming woman. The rural establishment that you will get will give you plenty of space

for pleasure. I am very pleased to have learned all of this, you promise me details. Send them as soon as possible.

Jean Baptiste then relates that he had met a wonderful woman:

I left London on the 7th of July to come stay in this area, the south of England, in a pretty thatched cottage near the sea and surrounded by delightful countryside. I spent an enchanting time with someone I adore and who embodies all that is amiable and good.

In closing Jean Baptiste writes,

I await your news with impatience my dear friend. In response I will give you news of my situation. We can boast that you and I are not the emigrants most to be pitied.[15]

The boast was well founded. The lives of the two French exiles, far from home, were transformed by the English women determined to marry them despite their fathers' disapproval. Letters in which Harriet divulges her feelings about Jean Baptiste have not survived, but her actions described in the next chapter attest to her devotion to him.

Chapter 4

From Domesticity to Dangers at Sea 1793–1796

> *I wish to persuade women to endeavor to acquire strength, both of mind and body.*
> —Mary Wollstonecraft, *A Vindication of the Rights of Woman* (1792)

Returning home to Berners Street, John Collins heard his daughter had eloped with Jean Baptiste. Immediately, he raced off in pursuit and caught up with them on their return journey. Heated words were exchanged, but in the end a reconciliation occurred. France and England were at war, but peace was restored within the family, and for this her practical father deserves credit.

To ensure the legality of the marriage and the legitimacy of any future children, Collins persuaded the couple to marry in England. The day after Harriet and Jean Baptiste were wed in 1793 by the Gretna Green blacksmith, they were married according to the Anglican rite in the Arthuret Church, Longtown, just across the Scottish border in England. Collins then convinced his daughter and son-in-law to accept his offer of a place to live—his country house in Willesden, north and west of London.[1] Harriet and Jean Baptiste's first child was born there on February 23, 1795. They named their daughter Cornelia Pauline Eugenia, after Harriet's sister.[2] The two years the couple spent in Willesden mark a rare period of quiet domesticity in their marriage.

William Cowper, one of the most popular poets in late eighteenth-century Britain, wrote "A Winter's Evening," that describes a tranquil scene. Picture the new parents with their baby by the hearth:

> Now stir the fire, and close the shutters fast,
> Let fall the curtains, wheel the sofa round....
> And, while the bubbling and loud hissing urn
> Throws up a steamy column, and the cups,
> That cheer but not inebriate, wait on each,
> So let us welcome peaceful evening in.[3]

Not long after Cornelia's birth, her father got news that his property in St. Vincent "had been laid waste, his buildings burnt to the ground." He returned to the island to repair his losses and restore order." The memoir notes that the damage was caused by "negroes," but in fact, the destruction was not caused by his slaves but by combatants in a civil war involving the indigenous Caribs and British and French colonists. While he was in St. Vincent, Collins wrote his son-in-law, "holding out the prospect that a part, and perhaps the whole, of his property might be placed under M. de Boinville's superintendence. This chance of an independence was not to be refused."[4]

Harriet knew her husband disliked being dependent on her father. The former soldier and leader of men had grown restless in England. He was ill-suited to inactivity in her country. Harriet had often described the island to Jean Baptiste, and she urged him to accept her father's proposal: a relocation of their family in St. Vincent. During this period of the French Revolutionary Wars, the battles between France and England were primarily at sea in the Caribbean islands, just where the new mother and father—and their year-old daughter Cornelia—planned to go.

Trouble en Route to Ireland

Late in 1796, the most ferocious winter recorded since 1708, the family boarded a merchant ship in Plymouth. On a two-masted, square-rigged brig, they sailed westward toward southern Ireland. In Cork they planned to join a convoy of ships for the long voyage to the Caribbean. At this time merchant ships never traveled alone. For protection, they sailed in a fleet accompanied by a British ship of war.[5] As Harriet and her family neared Cork, French naval forces approached Bantry Bay, not far from Cork on Ireland's southern coast. A second front in France's war against England—Expédition d'Irlande—had begun!

The war had not gone well for the British. France and its Austrian and Hessian allies had defeated the British at Dunkirk in the fall of 1793, an expedition lead by the Duke of York. Galvanized by the victory, leaders of the Irish resistance to British rule reached out to the French, who saw an opportunity to invade the British isles with support from local forces. Compounding the looming danger was a medical crisis. Cornelia was ill and growing worse. Harriet tried to comfort her wailing baby as the ship pitched in the wind and pounding rain. In Bantry Bay the British commander, Lord Jocelyn, was contacted. He knew John Collins and intervened to help. On shore Lady Jocelyn welcomed the baby and her parents "under her hospitable roof. M. de Boinville thus escaped suspicion." In typical understatement, the memoir noted that "a Frenchman's position under these circumstances was not a pleasant one."[6]

Badly damaged by the severe winter storms, the French fleet never entered Bantry Bay. British forces cheered the French retreat, and Harriet and her family embarked for the West Indies. Her emotions as she set sail are hard to imagine. Gratitude for Cornelia's recovery mixed with fear, realistic fear. She had traveled to and from the Caribbean before. She faced five weeks at sea. Anything could happen.

"Breasting the Atlantic"

Scotsman John Anderson, who sailed from Port Glasgow to St. Vincent in 1835 to assume his post as Special Magistrate, kept a journal that brings into vivid focus the hazards of seafarers. Only two days into the journey, a gale battered his ship, which veered wildly from point to point, tack upon tack, "scudding before the wind, under bare poles, for many a knot."[7] Days later, surrounded by water, he picked up his pen again and thus described "breasting the Atlantic":

> Column upon column rose the surge, —and rolling in majestic course in long and sinuoy [sic] piles of feathery white cord, as if to devour the ill-fated bark; —when suddenly

she would disappear into the boiling abyss—and again upheaved, stride with swanlike grace over the retreating waves...[8]

That record-breaking winter of 1796 Harriet sailed south from Ireland, passing Portugal and the Canary Islands near the western coast of Africa. Then catching the trade winds, her vessel turned west for the trans-Atlantic crossing. She made it to the Caribbean islands but not to safety. An alarm sounded. French ships!

Rapid preparations were made for an engagement. All the men on board volunteered their services, including Jean Baptiste who "ran the risk, had he been taken by the French, of being shot as a traitor to his country. This consideration did not, however, prevent him from doing what he felt in honour bound to do, and he took his part in the watch."[9]

Jean Baptiste prepared for battle on deck. Harriet also was put to the test. "Of the details of this anxious part of the voyage I remember little of what my grandmother told me," her grandson wrote, "but I know that on one occasion she was placed at the bottom of a boat, and heard the balls whistling across from the ships of the enemy."[10]

Harriet demonstrated her true colors during this hellish sail from Plymouth to St. Vincent. She was brave and resilient. At the turn of the century, femininity was equated with delicacy, and as the 1800s progressed, English women were increasingly viewed as nervous and frail. It was considered natural for them "to break down under all conceivable varieties of strain—a winter dissipation, a houseful of servants, a quarrel with a female friend, not to speak of more legitimate reasons."[11] Harriet was resilient and courageous. She little resembled the pampered wives, criticized by Mary Wollstonecraft, women who "supinely dream life away in the lap of pleasure" and "have nothing to do but to plume themselves, and stalk with mock majesty from perch to perch."[12] Harriet withstood serious challenges on this sea voyage: a sick baby, winter storms, and deadly warfare. And there were more such challenges to follow on St. Vincent.

Chapter 5

A Young Mother in a War-torn Colony 1797

I do not command in the name of anyone. I am not English, nor French, nor Spanish, nor do I care to be any of these. I am a Carib, a Carib subordinate to no one.
— A Carib fighter in St. Vincent, Summer of 1796, at the Surrender to the British

Born in St. Christopher after a devastating hurricane, Harriet returned to the Caribbean after another destructive tempest, the Second Carib War (1795-1796). She was twenty-four, the mother of a toddler, and pregnant. War marked her married life, war in Europe and war in the Caribbean. When she arrived in St. Vincent, the tiny island had not fully recovered from the civil war just ended.

At the beginning of the Second Carib War, the leader of the Caribs, Joseph Chatoyer, used the rhetoric of the French Revolution to rally the French to support his people. In 1795, when the Caribs reached Dorsetshire Hill near Kingstown, they pulled down the British flag and raised the tri-colored flag of the French Republic. "Where is the Frenchman who will not join his brothers at a moment when the voice of liberty is heard by them?" Chatoyer asked. "Let us then unite, citizens and brothers, round the colours flying in this island; and let us hasten to co-operate to that great piece of work which has been already commenced so gloriously."

Everything was at stake for the indigenous people—their land, their way of life, their very lives. In his speech, after this reminder of the glorious revolution in France, Chatoyer threatened his audience:

But should any timorous men still exist, should any Frenchm[e]n be held back through fear, we do hereby declare to them, in the name of the law, that those who will not be assembled with us in the course of the day, shall be deemed traitors to the country, and treated as enemies. We do swear that both fire and sword shall be employed against them, that we are going to burn their estates, and that we will murder their wives and children, in order to annihilate their race.[1]

The native Caribs ferociously defended their island, felling their enemies with their weapon of choice, a long pike with spear points. For a time it appeared that they had won the war. Britain's colonial militia was small and weak; "universal destruction threatened the whole colony and total extermination of the name of English from it." But the arrival of reinforcements from neighboring British

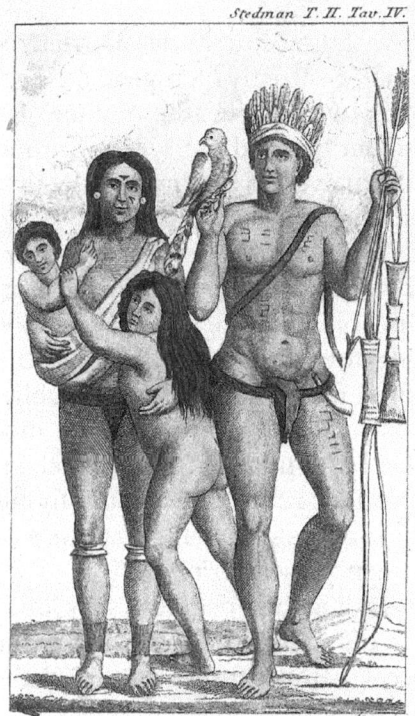

FAMIGLIA INDIANA CARAIBA.

Figure 5.1. Carib (Kalina or Galibi) Indian family after a painting by John Gabriel Stedman. Source: Public domain.

islands decimated the Caribs. Cannon fire rained down from land and sea. After Chatoyer was killed, his son addressed the remnant of his people: "It is no disgrace to us to surrender to a great nation, the subjects of France and all great nations, even of England, are obliged to submit to each other, when there no longer remains the means of resistance. What else is now left for us? Have we power to continue the war? No!" Accused of insurrection against the Crown, some 2,000 Caribs were corralled on the nearby island of Balliceaux. Hungry and disoriented, their numbers dwindled further. The last survivors were transported to Roatàn near the coast of Honduras in February 1797, about the time of Harriet's arrival in St. Vincent.[2]

Harriet's Return to the Tropics

After six weeks at sea, Harriet cried with relief at the sight of land. On deck she breathed in the fresh air and felt the sun on her back. Soon she would be welcomed by her father and sleep in a bed with clean sheets, not a pitching hammock in a stuffy cabin. The landscape coming into view was familiar. As a girl of twelve she had lived on her father's sugar estate, purchased in 1785.

A vivid depiction of scene comes from another European's journal: "My first view of St. Vincent scenery was well calculated to afford gratification. No European could pen the Emotions excited by the first glance of this windward Coast of beauty … luxuriant cane crops—overtopped by occasional dwelling houses, or windmills of dazzling white—and the beach lined with the tall Cocoa nut tree."[3]

Mrs. A. C. Carmichael, the long-time resident of St. Vincent, described "mountain heaped upon mountain, in that wild confusion that told of those awful convulsions of nature to which these tropical regions have been subject."[4] The island's rugged terrain included an active volcano, the Soufrière. Harriet landed at the Port of Caliaqua at the southern tip of the island, exactly where the Caribs had launched their assault on the British two years earlier.

According to historians and ethnographers, slaves probably were not the perpetrators of destruction on the British sugar estates in St. Vincent. The Caribs or—incredibly—the British, determined to deny their hated enemies any advantage, torched the properties. During the chaos of the burning buildings and smoking sugar

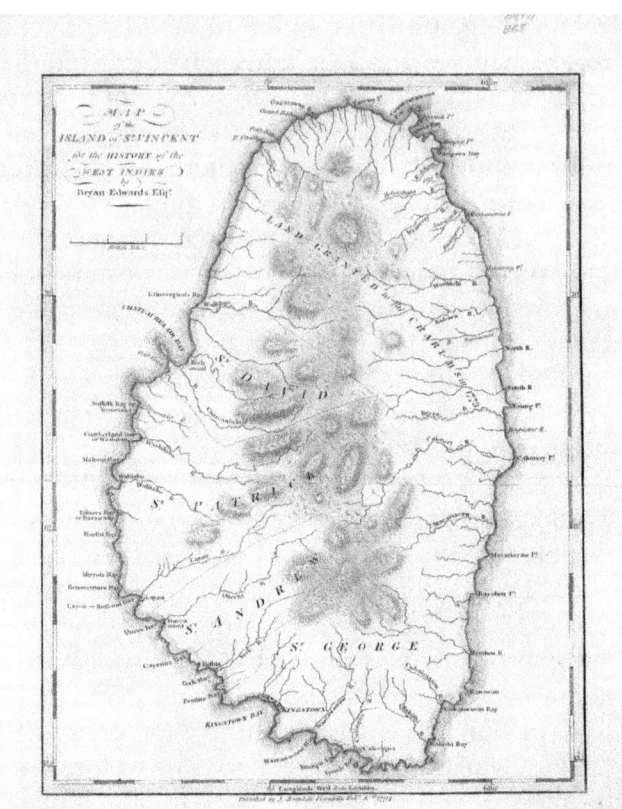

Figure 5.2. Map of St. Vincent created by Bryan Edwards in 1794. Source: Bryan Edwards, 1743-1800. Map of the island of St. Vincent, for the History of the West Indies, published in London in 1794. University of North Texas Libraries, The Portal to Texas History, https://texashistory.unt.edu; crediting University of Texas at Arlington Library

cane fields, the slaves tended to remain on the plantations of their masters, as hard as that is to believe. Slaves feared the Caribs, with their unfamiliar culture and traditions. Caribs painted their bodies, deformed the heads of their infants, buried their dead in a seated position, and believed in other practices. These customs, so different from the customs of the African slaves, may explain why they did not ally with the Caribs in the Second Carib War. Or slaves may have felt they had no place else to go, preferring the severe hardships they knew to hardships in the fearful unknown.[5]

The British victors of the deadly war in St. Vincent made clear their perspective: "a nation of 12,000 black slaves and 1,450 white masters had stood together and defended civilized life." According to this shocking view, enslaved Africans believed they were better off with the "civilized" British than with the strange and fearsome indigenous people.[6]

A Misfit in Colonial Society

Following extensive repairs after the fire, the property of Harriet's father "became more valuable than ever," the memoir states. Harriet and her husband had a comfortable home and everything they needed in terms of their physical well-being, but they felt like misfits in this British colony where their privileges contrasted sharply with the hard life of the slaves her father owned.

At some unknown date in 1797 Harriet labored and delivered her second child. It was a boy, named John Alfred—John after her father and Alfred after her brother.[7] The infant and his sister Cornelia were not the sole focus of their mother's attention. As the daughter of a wealthy planter, the highest stratum of the island's hierarchical society, Harriet was expected to pay and receive calls. Island society was even more stratified than back home in London with "rich versus poor, big planter versus small planter, master versus slave, white versus black."[8] A successful planter and medical doctor, Harriet's father also held positions of responsibility in the British colonial government: Assistant Justice—Common Pleas; member of the Assembly Parish of St. David; Aide De Camp to the General; and a member of the Commission of the Peace.[9]

Harriet was friendly and talkative by nature, never at a loss for words, but her social obligations in St. Vincent brought little pleasure. She had too much on her mind, not only her young children, but also her discontented husband. Jean Baptiste had expected that he would be given management responsibilities on his father-in-law's property, but this did not happen. Collins and his plantation manager continued to make all the decisions. As it turned out, "the true reason for Mr. Collins drawing M. de Boinville and his family to the West Indies," was for "the pleasure of their society."[10]

When Jean Baptiste left England in the late winter of 1796, he left a country inhospitable to the French, and when he arrived in St. Vincent, he found himself again in hostile territory. Collins's peers had not forgotten that the French sided with the Caribs against them in the war just concluded. Harriet became convinced that leaving England had been a mistake. Neither she nor her husband belonged in colonial society. The republican ideals that had excited her in 1789 when she was sixteen were still important to her. In St. Vincent, she was a misfit, a wealthy British woman with egalitarian principles.

Englishman Charles Shephard wrote *An Historical Account of the Island of St Vincent* and dedicated it to his countrymen who died in the Second Carib War. It is a heated account, more hysterical than historical in some passages. For example, Shephard called a French sympathizer with the Caribs an "infamous revolutionary zealot, bloated with the inhuman and wide wasting principles of the democratic system."[11] Harriet, always opinionated about government, embraced what Shephard so despised: "the principles of the democratic system."

Colonial society in St. Vincent, insular and conservative, did not suit broad-minded Harriet. When her father announced it was time to return to London, she willingly faced the daunting sea voyage. Harriet's wartime adventures continued. The conflict between Britain and France was far from over.

Chapter 6

A Bold Traveler Between Nations at War 1797–1800

> *The female character should possess the mild and retiring virtues, rather than the bold and dazzling ones.*
> —Erasmus Darwin, *A Plan for the Conduct of Female Education*, 1797, London: J. Drewry for J. Johnson, St. Paul's Churchyard

After the long sea voyage back to England, Harriet thought about the future more than the past disappointing year in St. Vincent. She hoped Jean Baptiste would settle down. Too often there was a distracted expression on his handsome face. She knew he was thinking of France. Harriet greatly admired her husband, seventeen years older than she. His interest in Cornelia, now beginning to talk, delighted her. Alfred was beginning to walk. Surely the children would help anchor her restless husband and keep him at her side.

These hopes were not realized. As their grandson explains:

> My grandfather ... remained in a great measure dependent on his father-in-law, and at last the situation became so irksome, that he determined, despite the entreaties of his wife, to seek some means of gaining his own bread, and of living independently... . [T]he "Reign of Terror" and of the Directory was over: Bonaparte was now First Consul. M. de Boinville returned to France to get his name struck off the Emigrant list, and found his way thither through Germany.[1]

The British government forbid travel between England and France. To avoid detection, Jean Baptiste took a circuitous route to Paris where his mother lived and his grown son. Eugene had been born shortly before the death of Jean Baptiste's first wife. His property, like his father's, had been taken by the revolutionaries. Eugene became an officer in Napoleon's army and died, without issue, in 1815 at Quatre Bras.

The lives of Jean Baptiste and his family in France and England, like everyone in Europe, were affected by Napoleon. *In Flight with the Eagle* by Raymond Horricks describes Napoleon's soaring ascendance to power—as well as his impetuosity. On March 2, 1796, Napoleon became commander-in-chief of the army of France. Seven days later he married. On the day of the wedding, Josephine, the love of his life, waited and waited:

> The general arrived late. He strode in at ten o'clock, his head still buzzing with plans for the Italian campaign, pulled Josephine's ear, kicked the registrar's [wooden] leg out of the fire and ordered: "Begin!" Josephine was thirty-three, he was twenty-seven, but the certificate recorded both as being twenty-eight. Two days later Napoleon set out for Italy and the battles which made him a hero.[2]

Napoleon defeated the Austrian army in Italy, signed a peace treaty with Austria, and returned triumphantly to Paris.

At her father's London home on Berners Street, Harriet waited for her husband to return, but he was gone "many months longer than he had intended." Harriet wanted to be with him. Taking the children, she crossed the Channel. As her grandson explains: "my grandmother determined, notwithstanding the opposition of her father, to join her husband in France."[3] Fearing for her safety and his grandchildren's, John Collins wanted her to stay. Harriet went anyway.

Harriet Stands Alone

"My own sex, I hope, will excuse me if I treat them like rational creatures, instead of flattering their fascinating graces, and viewing them as if they were in a perpetual state of childhood, unable to stand alone," Mary Wollstonecraft wrote in *A Vindication of the*

Rights of Woman. Harriet had "stood alone" before, without her father's approval, and she stood alone again. Harriet's decision to cross the Channel with her two children was more impetuous than rational. Love for Jean Baptiste drove her recklessly forward.

Harriet's journey began on land. Early in the morning, she boarded a stage coach with Cornelia and Alfred and probably a servant. The journey to Dover was a bumpy sixty miles. The next day they embarked on a neutral vessel. Unlike her husband, Harriet took a direct route to France. As she looked behind her at the white cliffs of Dover, she thought about the uncertainties ahead. She had notified Jean Baptiste by post of her expected arrival in Dunkirk, but the wartime post was unreliable. Would he be there?

After crossing the Channel with her children, Harriet embraced her husband waiting on shore, but immediately she was detained by the local police, suspicious of an English woman arriving on the French coast. This was Harriet's first imprisonment, though not her last. To secure his English wife's freedom, Jean Baptiste needed official permission for her to enter his country. He caught a stage coach that took him the 200 miles between Dunkirk and the French capital.

When he arrived in Paris, he used skills acquired during his military career as Lafayette's trusted aide. Articulate and charming, he knew how to work the back channels of the bureaucracy to obtain the requisite paperwork. He may have persuaded a senior military officer in Napoleon's service to write a letter. Or perhaps he convinced a sleepy bureaucrat to issue a faked passport. Whatever the nature of the papers he brought back to Dunkirk, they persuaded the police that his wife was not a British spy. Convinced that she posed no threat to France, or at least that she had official permission to enter, they let her and the children go.[4]

Reunited at last, Harriet and Jean Baptiste were ecstatic. Now they could travel together to Paris without fear of arrest. The exhausted children slept during the long coach ride, and their mother and father began to relax.

In Paris, Harriet met for the first time Jean Baptiste's mother, Lucie Françoise Dupasquier Chastel de Villemont. She had helped him when he arrived in London in the early 1790s "with no resources but such remittances as his mother, still living at Boinville, could occasionally send him." These small gifts of money at the beginning of his lonely exile meant everything.[5]

Meeting General Lafayette

Harriet met another person in Paris revered by her husband—General Lafayette. The hero of the American and French revolutions had returned after five years in captivity in Austrian prisons at Magdeburg and Olmütz.[6] Forced to flee France in 1792 with the remnants of his army when the Jacobins took control, Lafayette was released in 1797 as Napoleon's armies advanced through Europe.

All of Paris celebrated the aging general's long anticipated return. In a formal ceremony Harriet was presented to Lafayette, "who ever afterwards entertained toward her feelings of the highest and most friendly respect."[7] One reason why he thought so highly of her was the fund-raising letters she had written during his imprisonment. "Boinville and his wife attempted to secure Lafayette's freedom," notes a scholar of this period.[8] John Collins also contributed to the fund to free Lafayette. Many people in America, France, and England were part of this campaign to rescue Lafayette from prison, but it was Napoleon, unstoppable at the time, who succeeded where so many others had failed.

During his long captivity, Lafayette became very ill. Fearing he was dying, he wrote a letter in his own blood to thank those who had tried to help him. Jean Baptiste is mentioned by name in this blood-drenched epistle, now preserved among the papers of the first president of the United States, George Washington.[9]

Crossing the Channel Again

Harriet had a strong will but so did her father. On this occasion, financial necessity forced Harriet to bend her will to his. A section of the memoir titled "Matrimonial Vicissitudes" tells the story: "M. de Boinville did not conclude his business so soon as he had expected, and Mr. Collins steadfastly adhered to a threat of stopping his daughter's allowance until she returned to England, which she was thus forced to do, leaving her husband on the Continent."[10]

Under British law, Harriet as a married woman was a *feme co-*

vert. Her legal rights were subsumed by those of her husband. She could not own property or make contracts in her own name. Jean Baptiste did not have funds to support her continued stay with the children in France.

Before her marriage, as a *feme sole*, Harriet had access to money, the two hundred pounds a year given to her as a gift by John Collins's mother. These funds were not available to her now. Harriet's father was willing to support her. He used the lever of money to force his daughter and grandchildren to return to Berners Street. Reluctantly, Harriet had to leave her husband behind in France.

Crossing the Channel took nerve. Napoleon created an armée d'Angleterre in 1798, and that same year Admiral Horatio Nelson created the Sea "Fencibles," short for defensibles. This auxiliary French naval force of fishermen, bargemen, and other watermen provided a line of defense close to the English shore. A brilliant strategist, Napoleon calculated that "if he could frighten the British with a threat of an invasion, they might agree to peace terms favorable to himself."[11] Militarily, he had turned his attention to Europe, not the coastlines of France and England, but crossing the Channel remained risky.

With Cornelia and Alfred, Harriet returned home to her father, but she did not stay in England:

> Several times during the war, before and after the Peace of Amiens, she crossed the sea with her children, or with money; no easy matter in those troublous times, but her courage was great. On one occasion she was well-nigh shipwrecked with her little ones; on another she was taken prisoner at the Hague, but the jailer was so fascinated by her beauty, and moved by her sorrows, that he contrived to allow her to make her escape. On another occasion, when she had been to England, and was on her return to France on board of a smuggling vessel, rough weather came on, the vessel was driven ashore, and she had to get upon a sailor's back to land; just then, a huge wave threw them all down, and she had the sorrow of seeing most of her bank-notes floating upon the foaming sea, without any hope of rescuing them.[12]

In these adventures, Harriet resembles the amazing heroine of a modern-day movie thriller. She was nothing like the feminine ideal, docile and dependent. She ferries money back and forth between England and France, saves her children from drowning, and charms her jailer at the Hague. Determined to see her husband in France, she accepts a lift from smugglers. When their vessel founders in a storm, she clings to a sailor's back to try and reach shore. She sees her money float away. A wave knocks her down again. Struggling to her feet, Harriet goes forward.

Chapter 7

An Empathetic Friend to Frances Burney d'Arblay, 1800–1808

Not many of those who are happy enough to be personally & intimately acquainted with you, Madam, can have taken a deeper interest or greater share in all the painful feelings that have lately agitated you. The impertinence of unavailing condolence on a Mind full of such feelings, is, however, such that I should not certainly have presumed to address you at this moment, my dear Madam, had not M^r d'Arblay encouraged me...
—Harriet Boinville, Letter to Frances Burney d'Arblay, February 19, 1802[1]

At the turn of the century while Harriet crisscrossed the Channel, Frances Burney d'Arblay remained in the English countryside, enjoying a stable life of peaceful domesticity with her husband. This tranquil period was about to end. Writing from Watford, England, Harriet commiserated with her friend's "painful feelings" over the coming changes in her married life. Harriet knew what it was like to be pulled in two directions: toward France by your husband and toward England by your father. A marriage like that could exhaust your body, trouble your mind, and break your heart.

In February 1802 Madam d'Arblay anticipated leaving Camilla Cottage, her happy home in Sussex, built with proceeds from her third novel, *Camilla, or a Picture of Youth*. Her husband Alexandre, as soon as his name was removed from the list of emigrants, had obtained French passports for her and their seven-year-old son Alex. The coming move to France meant leaving behind in Chelsea her widowed and lonely father, Dr. Charles Burney. But what upset her the most was Alexandre's intention to return to military service. He had been offered a commission to go to the French colony of Santo Domingo (Haiti) to quell a slave rebellion led by the formidable black leader Toussaint L'Ouverture. Fanny feared for her husband's life.

"The expedition was every way frightful to me," she later explained, "not only for the *contention*, with a ferocious set of irritated, & probably ill used africans, but the risks of the stormy Voyage, and far greater risks of the pestilential climate."[2] Harriet could relate to her friend's concerns. She knew all about dangers in the Caribbean—the awful storms crossing the Atlantic and the sweltering climate upon arrival. As to the probable ill use of Africans, Harriet knew about that, too, having grown up on her father's sugar plantation in St. Vincent. John Collins's book on the management and medical treatment of slaves, published anonymously in 1803, presented his views and criticized the cruelty of bad masters in Britain's island colonies.[3]

Harriet empathized with Madam d'Arblay's worries. Although "personally & intimately" acquainted with the celebrated novelist, she always respectfully addressed her as Madam. The letter's twisting syntax and emotional language reflect the epistolary style of the day. In the "sentimental tradition," emotions tended to be "saturated in turbulent and disfiguring excess."[4] Harriet writes that she had received from Monsieur d'Arblay an assurance "that he had very kindly pre-disposed you to receive with indulgence these few lines, which are indeed a very imperfect expression of my sentiments: and of my earnest wish that you would before long indulge me with an opportunity of assuring you in person how truly I participate in your regret and anxieties." This was Harriet's "ardent hope." She signs the letter, "Your devoted humble servant, H. Boinville."[5]

Harriet's relationship with Madam d'Arblay comes into clearer focus in a later letter, praising her "piercing anatomizing eye," a reference to the novelist's acute powers of observation. "It has been my pride & my pleasure to tell those of my family who only know & admire you through your works, how soothingly kind you were to me in my Illness in Paris. How condescendingly good to my children in my absence." Eager to reciprocate Madam d'Arblay's kindness in this crisis, Harriet offers to forward her friend's mail. Through their deeds, more than words, the rapport of the two women is demonstrated.⁶

The d'Arblays in the Winter of 1802

Alexandre d'Arblay had had a distinguished military past, and he envisaged a military future as a way, perhaps the only way, he could help support his family. The d'Arblays had been scraping by entirely on his wife's literary earnings. Like Jean Baptiste, d'Arblay found financial dependence in exile, year after year, hard to bear, and so he said yes when the chance to lead a brigade to Santo Domingo was mentioned. Fanny did not want Alexandre to risk his life in the West Indies, but she understood his "military spirit of Honour, born & bred in him." She wrote Queen Charlotte, her former employer at Windsor Palace, on February 11, 1802, to try and explain why her husband was going to take up arms:

> Upon the total failure of every effort M. d'Arblay could make to recover any part of his natural inheritance, he was advised by his friends to apply to the French Government for half pay, upon the claims of his former military services. He drew up a memoir, openly stating his attachment & loyalty to his late King & appealing for this justice, after undeserved proscription. His RIGHT was admitted; but he was informed it could only be made good by re-entering the army; & a proposal to that effect was sent to him by Berthier, the Minister at War.⁷

Having applied to his country for back pay, Alexandre felt honor bound to serve it.

In Paris, ready to leave on the expedition for Santo Domingo, Alexandre learned he would not be going after all. Louis-Alexandre Berthier, his former army friend, had rescinded the proposal. Alexandre had made the mistake of telling him of a solemn promise he had made to Fanny: he would fight other foes of France, but he would *never* fight her compatriots, the British. Not surprisingly, the minister of war found this condition of d'Arblay's military service unacceptable. Fanny's fears proved to be well-founded. More than 20,000 members of the French expeditionary force died, in large part due to yellow fever.

The Peace of Amiens

A month after Harriet wrote Madam d'Arblay from Watford, she was still in that town, north and west of London in Hertfordshire. She was staying in a house with several Frenchmen. One she loved, Jean Baptiste; one she admired, Alexandre d'Arblay; and some were their friends, "nos camarades d'infortune," as Jean Baptiste had called his fellow French exiles.[8] Fanny was back at Camilla Cottage, preparing it for new tenants.

After nine years, eleven months, and five days (April 20, 1792 to March 25, 1802), the French Revolutionary Wars ended. In the French town of Amiens, a representative of Britain (First Marquess Cornwallis) and a representative of France (Napoleon's brother Joseph Bonaparte)—as well as representatives of Spain and the Batavian Republic (the Netherlands)—signed "A Definitive Treaty of Peace."

Throughout Britain, church bells rang. Mail coaches, decorated with sprays of laurel and British flags, raced from town to town sounding their horns. One such coach rattled through the streets of Watford. Harriet and Jean Baptiste's grandson Charles tells the story:

> The postmaster was the first to receive the joyful tidings, and wishing to have the pleasure of communicating the intelligence in person to my grandfather, he went to the home where the whole family were assembled, together with some French gentlemen, amongst them M. d'Arblay.... Deep was the impression produced on all by the reading of the official announcement of the blessings of peace—to be alas! of short duration. M. d'Arblay was so moved that he went down on his knees and thanked the Author of Every Good Gift.[9]

Harriet may have jumped for joy. The war, over at last. She remembered all she had been through. Her detention at Dunkirk, accused of being a British spy. Her many illegal trips to France to be with Jean Baptiste. She did not regret her marriage, but it had involved constant travel, unwanted separations, and years of uncertainty.

After the announcement of the peace, Alexandre went back to Paris to assume an administrative post in the French Ministry of the Interior—a desk job related to buildings, particularly prisons. Fanny and Alex followed in the spring to begin their new life together. Alexandre had long been exiled in her country and now it was her turn to live in his. As Fanny wrote her husband before her departure in the spring of 1802, "The more I reflect, the more I feel I can know no *happiness* but yours!--*misery* I may taste in many shapes; but *Happiness & you* are linked, for me, inseparably."[10]

Jean Baptiste also left England after the Peace of Amiens was announced. In Paris he pressed his case in the courts for restoration of his land and property. He worked his diplomatic connections and began to explore possibilities for military service. Many French Constitutionalists who had served the Bourbon king transferred their military allegiances to Napoleon, then First Consul of the republic.

The British flooded into France:

> The curious wanted to inspect the enemy's heartland, the artistic wished to see the looted treasures of Europe now in the Louvre; the sociable anticipated the ballrooms, dance halls, and two dozen theatres; the morbid sought scenes of horror in the Reign of Terror; libertines, the cocottes in the arcades of the former Palais Royale; gourmets anticipated delicate new cooking and rare wines; and men of business looked for the new, hitherto unexploited trade. Above all, Paris was again becoming a fashionable destination for the rich, and the aristocratic; it was estimated that, in that year two-thirds of the House of Lords arrived, including five dukes, three marquesses, and thirty-seven earls.[11]

Royals and common folk arrived; "idle captives of the land of fog shook their damp wings and prepared to take their flight towards the regions of pleasure and brightness."[12]

While the British people, rich and poor, rejoiced, Tories in Parliament grumbled. The terms of the treaty were too lax. In *That Sweet Enemy: Britain and France: The History of a Love-Hate Relationship*, Robert and Isabelle Tombs contend that "no agreement in British history, except that in Munich in 1938, has been so vilified and so welcome. As with Hitler at Munich, the hope was that Napoleon would be satisfied with his gains. Britain agreed to return its maritime acquisitions, including the Cape and Malta, whose inhabitants had requested British aid to expel the French. France in effect gave nothing in return."[13]

Fanny's father was aghast at the terms and wrote William Windham, the previous defense minister, to complain: "I had always seen the danger of making peace with France under her present rulers.... With all Europe at her feet, except this country; in actual possession of half Germany, the Netherlands, Switzerland, Savoy, Piedmont, Lombardy, Genoa, the Ecclesiastical States... as are Naples, Spain and Portugal as well as Holland: and all this territory and its inhabitants under the direction of such Miscreants, Regicides, Assassins, Plundererers, Jacobins, Atheists and Anarchists! –what had we to expect?"[14] Fanny's father hated the new French regime as much as the revolutionary one. Fortunately, however, his opposition to her husband had softened, and he did not direct these epithets at Alexandre.

War Resumes

On May 18, 1803, just fourteen months after the peace treaty was signed, the war between England and France resumed. The continuation of the war had disastrous consequences for Madam d'Arblay. She would become stranded in France, unable to visit her ailing father, for more than ten years. In August 1802, Napoleon was elected Consul for Life by a massive majority. He had direct control of the military. Although not called a king, he had more power than any Bourbon monarch, and cleverly "steered his way between the republicans and the royalists, offering concessions, promising concessions, promising favors, and flattering everyone...."[15]

During the Napoleonic Wars, Harriet's loyalties remained divided between her father, who wanted her to stay in England, safe and near him, and the husband she loved, who preferred to live in his native country. She traveled constantly, endured loneliness, and bravely faced illness. Harriet became ill in Paris, where Madam d'Arblay came to her rescue, and Cornelia Boinville became ill in London. As in past crises, Harriet had to act decisively—and independently.

Doctors recommended that Cornelia recuperate in a warm climate, Lisbon. Harriet, Cornelia, and Alfred left Plymouth and sailed to Nantes, a French city on the Loire River, where Jean Baptiste met them. At this anxious time, Harriet had the comfort of his reassuring presence, but the reunion was, by necessity, brief. Cornelia was ill. Harriet and Jean Baptiste made plans to meet later in Paris, when their daughter recovered. With that hope in mind, the couple parted. Harriet traveled on with the children to Lisbon. Cornelia regained her strength, and, as planned, the family was reunited with Jean Baptiste in Paris, a city Harriet loved. This happy reunion was abruptly cut short. She learned her father had died, and she hurried back to England. Once again, she and her husband had to part. Harriet's war was one of unwelcome surprises and fits and starts.[16]

The death of John Collins marked the start of a new phase of Harriet's life in London. Her friendship with the now famous author William Godwin began to flourish in 1809. Her circle grew to include Godwin and Mary Wollstonecraft's daughter Mary, the future author of *Frankenstein,* and Percy Bysshe Shelley, a young man with radical ideas and a way with words. Harriet's friendship with Shelley in the second decade of the 1800s became one of the most important in her life and his.

PART II
Life in London

Chapter 8

With the Proponent of Political Justice, William Godwin, 1809–1811

> *He blazed as a sun in the firmament of reputation; no one was more talked of, more looked up to, more sought after, and wherever liberty, truth, justice was the theme, his name was not far off.... No work in our time gave such a blow to the philosophical mind of the country as the celebrated* Enquiry Concerning Political Justice.
> —William Hazlitt on William Godwin, The Spirit of the Age, Or Contemporary Portraits[1]

H. Boinville visits, William Godwin wrote after Harriet called on him August 8, 1809. He was fifty-three. Between that date and 1827, the year she moved to Paris, they met an astonishing seventy-two times. He was one of her closest friends in London. Thanks to Godwin's diary, a terse record he meticulously kept of the people he saw and what he did, a picture comes into focus of Harriet the sociable Londoner in her thirties.[2] No longer crossing seas, she crosses streets—from her home in the Pimlico district of London to Godwin on Skinner Street.

Harriet first heard of Godwin as a child of eleven, when his friend James Marshall made the long sea voyage to St. Vincent to meet with her father. In 1784 Marshall tried to persuade John Collins to fund Godwin's writings. Harriet's father declined to finance the work of this unknown young writer, but the close ties between Harriet's family and Godwin's family continued.

Not until 1793 did Godwin write the 835-page treatise that made him famous, *An Enquiry Concerning Political Justice and Its Influence on Morals and Happiness*. The author wrestled with big ideas: justice, morals, and happiness. He envisioned the regeneration of society, not by government but by individuals. "If it could be proved that a sound political institution was of all others the most powerful engine for promoting individual good," he wrote, "or on the other hand that an erroneous and corrupt government was the most formidable adversary to the improvement of the species, it would follow that politics was the first and foremost subject of human investigation."[3]

Politics interested Harriet intensely. She had strong opinions about events going on in Britain and freely expressed them, both at Godwin's house and her own. Harriet took her duties as a wife and mother seriously. In this respect she conformed to the prevailing norms of how a woman should behave. But she was unconventional in the close attention she paid to developments outside the domestic sphere.

Harriet's Inheritance

Harriet may have loaned Godwin money. The diary shows that when Harriet and Godwin conferred, just the two of them, a lawyer or bookkeeper was sometimes present. Many of his relationships frayed and ripped over money. He had the tendency to shake a prospective benefactor like a fierce terrier, determined to wrest away a bone. Harriet and Godwin may have had financial interactions, but their warm rapport lasted.

Harriet's wealth came from the sugar estate that John Collins had once owned in the British island colony of St. Vincent. Her father sold this property at some time before 1806. (Slavery was abolished in Britain in 1807. Not until 1834, when the Abolition of Slavery Act of 1833 took effect, was slavery outlawed in British colonies.) The terms of her father's will were specified (or proved, to use the legal language of the day) on March 15, 1806. Collins is identified as a retired planter of Berners Street and a signatory of the 1783 address to George III by absentee owners and merchants. This legal document makes no mention of property in St. Vincent.[4]

After her father died in 1808, Harriet and her siblings received the money specified in 1806. Harriet received an annuity of 200 pounds per year, and 5,000 pounds for her children, Cornelia and Alfred, at her death. This sum was more than enough to live on.

Consider the inheritance of Dorothy Wordsworth. When her father died, she and her four brothers each received about 24 pounds a year. At that time, the minimum for living was about sixty-five pounds a year.[5]

Harriet's brother Alfred suffered from mental illness and is referred to in the will as my unfortunate son. Collins bequeathed him 500 pounds per year. Harriet's sister (Cornelia Newton, wife of John Newton of Grosvenor Place) received a generous 16,000 pounds in trust. Perhaps Harriet's choice of Jean Baptiste, against her father's wishes, explains why he left her less money than her sister. In 1808, Harriet and Jean Baptiste, and their children, sued her sister and brother-in-law and their children in London's Court of Chancery, a court made famous by Charles Dickens in *Bleak House*. At issue was how a trust of 200 pounds a year established for Harriet by her paternal grandmother (Anna Collins) was handled in her father's estate. While Collins was alive he managed this trust. After he died, Harriet expected to have access to the principal of the trust, but she received only the interest. The outcome of Harriet's suit against her sister and brother-in-law is not known, but the truly remarkable truth is that Harriet maintained very cordial relations with Cornelia and John Frank Newton until their deaths, and later with their children.

In his thorough and insightful biography of Godwin, Peter Marshall explains an important point about Godwin's unconventional view of property (money):

> Godwin believed that property is a trust which should be distributed according to need. He lent to those worse off when he could, and expected others to do the same. He may have been more on the receiving than the giving end, but this was the result of having a large family and an unsteady business rather than personal profligacy.[6]

The son of a Trinitarian minister and one of twelve children, Godwin did not inherit any wealth. A disciplined scholar, he stayed at his desk reading and writing hour after hour. He was a frugal person of simple tastes—and habitually broke.

Godwin and Mary Wollstonecraft

Harriet never met Godwin's first wife, Mary Wollstonecraft (1759-1797), but the extraordinary daughter they had together, Mary Godwin, became a member of Harriet's circle in London when she was a pre-teen and in Paris when she was an adult. Mary Wollstonecraft's determination and achievements are well presented in this portrait of her by Peter Marshall:

> A self-taught farmer's daughter, she had decided at the age of fifteen never to marry for interested motives or to endure a life of dependence. Consequently, she was obliged to work at different times as a lady's companion, school-teacher, governess and even seamstress. Her ambition was to be the first woman to achieve economic independence through writing, and with the help of the publisher Joseph Johnson she eventually became novelist, historian, essayist, reviewer, translator, and philosopher.[7]

Wollstonecraft and Godwin met for the first time in 1791. They both attended a goodbye dinner for Thomas Paine, who was about to leave London for Paris, where he had a seat as a delegate to the French Revolutionary Convention. Godwin was eager to talk to Paine and became annoyed by Wollstonecraft, whom he thought monopolized the attention of the guest of honor. Despite this inauspicious first meeting, Wollstonecraft decided to renew her acquaintance with Godwin in 1796. By then they each had written their masterpieces: *An Enquiry Concerning Political Justice* (1793) and *A Vindication of the Rights of Woman* (1792).

On April 14th Wollstonecraft called on Godwin at his house on Chalton Street. Uninvited and unchaperoned, she breached eighteenth-century proprieties by knocking on his door. A stunning woman, thirty-six years of age, stood on the doorstep, "her face fuller and softer than he remembered but with the same large brown eyes and striking mass of auburn hair worn short, unpowdered, and falling carelessly over her left brow. Wollstonecraft saw a stocky, energetic, balding man whose eyes sparkled behind round gold spectacles."[8]

They became lovers, an event noted in Godwin's diary. August 21, 1796: chez moi toute (at my house, everything). The celibate Godwin experienced passion and profound happiness in her company. He also welcomed into his life Wollstonecraft's two-year-old daughter Fanny, the result of an unhappy affair with an American named Gilbert Imlay.

When Wollstonecraft became pregnant with Godwin's child, the couple discussed what to do. They each had written disparagingly about the institution of marriage in the past, but now they wanted to marry. Godwin's best friend, James Marshall, witnessed their vows in London's St. Pancras Church on March 31, 1797.[9]

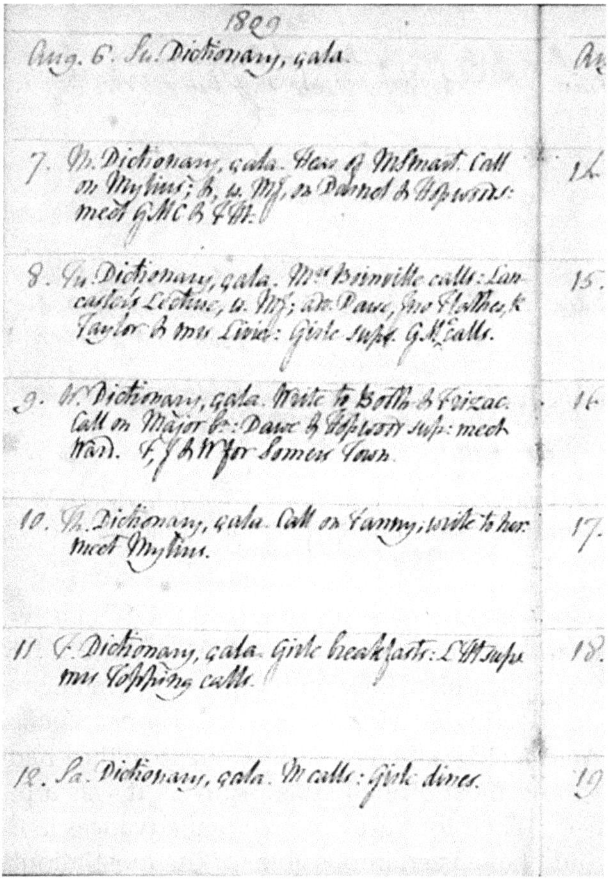

Figure 8.1. "Mrs. Boinville calls," William Godwin's diary, August 8, 1809 (numbered 8).

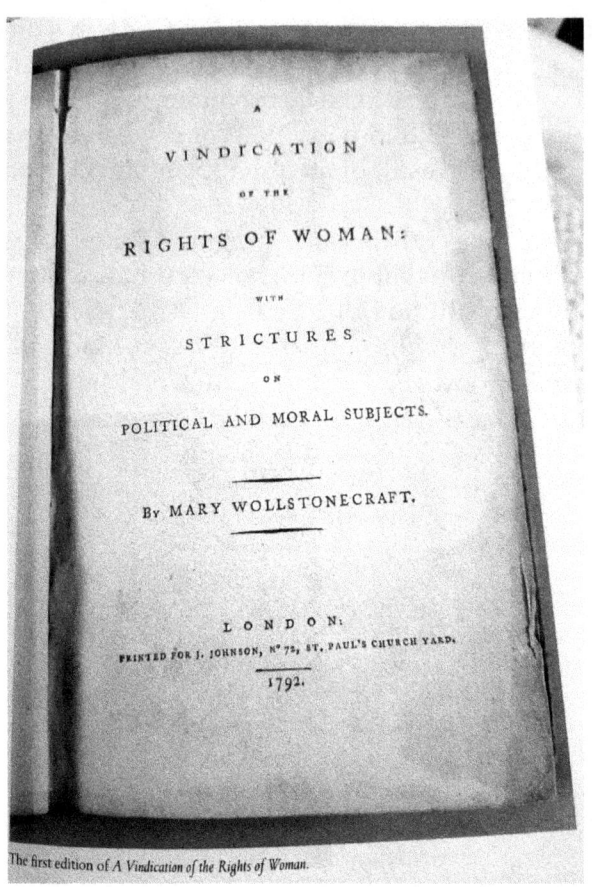

Figure 8.2. *A Vindication of the Rights of Woman* by Mary Wollstonecraft, first edition printed in London in 1792 for J. Johnson, No. 72, St. Paul's Church Yard.

Mary Godwin was born on August 30, 1797. Eleven days later the tiny infant's mother was dead. Wollstonecraft died from childbirth complications. Raw with grief, Godwin began to write a tribute to his dead wife: *Memoirs of the Author of a Vindication of the Rights of Woman* (1798).[10] He described the love they had shared as "the purest and most refined style of love." It was a partnership, he explained. "Their love grew with equal advances in the mind of each. It would have been impossible for the most minute observer to have said who was before, and who was after.... It was friendship melting into love."[11]

Godwin praised Wollstonecraft's literary accomplishments. He also revealed personal details: that she had a child out of wedlock, that she attempted suicide after Imlay deserted her. In the Preface, Godwin tried to explain why he revealed so much: "The more fully we are presented with the picture and the story of such persons as the subject of the following narrative, the more generally shall we feel in ourselves an attachment to their fate and a sympathy in their excellencies." Readers, however, did not focus on Wollstonecraft's excellencies.

Progressives, who revered Wollstonecraft for her championship of women, slammed the memoir as a betrayal of their idol.[12] The Conservative *Anti-Jacobin Review* was outraged: "This account of his wife's adventures as a kept mistress … informs the public that she was concubine to himself before she was his wife."[13] Godwin had hoped his book would be a lasting tribute to his beloved wife. Instead, it damaged her reputation and his. It also irreparably harmed Wollstonecraft's biological daughters, Fanny Imlay Godwin and Mary Godwin.

Godwin and Mary Jane Clairmont

One May evening in 1801 the forty-five-year-old widower was sitting on his balcony when a plump, smiling woman waved from a window in the building next door and called out, "Is it possible that I behold the immortal Godwin?"[14] She knew perfectly well who he was. Her flattering approach had the desired effect. Godwin became acquainted with the feminine and flirtatious Mary Jane Clairmont. Three weeks later the couple brought the children together. Fanny, age seven, and Mary, age three, met Charles, age five, and Clara Mary Jane (Jane for short), age three.

Godwin's neighbor had introduced herself as the widow Mrs. Clairmont, but, as Janet Todd explains,

> she was in fact Miss Mary Jane Vial and her two children were illegitimate, with different fathers. More circumspect than her predecessor [Mary Wollstonecraft], she had not allowed the circumstance to be generally known—and possibly Godwin was unaware of the unconventional parentage

of the children—but it did mean that, when she too became pregnant, and wanted marriage, she had to marry twice, once for public consumption as the widow Clairmont and an hour later for legal purposes as what she was: the spinster Mary Jane Vial.[15]

Mary Jane miscarried. Godwin was fond of his wife, although many of his friends were not, and rejoiced when a son was born, William Jr., in 1803. Hoping to pay their mounting bills, the couple created a publishing company called the Juvenile Library, which developed and sold children's books.[16] The family—and the book business—moved to 41 Skinner Street, a tall corner house with five stories and large bay windows perfect for displaying books on the ground level.[17] In addition to managing the bustling household, Mary Jane wrote publications for sale, met with customers, and reached out to prospective buyers. With her excellent French, she was able to form useful ties with the French émigré community. Godwin's literate and hard-working wife lost her temper easily. She also favored her biological children. Mary Godwin detested her stepmother, the usurper of her father's affections.

The looks and the temperament of the three girls differed greatly. Fanny, the oldest, tried to obey her mercurial stepmother and to be a peacemaker. She was plain in appearance, modest, and the least assertive about her own needs. Mary, a pale-skinned and fair-haired beauty, was serious and studious. Jane had flashing dark eyes, dark hair, and a flamboyant personality.

Mrs. Boinville on Skinner Street

Cornelia, fourteen in 1809, often accompanied her mother to Skinner Street. She was about the same age as Fanny and about two years older than Mary and Jane. With Mrs. Godwin snapping orders to her daughters, do this and do that, and Mary glaring at her stepmother with undisguised disdain, the presence of Mrs. Boinville, a calm and self-controlled adult, must have been welcome. In her well-researched and readable biography of Mary Godwin, Miranda Seymour speculates about how the three girls viewed Mrs. Boinville:

Perhaps Mary, Jane, and Fanny rather envied Cornelia a glamorous mother, who looked remarkably young, spoke French and Italian as easily as English and flaunted her views by tying a broad red sash around her slender waist. It must have been hard not to draw unfavorable comparisons with dumpy Mrs. Godwin in her green tinted spectacles and drab black velvet gown.[18]

A beauty by all accounts, Harriet in her late thirties still wore the red sash she had donned in 1789 at the beginning of the French Revolution. She wore it proudly, a way to demonstrate her republican ideals and her solidarity with her French husband as the war with France dragged on.

No portrait of Harriet at this age exists. Did she rouge her cheeks, a custom Mary Wollstonecraft had despised? Did she wear, like Madam d'Arblay, high hats? Harriet's contemporary Jane Austen commented on petticoats and headgear: "I am amused by the present style of female dress—the coloured petticoats and … enormous bonnets upon the full stretch, are quite entertaining." Harriet may have squeezed into tight corsets or preferred roomy gowns made popular by Rousseau's advocacy of loose clothing, but one thing is certain: ladies' fashions were not foremost in her inquiring mind. Many who knew her commented on her lack of vanity and gracious manners.

With Godwin and his interesting and intellectual guests, each one mentioned in his diary, Harriet had lots to talk about. Wars were fought across the globe: the Napoleonic Wars (1803-1815), the Anglo-Russian War (1807-1812), the Anglo-Swedish War (1810-1812), and the Peninsular War (1808-1814). In 1810, riots broke out in London. A member of Parliament who called for reform, Sir Francis Burdett, was charged with libel and imprisoned. King George III demonstrated symptoms of mania and was declared mad. His son assumed royal functions. "The Prince Regent upheld his father's Toryism, which favored continued war with France, while opposing Catholic emancipation and parliamentary reform. He was also a gambler, womanizer, begetter of bastards, and fat," writes Eric G. Wilson in a biography of Charles Lamb. The Triumph of the Whale, Lamb's political poem, did not land him in jail, the fate of Leigh Hunt for his libelous remarks about George IV.[19]

In the 1790s Godwin had attended the trial of Thomas Holcroft, imprisoned for his support of the French Revolution. Harriet met Holcroft's widow in 1810. Louisa Mercier Holcroft was French, and Harriet's fluency in French may have been why she was invited to that dinner. That same year she dined at Skinner Street with Henry Crabb Robinson, a notable barrister, journalist, traveler, literary socialite, and diarist.[20] He became one of the founders of London University.

Charles Lamb and his older sister Mary were among the learned and talented writers Harriet met at Godwin's table. Their *Tales from Shakespeare*, sold by the Godwins in their Juvenile Library, remain popular today. In August 1810 Mary Lamb had one of her recurring breakdowns and returned to the Hoxton House asylum. Her first manic episode had occurred a decade earlier, a day of horrors, when Mary killed their mother with a kitchen knife. Because of her brother's vigilant care, Mary was sometimes able to live at home with him. Harriet had a brother who demonstrated dangerous and erratic behavior—the unfortunate son mentioned in John Collins's will. On March 21, 1811, Harriet dined with the poet, lecturer, and sparkling conversationalist Samuel Taylor Coleridge.

Because of the terseness of Godwin's diary—names of people and places—the conversations on Skinner Street and Harriet's contributions to them are silent, but the seventy-two mentions of her name speak loudly of their friendship. Harriet looked up to Godwin, nineteen years older than she. Influenced by Jean-Jacques Rousseau and the French Enlightenment, Godwin was a rationalist and humanist. In his memoir, Harriet's grandson Charles, a minister, criticizes the false philosophy of the Enlightenment, but praises his grandmother for how she lived: "I have often heard her call herself *une enfant de la Révolution*. With this claim she had also unfortunately accepted the principles of the false philosophers of the age, but her general conduct, unbounded generosity, devotedness of character, and unfeigned modesty of nature, might well have put many professing Christians to the blush."[21]

Chapter 9

Harriet's Husband Rescues Madam d'Arblay, 1810–1812

In the year 1810, when I had been separated from my dear Father, & dear Country, & Native friends, for 8 years, my desire to again see them became so anxiously impatient, that my tenderest companion proposed my passing over to England alone, to spend a month, or two at Chelsea. [Many] Females at that period, & amongst them the young Duchesse de Duras, had contrived to procure passports for a short similar excursion; though no Male was permitted, under any pretence, to quit France, save with the Army.
—Frances Burney d'Arblay's recollection of events of 1810[1]

While Harriet was in London, going back and forth to William Godwin's home and meeting writers and radicals, her friend Frances Burney d'Arblay was in Paris. She had left England after the announcement of the Peace of Amiens, but when war with France resumed fourteen months later, she became stranded in her husband's native country. Her happiness with him and their son Alex did not assuage her longing to see her father, Dr. Charles Burney, and siblings again. With each passing year, she missed her family more. Her husband, her "tenderest companion," encouraged her to attempt a Channel crossing for a visit in 1810.

"There are few events of my life that I more regret not having committed to paper while they were fresher in my Memory, than my Police-Adventure at Dunkirk," Frances Burney d'Arblay wrote many years later. That she did not put pen to paper at the time is understandable, considering the dangers and uncertainties. Her record of her life (whether writing about recent events or events from her distant past) little resembled William Godwin's diary—a terse, emotion-stripped list of names of people and places. Her words skip along, page after page, as she describes in colorful detail conversations, characters, settings, and feelings. She possessed an exceptional memory, and "there was some element of hindsight at work in almost all her autobiographical writing," notes Burney biographer Claire Harman.[2]

By 1810 Napoleon had gained control of much of western Europe, including Spain, northern Italy, and large parts of Germany. Paris had become, in effect, the capital of Europe, as well as the capital of Napoleon's empire. When not planning and executing military campaigns, Napoleon directed his tremendous energy to the improvement of Paris. His domestic ambitions produced new roads, bridges, and monuments, including the Arc de Triomphe.

Napoleon's focus on Paris resulted in strict security measures. In her remembrance of 1810, Madam d'Arblay described herself as "a person known to have lived a life the most inoffensive to government & perfectly free from all species of political intrigue." She explained that when Napoleon was away from Paris, police enforcement of travel restrictions eased, and she managed to obtain a passport. She could not recall the destination on the passport, but "certainly not for England," enemy territory.

In his letter of September 24, 1793, to his compatriot Alexandre d'Arblay, Jean Baptiste concluded: "Adieu mon cher bon et ancien ami. Comptes bien à jamais sur moi," which is to say, "Goodbye my dear old friend. You can always count on me."[3] In 1810 he was as good as his word. Alexandre and Fanny both had reason to rely on him, their trustworthy neighbor in Paris. Once he had rescued Harriet at Dunkirk, when she was detained as a British spy. In 1810 Jean Baptiste came to the rescue of Madam d'Arblay. With characteristic flair, she tells the story of what happened:

> ... I prepared, quietly & secretly for my expedition, while my generous Mate employed all his little leisure in discovering where & how I might embark: when, one morning, while I was bending over my trunk to press in its contents, I was abruptly broken in upon by M. de Boinville, who was in my secret, & who called upon me to stop! He had re-

ceived certain, he said, though as yet unpublished information, that a universal Embargo was laid upon every Vessel, & that not a Fishing Boat was permitted to quit the Coast.

Confounded, affrighted, Disappointed—and yet, relieved—I submitted to the blow, & obeyed the injunction. M. de Boinville then revealed to me the new political changes that occasioned this measure, which he had learned from some confiding friends in office; but which I do not touch upon, as they are now in every history of those times.[4]

Having accepted a position with the wartime government, Jean Baptiste knew what was afoot. At this time, his wife and children were back in London. Jean Baptiste's business in Paris is explained in the 1880 memoir by Harriet's grandson Charles. "During his wife's absence, he determined to accept a good position in a Commissariat department of the army, and was named Directeur des Vivres, a high and lucrative position."[5] Jean Baptiste was one of the officers responsible for provisioning Napoleon's army, which may have been how he learned about the embargo on ships leaving the coast. His timely warning—"Stop!"—saved Fanny from undertaking a fruitless trip from Paris to Dunkirk, and what could have been a prolonged and unpleasant confrontation with the constabulary on the coast.

By 1811, the French people had grown restive from the long war. Short of men and money, Napoleon was forced to cancel arrears of pay owed soldiers killed in action. Veterans' families protested, and that summer terrible storms wrecked crops, creating flour shortages. "Bread, Work, or Death" appeared on posters throughout the country. Censorship tightened.[6] While France experienced these national shocks and struggles, Madam d'Arblay experienced a personal crisis. On September 30, 1811, she faced a danger far greater than hostile policemen. At the age of fifty-nine she underwent major surgery without anesthetic in her home in Paris. She had advanced breast cancer.

"My Heart Beat Fast; I Saw All Hope Was Over"

Six months later she wrote to her sister Esther about her mastectomy, a day of horror. In an essay on Frances Burney d'Arblay's journals and letters, John Wiltshire notes the letter's importance as an early example of pathography, "the story of an illness or medical intervention from the patient's viewpoint." Esther's letter, sent to England, "was copied for safekeeping in France, a communication simultaneously recognised as a piece of history."[7]

Dr. Baron Larrey, Napoleon's personal physician, performed the operation. His renowned surgical skills had been honed during battlefield amputations. On the dreaded day, the patient spared her husband, "her too sympathizing partner," from witnessing her ordeal. She had hoped to have female friends by her side, among them "Mademoiselle de Chastel belle soeur de Madame de Boinville." Fanny was friends with Harriet's sister-in-law and had wanted her to be there.[8]

The patient waited on the elevated table. "I assumed the best spirits in my power, *to meet the coming blow.*" When it was time, "my heart beat fast; I saw all hope was over." Seven men, draped in black, solemnly approached: Dr. Larrey and six assistants. Seven hours later, the operation ended. The patient survived.

Figure 9.1. Portrait of Frances Burney. Mezzotint by Charles Turner after Edward Francisco Burney, published 16 May 1840 by Paul and Dominic Colnaghi & Co. Source: https://victorianweb.org/previctorian/burney/gallery/1.html

Frances Burney d'Arblay's father was eighty-five and ailing. Esther learned from the letter how anxious her sister was to see her father again. And she was worried her family had heard about her ordeal:

> Separated as I have now so long—long been from my dearest Father—BROTHERS—SISTERS—NIECES, & NATIVE FRIENDS, I would spare, at least their kind hearts any grief for me but what they must inevitably feel in reflecting upon the sorrow of such an absence to one so tenderly attached to all her first and for-ever so dear & regretted ties—nevertheless, if they should hear that I have been dangerously ill from any hand but my own, they might have doubts of my perfect recovery which my own can obviate. And how can I hope they will escape hearing what has reached Seville to the South, and Constantinople to the East? From both I have had messages—yet nothing could urge me to this communication till I heard that M. de Boinville had written it to his Wife, without any precaution, because in ignorance of my plan of silence.[9]

Jean Baptiste had been told about the surgery. "Without any precaution," he wrote his wife about their friend. He knew she would be concerned. There is no evidence that Harriet ever said anything to members of the Burney family or to anyone else.

Frances Burney's novels had made her famous—and skittish, as the reference to "Seville to the South and Constantinople to the East" shows. She was an intensely private person and understandably upset. To the fragile patient, it felt like the whole world now knew about her personal business.

"My Second Attempt in the Year 1812"

Madam d'Arblay recorded her memories of 1812 many years later—in 1825. She had promised her husband she would write down all that she remembered of her past for the benefit of their son—and for posterity in general. Once she was "sufficiently recovered for travelling after a dreadful Breast operation," she prepared for her second attempt to leave France. There was no time to lose. "Buonaparte was now engaging in a new War, of which the aim & intention was no less than the Conquest of the World: this menaced a severity of Conscription." Alex was seventeen. His parents, fearing he would be called to arms against England, decided he must accompany his mother back to England.[10]

Again it was difficult to obtain passports. Monsieur de Saulnier was the head of the police in charge of issuing them. Upon learning that he admired her first novel, *Evelina, or The History of a Young Lady's Entrance into the World*, she decided to improve her chances. "I could do nothing more acceptable to M. de Saulnier than to present him with a Copy of *Evelina*, in English, for his little Daughter, who was then studying that language." By the time she applied for passports, "Buonaparte had left Paris to proceed toward the scene of his next destined Enterprise; & he was, I believe, already at Dresden when my application was made." Success required subterfuge. "For what place, Nominally, my Passport was assigned. I do not recollect; I think, for Newfoundland; but certainly for some Coast of America. Yet every body at the Police office saw and knew that England was my object."

Napoleon and the Grande Armée were headed toward Russia when mother and son prepared to depart. "General d'Arblay, through his assiduous researches, aided by those of M. de Boinville & some others, found that a vessel was preparing to sail from Dunkirk to Dover, under American Colours." Dunkirk, the famous port on the northern coast of France, was only twenty-one miles across the Channel from England, and the captain planned to make a surreptitious stop on the English coast before continuing on to New York.

After a delay of six weeks, the *Mary Ann* set sail. Soon it was boarded by *English* officers. They took possession of the vessel, "not as French, but American booty, War having been declared against America the preceding Week." What Americans called the War of 1812 was now under way.

Greatly relieved, Madam d'Arblay and Alex sailed home under English command. She thus described her first blissful moment on shore: "I took up, on one knee, with irrepressible transport, the nearest bright pebble, to press to my lips, in grateful joy at touching again the land of my Nativity, after an absence nearly hopeless of more than 10 Years."[11]

Jean Baptiste had helped facilitate the long-awaited reunion, but his military responsibilities precluded a reunion with his own family in England. In 1812 Jean Baptiste was unable to return to London to attend his daughter Cornelia's wedding, festivities that included the Godwins' daughters Mary and Jane as well as their American friend Aaron Burr.

Chapter 10

Aaron Burr and the London Wedding of Godwin's Protégé, 1812–1813

> *Let me come to your house and enjoy your conversation once a week or once a month. Let me in your company regain my love of wisdom.*
> —Thomas Turner, Harriet's future son-in-law,
>   Letter to William Godwin[1]

> *Cornelia is married to a man whose understanding and conduct satisfies entirely her mother.*
> —Harriet Boinville

Harriet liked her daughter's fiancé and was pleased on the cold winter day, January 24, 1812, when Cornelia married Thomas Turner, William Godwin's friend and legal adviser. She knew the groom well, having welcomed him often in her home. Turner was a ubiquitous presence at Godwin's house, where on fifteen occasions between 1800 and the wedding, Harriet saw him there.

Time has erased almost all details about the wedding. Information about the nuptial ball before the wedding comes from a surprising source, the journal of Aaron Burr. He is perhaps best known today as the American statesman who killed Alexander Hamilton in a duel and became the villain of the musical *Hamilton*. Fewer people are aware that Burr admired the views of Godwin's first wife, Mary Wollstonecraft, and put in practice her views on female education.

Aaron Burr visited Godwin and his second wife, Mary Jane, in 1808 and again in 1812. He was fond of their three daughters, Fanny, Jane, and Mary. Someone who should have had a key role in the wedding festivities was absent. On March 24, 1812, England and France signed a peace alliance, but it came too late for Harriet's husband. Jean Baptiste was already traveling east with Napoleon's Grand Armée toward Russia—and his death.

"Let Me Come to Your House"

Before her marriage, Cornelia became well acquainted with Tom Turner. According to Godwin's diary, she saw him at Skinner Street on ten occasions between 1810 and 1811.[2] Godwin knew something about her husband that Cornelia may not have known: a personal crisis in Turner's distant past.

On July 4, 1803, Turner wrote to Godwin, someone he had never met:

> Mr. Godwin
> I am confident that you are a man of benevolence and therefore entreat your assistance. I totter on the brink of perdition and call on you to save me. Two years ago by reading your works I was incited to study. Assiduous and happy I advanced with rapidity in the road to Learning. Last September an intimacy took place between me and two young men whom I proudly designed to guide to knowledge and virtue. Instead of this they are dragging me to ignorance and vice. I see my danger, I lament and condemn my folly but I go on. A violent affection for one of the youths reduces me to the most abject slavery. I have absented myself from them, I have shut myself up in my study, I have had recourse to my books in which I once found felicity; my books are dumb, my study is a dungeon and absence encreases [sic] the fire that consumes my soul. I must fall or I must go mad should you in whom is my last hope deny me the support I am soliciting. Let me come to your house and enjoy your conversation once a week or once a month. Let me in your company regain my love of wisdom. There may be presumption in this request but do not I conjure you do not refuse to grant it. If you do, the blossom which you

have called forth in me will be destroyed I shall wither like a blasted tree.
Thomas Turner
At 8 o'clock this evening I shall call at your house.³

"Let me come to your house" Turner had asked, and Godwin said yes right away. The philosopher believed that "patient discussion among individuals," rather than political protests, was the best means to effect positive change in the world. As William St. Clair notes, "the door of Skinner Street was always open. If Godwin was poor in money, he was rich in wisdom, and he redistributed without stint… . Strangers who called personally during the afternoon were shown straight in; and if they came in the mornings when Godwin 'was not at home', they were advised when he would be back."⁴

Godwin took the troubled young man under his sheltering wing. The July 4, 1803, letter reveals much more than Turner's inner conflict about a homosexual passion. It shows he was familiar with Godwin's publications and had a love of learning and desire for wisdom. Godwin's protégé wanted to lead a life worthy of Godwin's good example.

Between the summer of 1803 and the fall of 1809, Turner sought Godwin's company so often that his mentor suggested he visit less frequently, which he did. The friendship was not all one way, however. Godwin genuinely enjoyed his protégé's company, and he needed his financial advice. Turner spent many hours trying to unravel the tangled thicket that was Godwin's finances.

Aaron Burr, Mary Wollstonecraft, and Female Education

Godwin's hospitality brightened the sad exile of Aaron Burr in London. The former vice president of America was friendless and practically penniless when he visited London in 1808. A man adrift, he traveled in Europe on a shoestring budget, before returning to London in 1812. Years earlier, when Burr was an up-and-coming senator from New York, he read *Vindication of the Rights of Woman* by Mary Wollstonecraft. The minute he put down the book, he wrote his wife Theodosia, praising it as "a work of genius":

> I had heard it spoken of with a coldness little calculated to excite attention. But as I read with avidity and prepossession everything written by a lady, I made haste to procure it, and spent the last night, almost the whole of it, in reading it. Be assured that your sex has in *her* an able advocate. It is, in my opinion, a work of genius. She has successfully adopted the style of Rousseau's *Emilius*; and her comment on that work, especially what relates to female education, contains more good sense than all the other criticisms upon him which I have seen put together. I promise myself much pleasure in reading it to you.⁵

Theodosia was an intelligent woman, greatly respected by her husband. The couple put in practice Wollstonecraft's views about female education with regard to their daughter, born in 1783 and named after her mother. They wanted little Theo to have "all the advantages of education and expectation the well-to-do typically afford their male children but deny their girls."⁶

Wollstonecraft had criticized what girls were taught at the end of the eighteenth century. It was not very much. They learned to take care with their appearance and to acquire docile behaviors designed to attract a husband. "Not content with being pretty, they are desirous of being thought so; we see, by all their little airs," she wrote in *Vindication*. Burr was determined Theo would not be another fashion-conscious, ignorant flirt. He and Theodosia made sure she learned Latin, logic, higher mathematics, French, and other subjects. On one occasion, eager to buy Theo a book, Burr perused the offerings in a booksellers' shop: "fairy tales and such nonsense, … nothing that I could offer with pleasure to an intelligent, well-informed girl of nine years old." To his wife he made clear his high expectations for their beloved daughter:

> If I could foresee that Theo would become a *mere* fashionable woman, with all the attendant frivolity and vacuity of mind, adorned with whatever grace and allurement, I would earnestly pray God would take her forthwith hence. But I yet hope, by her, to convince the world what neither sex appear to believe: that women have souls."⁷

In 1794, Burr's wife died of cancer at the age of thirty-nine. In *The Heartbreak of Aaron Burr*, H. W. Brands brings to life this sorrow, the first of many deaths in Burr's family. He was thirty-eight when his wife died; their daughter Theo, eleven. Burr would outlive Theo as well.

"The mother of my Theo was the best woman and finest lady I have ever known, " Burr wrote soon after her death. Theo grew up, under her father's watchful eye, married, and had a son whom she named Aaron. As an adult she continued to benefit from her father's love and high expectations.

Before the duel, Burr wrote Theo's husband, Joseph Alston:

I have called out General Hamilton, and we meet tomorrow morning. If it should be my lot to fall, yet I shall live in you and your son. I commit to you all that is most dear to me—my reputation and my daughter. Your talents and your attachment will be the guardian of the one, your kindness and your generosity of the other. Let me entreat you to stimulate and aid Theodosia in the cultivation of her mind.

Before the duel, his daughter also received a parting word: "I am indebted to you, my dearest Theodosia, for a very great portion of the happiness which I have enjoyed in this life. You have completely satisfied all that my heart and affections had hoped or even wished."[8]

After he killed Hamilton, the former vice president fled out West. In the newly acquired Louisiana Territory, he got involved in land schemes of questionable legality. He also had dealings with foreign governments that alarmed his enemies. Accused of treason, he was arrested and tried in Richmond. The whole country followed his trial. George Hay led the prosecution, supported by President Thomas Jefferson, Burr's chief political enemy. Washington Irving joined the defense team; he was a lawyer before he became a famous author. The judge in the case was James Marshall. On August 31, 1807, the grand jury found Burr not guilty.[9]

Acquitted but disgraced and besieged, Burr eluded his numerous creditors and foes and escaped to London, where William and Mary Jane Godwin befriended him. Unpopular with many of Godwin's friends because of her irascibility, Godwin's second wife got along famously with the lonely exile. Skinner Street filled with the sound of laughter, as Burr and Mrs. Godwin teased each other and bantered in French. The American guest also paid attention to Fanny, Jane, and Mary. He called the three sisters "les goddesses."[10]

The Sisters, the Ball, and the Bride

While in London, barely scraping by, Burr scribbled in his journal. It contained a trove of information about Godwin and his family and about Burr's innermost feelings. On January 22, 1812, two days before Cornelia's wedding, Burr wrote about a present he had purchased for Fanny, Jane, and Mary. He knew the sisters were very excited about attending their first London ball, and he had bought them presents:

> three pairs of beautiful stockings.... I have never given them anything, and they all love me so; and this night they all go to a great ball... So went to Godwin's with the three pairs of stockings nicely rolled up. Went directly upstairs where the children set; but F. was not there. Waited a few minutes, but she came not; then came in Madame; all hard at work. Somehow the occasion did not suit, and I came off with the three pairs of stockings in my pocket. How ridiculous![11]

At seven that evening, Burr saw "the three lasses dressed for the ball; they were extremely neat." The next evening, while on his way home, he visited the Godwins to talk over the ball. Whether Burr attended the wedding on January 24, 1812, is not known. He may only have heard about it from "les goddesses."

On her wedding day, Cornelia Pauline Eugenia Boinville looked radiant, "one of the loveliest of girls" with "a look of eternal tenderness, trust, and well-wishing." A portrait of Cornelia shows "brown ringlets, falling over her faultless forehead, her blue eyes and delicate lips announcing perfect womanly sincerity and devotion."[12] This praise appears in a 1946 biography of Percy Bysshe Shelley by Edmund Blunden. Blunden's language is overblown, but there is no doubt: Cornelia, like her mother Harriet, was a striking beauty. A year later Cornelia's looks and sweet manner would bedazzle and confound Shelley.

About a month after the wedding, Burr visited the Godwins again, and in his journal he refers to Thomas Turner, "lately married to M'lle. Boinville, niece de Madame Frank Newton."[13] Burr was familiar with the most important members of Harriet's London circle: Godwin, perhaps her closest friend in London; her daughter Cornelia; her brother-in-law, John Frank Newton; and her sister, Cornelia Newton, a beautiful woman whom Shelley would also pay attention to in 1813.

The Godwins Visit Aaron Burr

On January 28th, William and Mary Jane Godwin visited Burr in his shabby lodging: "While I was writing the last sentence, Mr. and Mrs. Godwin came in and have sat an hour. They have news for me of a declaration of war by the United States, of which, however, I do not believe a word." The War of 1812 had begun. Burr did not believe it. Perhaps he was as astonished as Frances Burney d'Arblay who knew nothing of the war when British officers took possession of her American ship in French waters near Dunkirk.

William Godwin with two of his daughters, Mary and Jane, returned to Burr's room on March 5, 1812: "Mr. Godwin with Mary and Jane came in and sat an hour. Mr. G. will undertake to sell Bayle and Morreri, and Madame Godwin The Ring Watch." Broke themselves, the Godwins sold a few books, income Burr badly needed.

Other journal entries in the winter and early spring of 1812 reveal glimpses of home life on Skinner Street and Burr's attachment to the Godwins' children. On February 15th, William Jr., age eight, "gave his weekly lecture; having heard how Coleridge and others lectur'd, he would also lecture; and one of his sisters (Mary, I think) writes a lecture, which he reads from a little pulpit which they have erected for him. He went through it with great gravity and decorum. The subject was 'the Influence of Government on the Character of the People.' After the lecture we had tea, and the girls sang and danced an hour."

The family warmed Burr, far from his own family. He journaled about his visits when he returned alone to his room. Even small things are remembered. On March 8th he commented on his tea: "Fanny, whom of all the family I trust to make my tea, gave it rather too strong last night, and I was *vigil* til past 4." On March 13th he noted an outing to a school whose progressive principles interested him: "to Godwin's, to escort Fan to Lancasters School."

In his last month in England, Burr mentioned his debt to the Godwins, but "Mr. and Mrs. Godwin would not give me their account, which must be five or six pounds, a very serious sum to them" (March 25, 1812). On the next day he journaled: "That family really does love me. Fanny, Mary, and Jane, also little William."

Before he left London, Burr asked Godwin for a copy of the portrait of Mary Wollstonecraft displayed in his home. Even after Godwin married Mary Jane, he kept John Opie's painting of his first wife in a prominent position over the fireplace on Skinner Street.[14]

Fallen Founder is the fitting title of an excellent biography of Burr by Nancy Isenberg. After explaining the pitfalls of a biographer, she calls for a radical reassessment of her subject:

> History is not a bedtime story. It is a comprehensive engagement with often obscure documents and books no longer read… all of which reflect a world view not ours. We cannot make eighteenth century men and women "familiar" by endowing them and their families with the emotions we prefer to universalize; nor should we try to equate their politics with politics we understand. But this is what popular biographers do, and as a result, everything we think we know about Aaron Burr is untrue. It is time to start over.[15]

Burr is thought of today as a womanizer and a villain. He has been rightly judged for his faults, but too seldom recognized for his accomplishments as a father, a friend, and a champion of female education.

Once Burr made disparaging comments about Thomas Turner, calling him "un fils d'un bucher" (the son of a butcher), but Harriet was delighted with her son-in-law, as this comment in a letter to Madam d'Arblay makes clear: "Cornelia is married to a man whose understanding and conduct satisfies entirely her mother." Then she added the good news that Cornelia "is about to present us with a little one."[16]

Chapter 10

Harriet became a proud grandmother with the birth of Oswald Turner. Holding the baby, hearing him coo, seeing his first smiles distracted her from her fears about Jean Baptiste, far away and in danger with Napoleon's army. Cornelia, a teenager with a new baby, often stayed with her mother at Harriet's country home at Bracknell, twenty-seven miles from London in Berkshire. Thomas Turner owned a house in the village of Binfield, not far from the law courts and only two miles from Bracknell. Percy Bysshe Shelley entered Harriet's life at this time, a friendship that flourished at Bracknell and in London. When they met, he had not yet achieved fame, but he quickly interested her and was welcomed into her illustrious circle.

Chapter 11

Percy Bysshe Shelley Meets "Miamuna" Spring 1813

>He found a woman in the cave,
>A Solitary woman,
>Who by the fire was spinning,
>And singing as she spun.
>The pineboughs were cheerfully blazing,
>And her face was bright as the flame;
>Her face was as a Damsel's face,
>And yet her hair was gray.
>*Thalaba the Destroyer* (1801)
>—Robert Southey

Percy Bysshe Shelley met Harriet in the spring of 1813. He was twenty; she was forty. He called his new friend by a special name, "Miamuna," the name of the lonely spinner in the Robert Southey poem *Thalaba the Destroyer*. It was her face, rosy and fresh like a damsel's, that made Shelley think she looked like the spinner in the poem. Another friend of Harriet's, Thomas Love Peacock, described her as "a young-looking woman for her age" with hair "white as snow."[1] Worry about Jean Baptiste, gone for many months, had prematurely whitened her locks. One Shelley scholar, James Bieri, has described Harriet as "startlingly attractive." Across her dress, she wore a bright red sash, a symbol of solidarity with her French husband and her unwavering belief in the republican ideals of the French Revolution.[2]

Shelley noticed Harriet's beauty, but he soon became aware of her intelligence and charm. In *The Young Shelley: Genesis of a Radical*, Kenneth Neill Cameron correctly notes that "through Mrs. Boinville and the circle centered around her, Shelley made his first living contact with the traditions of the French Revolution.... It was his first introduction to a society of intellectual radicalism, a society presided over by a lady of intelligence and charms."[3]

Shelley also met Harriet's sister and brother-in-law, Cornelia and John Frank Newton. As Cameron explains, "It was apparently through Mrs. Boinville that William Godwin met the Newtons. And it was Godwin's friendship with the Newtons that led to Shelley meeting them."[4] Influenced by Harriet and her circle, Shelley became a vegetarian.

The Captivating "Mrs. B"

Harriet—or "Mrs. B" as he called her—captivated Shelley, just as Miamuna captivated the hero in Southey's poem. She was completely unlike other women he had known. "I had been unaccustomed to the mildness, the intelligence, the delicacy of a cultivated female," he wrote his friend Thomas Jefferson Hogg.[5]

Harriet found Shelley fascinating. He said exactly what he felt and thought. He seemed electrified by the thoughts swirling around in his brain. Shelley had the ability to transfuse excitement into the lives of all around him. Harriet felt his magnetic pull.[6]

Born in 1792, the son of a squire, Shelley was a member of Britain's privileged class. He had an easygoing way about him. His manners were gracious. He was unassuming and friendly, not conceited or proud. Harriet noticed these appealing qualities. A young military officer named Captain Kennedy also was impressed by Shelley's manners when they met on the grounds of Field Place, the Shelley family estate in Sussex. "There was an earnestness in his manner and such perfect gentleness of breeding and freedom from everything artificial as charmed everyone," Kennedy later remembered.[7]

The prospective heir of Field Place and Captain Kennedy met under unusual circumstances. Shelley wanted to return home to see his mother and sisters, but he had been banned from the house by his father. Sir Timothy had lost patience with his son's radical opinions and virulent criticisms of his way of life in Sussex. One day, walking on the grounds of Field Place, Shelley approached

Kennedy and asked politely if he could borrow his cap and jacket. The officer handed over the items, and Shelley, in disguise, was able to slip undetected into the ancestral mansion.

Shelley's Earlier Relationships with Women

"The contemplation of female excellence is the favorite food of my imagination," Shelley correctly said of himself.[8] Before he met Mrs. Boinville, three women had fed that active imagination: Harriet Grove, his first crush; Elizabeth Hitchener, an intellectual schoolteacher; and Harriet Westbrook, the girl he would marry.

When he was seventeen, a bookish student at Eton, Shelley met Harriet Grove. She lived in the same county and came from the same social class. He took her to dinners and dances. They walked in the moonlight and wrote each other letters. He discussed with her the books he was reading and sent her unromantic letters, "packed out with Shelley's strange mixture of grim, gothic fantasies and poems, and lumps of ill-digested Condorcet and Lucretius."[9] The relationship soon came to an end. After reading William Godwin's *Political Justice*, Shelley became "fully convinced that formal marriage was an evil social institution," views the conventional Miss Grove did not share.[10]

Elizabeth Hitchener was more than ten years older than Shelley and "the daughter of a smuggler turned publican."[11] She rose above her class, an unusual accomplishment in England's stratified society. Intelligent and hard-working, Elizabeth became the head of a school at Hurstpierpoint where Shelley's uncle, Captain Pilfold, sent his daughter. Shelley and Elizabeth shared a consuming interest in ideas. He called her "sister of my soul" and in 1810 and 1811 wrote her more than forty fevered letters.

The schoolteacher from a lower social class sympathized with Shelley's tirades against "aristocratical *insipidity*."[12] He told her he hated "more and more the existing establishment of every kind. I gasp when I think of plate & balls & tables & kings." Shelley had observed the misery of workers in the manufacturing North, "reduced to starvation."[13] The son of a Sussex squire was evolving into a radical activist.

Shelley's interest in Elizabeth Hitchener overlapped with his interest in Harriet Westbrook, a fifteen-year-old who attended the same school as his sisters. Like many adolescents, this Harriet was miserable at home and at school. "My little friend Harriet W is gone to her prison house," Shelley wrote Hogg, referring to her school, Miss Fennings in Clapham. Mr. Westbrook "has persecuted her in the most horrible way & and endeavors to compel her to go to school. She asked my advice: resistance was the answer."[14]

Miss Westbrook was unhappy at her school. Shelley had been expelled from his, Oxford University. A tract he wrote, "The Necessity of Atheism," was the reason. Like every student admitted to Oxford in 1810, Shelley had signed an oath of allegiance to the Church of England. Shelley and Hogg blanketed the campus and town with the inflammatory pamphlet.

Banned by his conservative father from Field Place and kicked out of Oxford, the unapologetic teenager made matters worse by writing his father's lawyer about money he expected to inherit. Shelley announced he would accept an annuity of 2,000 pounds, under certain conditions, but he intended to resign his claim to his inheritance. This renunciation had no legal effect. He had not yet reached twenty-one. His brash declaration "accorded with his egalitarian principles, and besides those, he had little else left."[15]

Shelley kept thinking about the lovely Harriet Westbrook, a modest and sweet girl. He and Hogg often conferred about what he should do. Shelley had a problem. He was opposed to marriage, on principle, but Harriet would not be his without being wed. In the end, Shelley decided to abandon his antimatrimonial principles, something Godwin, his idol, had done years earlier. Shelley explained his reasoning to Hogg:

> The ties of love and honor are doubtless of sufficient strength to bind congenial souls, they are doubtless indissoluble but by the brutish force of power; they are delicate and satisfactory, —yet the arguments of impracticability, and what is even worse the disproportionate sacrifice which the female is called upon to make, these arguments which you have urged in a manner immediately irre[sis]tible I cannot withstand....I am become a perfect convert to matrimony.[16]

Harriet had a sister, seventeen years older, named Eliza Westbrook. Eliza liked the idea of her sister enjoying a comfortable life as the wife of a Sussex gentleman. Their father owned a coffee house, and the Westbrooks, a respectable middle-class family, were beneath Shelley's social class.

Shelley kept Hogg apprised of courtship developments; "she would fly with me & threw herself on my protection. We shall have 200 £ a year, and when we find it run short we must live, I suppose, upon love. Gratitude and admiration all demand that I should love her *forever*."[17] Naïve and impressionable, Harriet Westbrook agreed to elope with her charming and persistent suitor. He promised her a wonderful new life at his side.

Short on cash, and not speaking to his father, Shelley borrowed twenty-five pounds from his cousin's father. On the pre-arranged day and at the chosen hour, he waited for Harriet. He paced back and forth and ran his hands through his hair, which looked wilder than usual. The morning coach to Edinburgh came and went. Had she had second thoughts? At last Harriet appeared, breathless and beautiful. She took Shelley's arm in the darkness, and they boarded the night coach on August 25, 1811. Three days later they arrived in Edinburgh.

In 1793 Harriet Collins and Jean Baptiste Boinville had eloped to Scotland because they could not marry in England without her father's consent. Similarly, Percy Bysshe Shelley and Harriet Westbrook could not legally marry in England. Obtaining a certificate of union in Scotland was easy, only a matter of paperwork. On the form that asked for profession, Shelley, who would become one of the greatest poets in the English language, scrawled "Farmer of Sussex."[18]

"I am not so frugal as could be wished"

Money quickly became a problem on Shelley's honeymoon. "I am not so frugal as could be wished," he reluctantly wrote his father and asked for 50 pounds. He said nothing about his marriage, hoping to keep it a secret. Sir Timothy, however, found out and was furious. Upon learning that his son was in Scotland with Hogg and a young woman, Sir Timothy dashed off a letter to Hogg's father to warn him of the scandal: "from one Parent to another.... God only knows what can be the End of all this Disobedience."[19]

Shelley, Hogg, and the new bride left Edinburgh and traveled on to York. A shortage of cash and other necessities prompted Shelley to write to his father again. It was a difficult letter to write. On the one hand, he wanted to reconcile with his father; on the other, he was not willing to apologize for deceiving him about his marriage. Nor was he willing to tone down his radical opinions about church and the state to appease Sir Timothy. The letter, with its mixed messages, concluded:

> Obedience is in my opinion a word which should have no existence—you regard it as necessary... . Adieu. Answer this. I wd be your aff. Dut [affectionate Dutiful] Son,
> —Percy B. Shelley[20]

His father did not answer the letter, but handed it to William Whitton, his lawyer.

As biographer Richard Holmes has noted, Shelley had a "genius for disturbance."[21] Not surprisingly, Hogg became disturbed by Harriet's beauty. Although Harriet and Hogg both objected, Shelley left them alone in York and returned to London to see Whitton in the hopes of extracting some badly needed funds. While Shelley was gone, Hogg made passes at Harriet. She rebuffed him. When Harriet later told her husband what had happened, he got angry at Hogg—not for the sexual advances but for Hogg's refusal to take into account her feelings. "Your crime," he wrote Hogg, "has been selfishness." Ignoring Harriet Shelley's happiness, Hogg pursued his own desire.[22] Over this wrong to his wife, Shelley parted company with his best friend for a year.

In York, Shelley invited Eliza Westbrook to come and stay with them. Once friends with Harriet's older sister, Shelley now found her bossy and irritating. Winter approached and the tense household felt the chill. "We are so poor as to be actually in danger of every day being deprived of the necessaries of life," Shelley wrote his cousin Tom Medwin, who once again sent money—as did Mr. Westbrook, Harriet's obliging father.

The Itinerant Shelleys

The itinerant newlyweds moved on to Keswick in the Lake District, where Shelley saw Southey, the author of *Thalaba*. From him he learned that Godwin was not dead, as he had mistakenly thought, but very much alive. Shelley and Godwin began to correspond. Harriet Shelley was not focused on poetry or philosophy. She was very worried about her husband. He walked in his sleep. He kept pistols by the bed. He suffered crippling headaches. He regularly dosed himself with laudanum, which gave him "morbid trains of fantasy, suspicion and fears."[23]

Shelley told the press he had been the victim of an assassination attempt, but some suspected the attack was a figment of Shelley's overheated imagination. To spare Elizabeth Hitchener anxiety, in case she had read about the attack in the paper, Shelley's wife wrote to her. Harriet Shelley was a considerate person, as her letter to the schoolteacher (formerly, the sister of Shelley's soul) demonstrated: "I was afraid you might hear the circumstance much more dreadful than it really was; but do not my dear Madam suffer yourself to be alarmed at it.... he is much better than he has been for some time and I hope as he gets stronger he will outgrow his nervous complaints—next week we think of going to Ireland."[24]

In Dublin, Shelley and his Irish manservant Daniel Healey disseminated political pamphlets in favor of "Catholic Emancipation" from the tyrannical British. Shelley admired Thomas Paine, whose pamphlet *Common Sense* (1776) had stirred up support for the American Revolution, and he hoped his pamphlets would spark an uprising. One was entitled *An Address to the Irish People*. Another, *Proposal for an Association of Philanthropists, who Convinced of the Inadequacy of the Moral and Political State of Ireland to Produce Benefits which are Nevertheless Attainable are Willing to Unite to Accomplish its Regeneration*. At twenty, Shelley had overblown ideas and big plans. Incredibly, he believed he could change a whole country.

Harriet Shelley feared repercussions. She confided in her Irish friend Catherine Nugent, "Percy's having made himself so busy in the cause of this poor Country, he has raised himself many enemies who would take advantage of such a time & instantly execute their vengeance upon him."[25] There was talk that the Habeas Corpus Act, which prevented unlawful imprisonment, might be suspended. Harriet feared her husband might be arrested at any minute. Godwin wrote Shelley and pleaded with him to act with more restraint.

By the end of 1812, the Shelleys had moved to Wales. Harriet Shelley hoped Sir Timothy would forgive his son and welcome them to Field Place. After all, Sir Timothy was a member of Parliament, and Percy's grandfather, Bysshe Shelley, had been a baronet. Her husband was the rightful heir of an entailed estate. As the young woman looked forward to the birth of their first child in June, she imagined aristocratic comforts that were not to be.

Queen Mab

Soon after Shelley met Mrs. Boinville in London in the spring of 1813, she became good friends with his wife as well. Shelley completed *Queen Mab: A Philosophical Poem with Notes* early in 1813. Previously he had written the pamphlets in favor of atheism and Catholic emancipation and two Gothic novellas, *Zastrozzi* (1810) and *St. Irvine; or the Rosicrucian: A Romance* (1811). Shelley considered *Queen Mab* his most important work. He was very proud of it and presented Mrs. Boinville with one of the original copies—a copy she would loan Shelley's widow twenty-six years later. (This letter of January 26, 1839, is on page 248.)

"*Queen Mab* is no less than an attempt to state the basis for an entire philosophy of life, an active and militant view of man confronting his society and his universe," wrote Holmes. Argumentative in tone, sprawling in length, and ambitious in scope, *Mab* attacked four targets: established religion; political tyranny; the destructive forces of war and commerce; and the perversion of human love.[26]

When Shelley returned to London with his wife, the police closely monitored his activities. He had tried to rally the lower classes in Ireland, and the police suspected him of fomenting rebellion in his native country. Shelley knew his arrest was a real possibility, and for safety reasons limited the first printing to 250 copies. Even fewer were actually distributed. Shelley removed any reference to where he lived, to avoid detection, and he removed the beautiful dedication to Harriet Shelley, perhaps to shield her or perhaps because of a change in heart.

© Bodleian Library, University of Oxford   Abinger Dep. c. 516/1

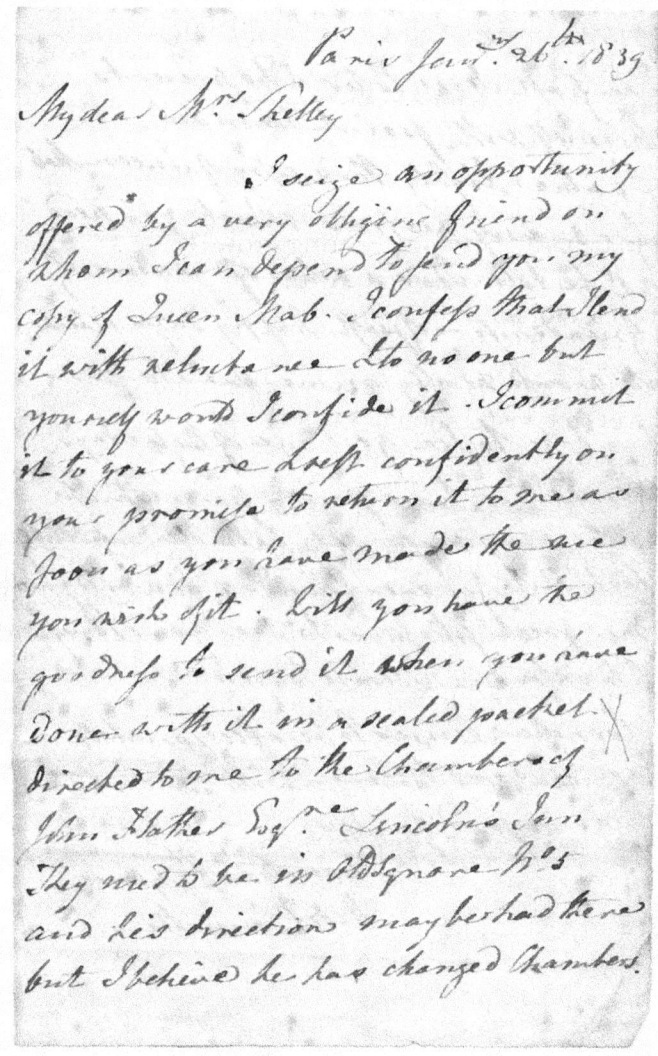

Figure 11.1. Mrs. Boinville agrees to loan Mary Shelley her own copy of *Queen Mab*; January 26, 1839, letter. Source: Bodleian Library, University of Oxford, Abinger Dep. c. 516/1.

The poet praises his wife—her eyes, her purity, her transforming love. She revived his soul and inspired his song.

> Whose is the love that gleaming through the world,
> Wards off the poisonous arrow of its scorn?
> Whose is the warm and partial praise,
> Virtues most sweet reward?
>
> Beneath whose looks did my reviving soul
> Riper in truth and virtuous daring grow?
> Whose eyes I have gazed fondly on,
> And loved mankind the more?
>
> Harriet! On thine—thou wert my purer mind;
> Thou wert the inspiration of my song;
> Thine are these early Wilding flowers,
> Tho garlanded by me.

By the spring of 1813, Shelley had reconciled with his best friend Hogg but remained estranged from his father. Shelley increasingly sought the company of Mrs. Boinville and her circle. He approved of the vegetable diet of her sister and brother-in-law and mentioned their vegetable-fed children in his Notes to *Queen Mab*.

Chapter 12

Vegetarians and Egalitarians "Return to Nature," Summer 1813

At Bracknell, Shelley was surrounded by numerous society, all in a great measure of his own opinions in relation to religion and politics, and the larger portion of them in relation to vegetable diet.
—Thomas Love Peacock, *Memoir of Percy Bysshe Shelley*[1]

In July 1813, with *Queen Mab* just published and his daughter Ianthe only a month old, Shelley decided to leave London and move near Mrs. Boinville, then residing at Bracknell in the Berkshire countryside. Thomas Jefferson Hogg and a new friend, Thomas Love Peacock, often accompanied Shelley to her home. The Boinville circle also included Harriet's sister and brother-in-law, Cornelia and John Frank Newton, and her son Alfred's future father-in-law, William Lambe, a renowned London physician.

That summer Shelley expanded his notes about diet in *Queen Mab* into a book, *A Vindication of Natural Diet*. He made this impassioned plea: "By all that is sacred in our hopes for the human race, I conjure those who love happiness and truth to give a fair trial to the vegetable system."[2] John Frank Newton's *The Return to Nature, Or; A Defense of the Vegetable Regimen* (1811) had convinced Shelley to adopt a vegetable diet. Today the International Vegetarian Union extolls Newton as one of the very first vegetarians.

Newton's Natural Program

Newton dedicated *The Return to Nature* to William Lambe, the person whose ideas about diet changed his life. Since childhood, Newton had been an "habitual invalid" who "vainly hoped for relief from drugs." After taking a scientific and empirical approach to diet, he became well. With the zeal of a recent convert, Newton appealed to his readers: "All that I petition for is a fair experiment of Dr. Lambe's system."[3] He contrasted Britain's "civilized unhealthy race" with the ancient Brahmins and their "peaceful and respectable existence." Newton found in the Latin classics "many passages which prove that living on the fruits of the earth was considered by the ancients as natural to man, and best adapted to the preservation of his health, his life, and his morals."

Newton subtitled his book *With Some Account of an Experiment Made During the Last Three or Four Years in the Author's Family*. The domestic experiment involved his wife and children and concerned the health benefits of fresh air and sunshine. In the privacy of their London home on Chester Street, Cornelia Newton spent part of every day in the nude. She basked in the sunlight with the windows open. The couple's children (eventually there were five) ran around in lightweight clothing—or none at all. Shelley was often greeted at the door of Chester Street by little naked Newtons.

Harriet's brother-in-law, the former invalid, rebutted the prevailing view that drafts were deadly:

> I will now say a few words on the state of the invalid, who would, I believe, eagerly relinquish his erroneous diet, if he could look into his frame and observe the ravages which disease is making there. Rather than contemplate the real source, rather than think of foregoing his accustomed indulgences, the unhealthy man is for ever attributing his suffering to slight and inadequate causes. He cases himself in fleecy hosiery, he lists his double doors at top and bottom; he lays cushions on his window sashes, and at length injures himself by excluding too carefully the external air from his apartment.

Newton proudly reported the results of his domestic experiment, lasting three or four years: a drastic reduction in his large family's apothecary bill to sixpence.[4]

An Estimable Society of Persons

"For some months, for some years, I was in the thick of it, for I lived much with a select and most estimable society of persons, who had returned to nature, and of course I heard much discussion on the topic of vegetable diet."[5] Shelley's friend Hogg wrote these words years later in a memoir published after Shelley's death. In the summer of 1813, Hogg was not a convert to the healthy diet served at Bracknell:

> Flesh, fowl, fish, game, never appeared, nor eggs bodily in their individual capacity, nor butter in the gross: the two latter were admitted into cookery, it is true, but as sparingly as possible, and their presence was provisional, under protest, as culinary aids not approved of, and soon to be dispensed with. The injunction extended to shell-fish..... Cheese was under the ban.... Milk and cream might not be taken up unreservedly; however, they were allowed in puddings, and to be poured sparingly into tea as an indulgence...[6]

Hogg did have a good word for the tea served by Mrs. Boinville, Mrs. Turner, and Mrs. Newton: "The ladies were never weary of the sweet courtesies of making tea and of handing it about to us graciously and gracefully." After tea, there was dinner, but not soon enough: "At some hour of the day we had dinner; but it was not much; it was irregular, unpunctual, uncomfortable, inconclusive, according to the ordinary course of proceedings in such matters, which were slightly regarded by this family."

A British gentleman who enjoyed a hearty traditional dinner, Hogg saw no reason why Mrs. Boinville offered such meager fare: "The simple fare of the poorest old woman, of the starved labourer, and his children, through a stern iron necessity, was the diet, through free will and deliberate choice of the most refined, elegant, accomplished, intellectual specimens of humanity."

Shelley, who ate and drank little, never commented on cuisine at Bracknell. He enjoyed Harriet's engaging conversation and boating, one of his favorite pastimes. A tributary stream of the Thames meandered at the end of her garden. "Bysshe went to sea upon it stealthily in one of the washing tubs of his amiable hostess, rowing, or punting his frail bark with a stick used in washing, until the bottom came out. He then freely took possession of another vessel, until the whole fleet of tubs had suffered shipwreck" On washing day it was discovered that Shelley had been "the too fearless navigator."[7]

The Empire of the Nairs

Mrs. Boinville had a fascinating friend named James Henry Lawrence, an Etonian, a writer, and a world traveler. Like her, he was born in the Caribbean in 1773 and was detained during the war in France because of his English nationality. For a time he lived among the Nairs, a caste of Hindus on the southwestern coast of India. Based on his close observation of them, he wrote an internationally acclaimed novel: *The Empire of the Nairs, or The Rights of Women. An Utopian Romance in Twelve Books*.[8] Lawrence believed British women were forced into prostitution because of discriminatory laws governing marriage and property. As the title suggests, he admired Mary Wollstonecraft, the author of *A Vindication of the Rights of Woman*.

Lawrence's utopian novel was published first in Germany, then in France, and finally in Britain in 1811. Prostitution was a skyrocketing problem in London, much worse than in France. Lawrence sympathized with victims of seduction, "poor creatures" who "force their lips into smiles when grief preys upon their hearts." The abuses married women suffered also outraged him; they, too, had few rights under British law. Lawrence became convinced that the Nairs were wiser, happier, and healthier than civilized Westerners.

In *The Godwins and The Shelleys: A Biography of a Family*, William St. Clair ridicules Harriet and her sister and brother-in-law as wacky practitioners of "nakedism" and "naturism." Referring to the philosophy of the Enlightenment, St. Clair states, "The New Philosophy had always been prey for cranks.... In the 1800s it was the Newton and Boinville families and their friends who provided the eccentricity. The wives, who were sisters, were the initial link."[9]

St. Clair considers Mrs. Boinville eccentric for several flimsy reasons. Lawrence (known as "Chevalier" Lawrence) was her friend. Her sister was sometimes nude in the privacy of her own home. Her brother-in-law, John Frank Newton, was interested in the Zodiac. In his biography, St. Clair refrains from criticizing Shelley or William Godwin for their association with Lawrence. Godwin recorded in his diary numerous meetings with Lawrence in 1813. After reading *Empire of the Nairs*, Aaron Burr also numbered among Lawrence's admiring readers.[10]

Harriet little resembled the women in the primitive culture Lawrence studied and respected, a culture where men and women had multiple sexual partners and lived free from laws governing marriage and property. Lawrence's attacks on marriage probably did not resonate with her, a married woman who stayed married to the same person all her life. On the other hand, what Lawrence had to say about British women she probably endorsed; they had no legal rights or legal autonomy and were dependent on male relatives. Harriet Boinville was a strong, self-reliant person who often made decisions without male advice. She had disobeyed her father to marry the Frenchman she loved. Against her father's wishes, she had crossed the Channel in wartime to be with Jean Baptiste. And that summer of 1813, when her husband was far away with Napoleon's army, somewhere, she did not know where, she carried on at Bracknell, pouring cups of tea with a gracious smile and an aching heart. One of the recipients of her kindness and hospitality was Harriet Shelley.

Harriet Shelley at Bracknell

In August of 1813 Harriet Westbrook Shelley turned eighteen. She and Shelley and their baby daughter Ianthe Eliza, as well as her sister Eliza Westbrook, lived near Mrs. Boinville at High Elms in Berkshire. "We are now in a house thirty miles from London merely for convenience," Mrs. Shelley wrote her friend Catherine Nugent. "How long we remain is uncertain, as I fear our necessities will oblige us to remove to a greater distance." Those "necessities" were financial:

> Mr. S is of age, but no longer heir to the immense property of his sires. They are trying to take it away, and will I am afraid succeed, as it appears there is a flaw in the drawing up of the settlement, by which they can deprive him of everything.... . Our friends the Newtons are trying to do everything in their power to serve us; but our doom is decided. You who know us may well judge of our feelings. To have all our plans set aside in this manner is a miserable thing. Not that I regret the loss, but for the sake of those I intended to benefit.[11]

On August 4, 1813, four days before Harriet Shelley wrote this letter, her husband turned twenty-one. She had hoped their finances would improve when he came of age, but this did not happen. Sir Timothy did not forgive his estranged son. As she predicted, mounting debts and angry creditors would soon force another move.

Harriet considered Mrs. Boinville a good friend and liked to visit her. At Bracknell, she kept her distance from Hogg, who had made unwanted sexual advances on her honeymoon, but she got along well with Shelley's friend Peacock, who also frequently visited Mrs. Boinville. Years later, in his posthumous memoir of Shelley, Peacock wrote about the debates he overheard. "At Bracknell, Shelley was surrounded by a numerous society, all in a great measure of his own opinions in relation to religion and politics, and the larger portion of them in relation to vegetable diet. But they wore their rue with a difference." Peacock then makes a few disparaging comments about Harriet's other guests:

> Every one of them adopting some of the articles of the faith of their general church, had each nevertheless some predominant crochet of his or her own, which left a number of open questions for earnest and not always temperate discussion. I was sometimes irreverent enough to laugh at the fervor with which opinions utterly inconducive to any practical result were battled for as matters of the highest importance to the well-being of mankind. Harriet Shelley was always ready to laugh with me, and we thereby lost caste with some of the more hot-headed of the party.[12]

Peacock's host at Bracknell was too idealistic and impractical. He was interested in parliamentary reform and the talk at Bracknell was theoretical, "inconducive to any practical result." It was also too fervent for his taste. Shelley biographer Richard Holmes refers to "the slightly rarified intellectual air of Madame Boinville's salon."[13] Hogg, however, found little that was "rarified" about the people at her gatherings. Like Peacock, he belittles her guests:

> The greater part of her associates were odious. I generally found there two or three sentimental young butchers, an eminently philosophical tinker, and several very unsophisticated medical practitioners, or medical students, all of low origin, and vulgar and offensive manners. They sighed, turned up their eyes, retailed philosophy, such as it was, and swore by William Godwin and *Political Justice*.[14]

Hogg confirms his host's enthusiasm for political justice—and he reveals his own prejudices. To make his anecdote more entertaining, he came up with a comic triumvirate (a butcher, a tinker, and a medical practitioner). Persons from those walks of life may or may not have been her guests, but the truth underlying his caricature is that Harriet extended her hospitality to persons of all social classes. They were not all well-born gentlemen.

The meritocracy in Britain was growing. The "aristocratic privilege" that Shelley benefitted from, and railed against, was lessening. Harriet Boinville welcomed these developments. The British government still feared the effects of the French Revolution, with its emphasis on equality, fraternity, and liberty. She remained steadfast. She looped a red sash over her dress in solidarity with egalitarian ideals.

Mrs. Boinville's Return to Nature

At forty, Harriet was wiser about life than the young men who returned again and again to her home: Percy Bysshe Shelley, Thomas Jefferson Hogg, and Thomas Love Peacock. In a reply to "an agreeable and welcome letter" from Hogg after one visit, she questioned, in a jocular way, his ideas about human happiness: "What you say

I maintained the other night," she could not confirm. She assured Hogg that she *did not say* "that to follow our inclinations *on all occasions* is the first and great commandment."¹⁵ What she meant was something else: "Perhaps the following precept of Champfort [sic] taken in its best sense will satisfy you and certainly comes much nearer to my meaning: Jouis et fais jouir sans faire de mal à personne voila toute la morale." Harriet liked the maxime of French writer Sébastien-Roche Nicolas Chamfort: Be happy and give happiness without hurting anyone. This is morality in a nutshell.

She tells Hogg that he should not shut his heart "against every feeling that can possibly bring with it any pain." To make her point, she describes roses:

> When I have been delighted by the beauty and fragrance of the rose I have sometimes doubted whether we could strip it of its thorns without injuring its beauty, and certainly I have never doubted whether it would be wise to renounce such beauty and fragrance because of the thorns that guard it. Alas! Yes. Joys can and do pass away, and we must lament over them for ever; but that which does not pass away is the susceptibility of pure joys; which, with a lavish hand, nature scatters everywhere around her favoured children, to whom she gives, to make amends for all their sorrows, the power of going out of themselves for pleasure.¹⁶

Instead of always following his own inclinations, Harriet suggests to Hogg, the hedonist, the pleasure seeker, that he should try something very different: going out of himself for pleasure. The fruit of unselfishness can be happiness. In her experience, "a loving Soul, bears about within itself a living spring of Affection which keeps it fresh in spite of blights from evil things & evil Men and suffers no good feeling to wither & to die."¹⁷

Shelley returned to Bracknell at the beginning of 1814. At that time he was in desperate need of Mrs. Boinville's loving soul and living spring of affection.

Chapter 13

Shelley Retreats to Harriet's Home at Bracknell, February and March 1814

> *I have been staying with Mrs. B for the last month; I have escaped, in the society of all that philosophy and friendship combine, from the dismaying solitude of myself. They have revived in my heart the expiring flame of life. I have felt myself translated to a paradise, which has nothing of mortality but its transitoriness; my heart sickens at the view of that necessity, which will quickly divide me from this happy home—for it has become my home.*
> —Percy Bysshe Shelley, Letter to Thomas Jefferson Hogg
>   March 16, 1814[1]

In February and March 1814, Percy Bysshe Shelley retreated to Mrs. Boinville's home after a physical and emotional breakdown precipitated by the painful realization that he no longer loved his wife. The sad realities of Shelley's married life clashed resoundingly with his ideal of romantic love.

Mrs. Boinville's response to Shelley at this time of crisis was patient and kind. "Seriously I think his Mind & body want rest," she wrote Hogg. "His journies [sic] after what he has never found have racked his Purse & his Tranquility. He is resolved to take a little care of the former in pity of the latter which I applaud and shall second with all my might." She understood the restlessness at the root of Shelley's character. Constant traveling and constant spending were undermining his health. As his debts mounted, so did his anxieties. Mrs. Boinville gave Shelley motherly advice and hoped he would find respite in her home. They got along extremely well. "Excuse a thousand blunders & confusion of expression," she concludes the letter. "I write talking occasionally to Shelley of twenty different subjects."[2]

In her company, Shelley found "all that philosophy and friendship combine." He felt "translated to a paradise" he wrote March 16th. Even his surroundings delighted him: "The trees, the bridge, the minutest objects have already a place in my affections." Many signs of Shelley's mental imbalance appear in this letter. To Hogg he spills every roiling emotion. The "happy home" has become "his home." He feels sick. He wants to stay at Bracknell but must leave. "My friend, you are happier than I," he says because Hogg has "the pleasures as well as the pains of sensibility," whereas he has "sunk into a premature old age of exhaustion, which renders me dead to everything, but the unenviable capacity of indulging the vanity of hope, and a terrible susceptibility to objects of disgust and hatred."[3]

Eliza Westbrook, his wife's sister, was just such an object. He could not stop obsessing about her, then a few miles away in Windsor with his wife and Ianthe:

> Eliza is still with us — not here — but will be when the infinite malice of destiny forces me to depart. It is a sight which awakens an inexpressible sensation of disgust and horror to see her caress my poor little Ianthe, in whom I may hereafter find the consolation of sympathy. I sometimes feel faint with the fatigue of checking the overflowings of my unbounded abhorrence for this miserable wretch. But she is no more than a blind and loathsome worm that cannot see to sting.[4]

At this time the extremely unattractive side of Shelley's complex nature is on shocking display. It was in the spring of 1813 that he had become captivated by Mrs. Boinville, his white-haired Miamuna. He put her on a pedestal of womanly perfection. Her married daughter stirred up much more intense feelings.

"All the Divinity of Her Mother"

Contrary to what Shelley had written Hogg, he was *not* "dead to everything" but alive to Harriet's sweet and beautiful daughter. Scholars have commented on Cornelia's age, eighteen, and her loveliness, but her pregnancy by her husband has not been mentioned, a fact revealed in Harriet's letter from Bracknell to Frances Burney d'Arblay on March 7, 1814:

> Cornelia is married to a man whose understanding and conduct satisfies entirely her mother. She's about to present us with a little one. This anxiety occupies me very much just now and will take us to Town next month for a few weeks. I trust you will then be in Town and that you will open your arms to receive us.[5]

Cornelia and Shelley spent many hours together during his stay in February and March 1814. They read Plutarch's love sonnets together and weighty prose, an essay that condemned capital punishment and torture and advocated improvements in education as a means to lower crime: Cesare Marchese di Beccaria's, "Tratto dei Delitti e delle Pene" (1764). In the letter to Hogg ranting about his sister-in-law, Shelley raved about Cornelia:

> I have begun to learn Italian again. I am reading Beccaria dei delitti e pene. His essay seems to contain some interesting remarks, though I do not think it deserves the reputation it has gained. Cornelia assists me with this language. Did I not once tell you, that I thought her cold and reserved? She is the reverse of this, as she is the reverse of anything bad. She inherits all the divinity of her mother.[6]

A personal notebook that Shelley kept at Bracknell makes it clear that he was driven wild with desire for Cornelia Turner. Shelley biographer Richard Holmes comments on the notebook and Shelley's "rather stumbling Latin dog prose." In one Latin passage that Holmes translates, the gender of the narrator cannot be determined, hence the bracketed pronouns:

> [She] pressed kisses upon my lips! Suddenly the whole world was clothed with the everlasting colours of heaven... . Out of a terrible solitude I contemplated love as if I were a prisoner, both wretched and content... . I rose up from sleep, denied all delicious desires... . [She] held me in

[her] arms in bed. I nearly died from delirium of madness and delight. Sweet lips called back the mutual kisses of life! [She] calmed my fears.[7]

Shelley copied into the notebook a favorite passage from St. Augustine's *Confessions:* "I was not yet in love, but I was in love with love itself; and I sought for something to love, since I loved loving."[8]

We do not know exactly what happened in Shelley's bedroom in Mrs. Boinville's home. Shelley biographer James Bieri mentions a torn-out page in the notebook and the fact that someone burned out words from three of the lines.[9] Mysteries remain, but the appearance of the bedroom was described by Hogg in his memoir of Shelley. He remembered one visit to Bracknell when Shelley (he called him by his middle name) was absent:

> Bysshe was not there; he was absent in London..... Why we parted; how we got to bed; why the party ever broke up, and are not sitting together in Bracknell at this hour, is a mystery which I could never unravel. Nevertheless, I found myself, somehow or other, in Bysshe's room. His clothes were scattered about; there was much to remind me of him, although I could never forget him; in particular, there were books on all sides; wherever a book could be laid, was an open book, turned down on its face to keep his place.[10]

Shelley composed eight lines of verse about Cornelia, a secret poem addressed to her that he tucked into his March 16th letter to Hogg, the messenger. Before sealing the letter, he added these words to Hogg: "This is the vision of a delirious and distempered dream, which passes away at the cold clear light of morning. Its surpassing excellence and exquisite perfections have no more reality than the colour of an autumnal sunset. Adieu!"[11]

As Holmes has astutely observed, "At Bracknell Shelley moved in a dream world, totally disillusioned with Harriet's [his wife's] love, but desperately seeking some alternative relationship."[12] In the "dewy looks" and "gentle words" of Cornelia Turner, the wayward Shelley imagined he had found it. The following fragment of verse, dated March 1814 and titled only "To—," appeared in *Alastor: Or, the Spirit of Solitude, and Other Poems by Percy Bysshe Shelley* (1886).

> Thy dewy looks sink in my breast;
> Thy gentle words stir poison there;
> Thou has disturbed the only rest
> That was the portion of despair!
> Subdued to duty's hard control,
> I could have borne my wayward lot:
> The chains that bind this ruined soul
> Had cankered then—but crushed it not.

"Subdued to Duty's Hard Control"

For a time, Mrs. Boinville was in the dark about Shelley's dangerous passion for her daughter. Eventually, however, she became enlightened; exactly when is disputed. Word traveled in her circle. Harriet Shelley, very upset, went to visit the Godwins and reported that her husband was falling in love with Cornelia. Mrs. Godwin passed on this information in a letter to her friend Lady Mount Cashell, adding the news that Thomas Turner had taken his wife away from Bracknell to Devon.[15] Cornelia never saw Shelley again, but in the 1870s, shortly before her death, she wrote about their relationship (see Chapter 26).

The turbulent feelings and dramatic circumstances surrounding Shelley's departure from Bracknell appear in his "Stanzas, April 1814." Every voice, he wrote, cried "Away!" Mrs. Boinville, "the friend" with an "ungentle mood," wanted him gone. Cornelia, "the lover" whose eye was "glazed and cold," dared not ask him to stay.

"Stanzas, April 1814" has been called Shelley's "first successful lyric."[16] At the end of the poem the poet envisions his own death and concludes with a nostalgic remembrance of the mother and the daughter he cannot forget:

> Away! the moor is dark beneath the moon,
> Rapid clouds have drank the last pale beam of even:
> Away! the gathering winds will call the darkness soon,

And profoundest midnight shroud the serene lights of heaven.
Pause not! The time is past! Every voice cries, Away!
Tempt not with one last tear thy friend's ungentle mood:
Thy lover's eye, so glazed and cold, dares not entreat thy stay:
Duty and dereliction guide thee back to solitude.

The cloud shadows of midnight possess their own repose,
For the weary winds are silent, or the moon is in the deep:
Some respite to its turbulence unresting ocean knows;
Whatever moves, or toils, or grieves, hath its appointed sleep.

Thou in the grave shalt rest—yet til the phantoms flee
Which that house and heath and garden made dear to thee
    erewhile,
The remembrance, and repentance, and deep musings are
    not free
From the music of two voices and the light of one sweet smile.

Shelley hurried away from that "house and heath and garden" that had become so dear to him. He returned to his wife and remarried her, for legal not romantic reasons, on March 24, 1814, at St. George's Church, Hanover Square, where their daughter Ianthe had been christened the previous year. Harriet Shelley was in the early stages of pregnancy with his second child. (Charles Shelley would be born prematurely, "an eight-month's baby," in November.)

John Westbrook, a witness at the marriage ceremony, may have requested the marriage. He wanted his daughter's legal position clarified, "especially since the emotional position was steadily deteriorating for all to see."[17] The marriage ensured that if the baby was a boy, he would have a legal right to the entailed estate of the Shelley family. The marriage in England obviated any legal problems arising from the 1811 Scottish elopement. Similarly, in 1793, John Collins had been concerned about the legal status of any future heirs. After his daughter eloped to Scotland and was wed by the Gretna Green blacksmith, Collins insisted she remarry Jean Baptiste in an English church.

While Shelley's own inheritance was tied up in Chancery, he

could still borrow, and borrow he did, resorting to financial instruments called post-obituary bonds with ruinously high rates of interest. The lender would be paid back when Shelley died. As Shelley's widow discovered years later, by that point there was little left of the inheritance.

The post-obit transactions in March 1814 were necessitated by Shelley's desperate need for cash. He promised the debt-ridden Godwin, whom he had idolized since his youth, a sizable sum from this transaction. At Skinner Street they met often to discuss philosophy, political justice, and money matters.

Shelley Reflects

In a letter to Hogg on October 4, 1814, Shelley reflected on his stay at Bracknell, calling those two months "probably the happiest of my life: the calmest, the serenest, the most free from care." (He added a caveat—they were the happiest if the "succeeding period," between the spring and the fall, was not taken into account.) At Bracknell he had discovered "ample scope for admiration.... . The presence of Mrs. Boinville and her daughter afforded a strange contrast to my former friendless and deplorable condition."[18]

The last poem Shelley wrote about Cornelia refers to her as "another's wealth," a recognition that she was Thomas Turner's treasure.[19] See below the introspective final stanza:

> Oh! there are spirits of the air
>
> And thou hast sought in starry eyes
> Beams that were never meant for thine,
> Another's wealth:—tame sacrifice
> To a fond faith! still dost thou pine?
> Still dost thou hope that greeting hands,
> Voice, looks, or lips, may answer thy demands?

Shelley made a number of admissions about his behavior in the letter to Hogg written on October 4, 1814. Courting and "cultivating" Harriet Westbrook had resulted in a "rash & heartless" union. He now saw "the full extent of the calamity" that resulted.

Referring to the act of love with his wife, he said he deceived her. Intercourse with her when he did not love her was a "revolting duty." Presumably referring to the period after he left Bracknell and returned to his wife, Shelley wrote: "I believed that one revolting duty yet remained: to continue to deceive my wife."

About Shelley's admissions to Hogg about his marriage, Holmes wrote: "Shelley had at last managed to do the thing that all his life he found most difficult: to face up to one of the deep and often unpalatable truths of his own feelings and temperament. But this he achieved only in retrospect: in October 1814, and not in April or May."[20] In the fall of 1814, while Shelley was making confessions to Hogg about his marriage, Mrs. Boinville was dealing with a terrible personal tragedy of her own—and the aftermath of Shelley's desertion of his wife for Godwin's daughter Mary.

Chapter 14

Broken Hearts and a Mourning Widow Spring and Summer 1814

Mrs. Boinville deeply knows the human heart.
—Percy Bysshe Shelley, Letter to Harriet Shelley
July 14, 1814

Mary Godwin amazed Shelley on May 4, 1814. They had met briefly two years earlier, but that day, when he saw her in her home on Skinner Street, it was as though for the first time. He studied her beautiful face and golden hair. He listened intently to her soft voice. It seemed as if Mary combined the attributes of her parents: William Godwin's "intellectual force" and Mary Wollstonecraft's "keen sensibility." Shelley later wrote: "They say thou wert lovely from thy birth, of glorious parents, thou aspiring Child."[1]

Beginning in mid-June, Shelley saw Mary nearly every day at the Godwins' home. After a meal with the family, he often walked with her to the churchyard of St. Pancras where Godwin and her mother had married in 1796 and where her mother had been buried in 1797, shortly after Mary's birth. At the cemetery, Mary's sister Jane, an unwanted chaperone, would look on from a distance. On June 27th, under a willow by her mother's grave, Mary told Shelley she loved him. He recorded this momentous news in his journal and called that day his new birthday, the day he was reborn.

What happened next shook the Boinville circle and made literary history. Shelley, Mary, and Jane made life-changing decisions that deeply upset the people who loved them. Tragic consequences followed.

"Something Dreadful Has Happened"

"Will you write by return post and tell me what has become of him, as I always fancy something dreadful has happened if I do not hear from him?" Harriet Shelley wrote Thomas Hookham, a publisher and friend, on July 7, 1814. She had had no word from her husband for four days, "which to me is an age." She wrote from Bath, where she was staying with her baby Ianthe and her sister Eliza Westbrook.[2]

Upon her return to London, Harriet Shelley went to her parents' home. Her husband visited her there. He told her stunning news: he was in love with Mary Godwin. Because his wife did not make a scene after this revelation, he felt relieved. On July 14th he wrote to her, "I dreaded lest the shock might inflict on you some incurable unhappiness" — words that would prove to be true. Shelley then mentioned Mrs. Boinville in this letter to his wife. To persuade her to view their marriage as he viewed it, he used their mutual friend to achieve his purpose. Knowing how much Harriet respected Mrs. Boinville and valued her opinion, Shelley presented her as sharing his opinion, which she did not. Mrs. Boinville, he wrote,

> deeply knows the human heart: she predicted that these struggles would one day arrive; she saw that friendship & not passion was the bond of our attachment. But I derided her short-sighted prophecies—I! who was so soon to become the object of their completion.[3]

Shelley may have confided in his host about his marital unhappiness. It is unlikely, however, that she prophesied the marriage would end or specified the exact reason. She described Shelley's wife as his "beauteous half" in a letter to Hogg on April 18, 1814 (see page 235), which is not something she would say if she was sure the marriage was irreparable.

"Ever Most Affectionately Yours"

Shelley truly believed he could be Mary's lover and his wife's friend, as incredible as that belief appears. No matter what "vulgar minds regard as so important," the ties that connected them were now of a "deeper and more lasting character," he told her, since they were not based on passion and impulse. He misinterpreted his wife's dignified response to the bombshell that he loved Mary: "Feeling still persuaded that my affection for you was undiminished: you offered to my view, & anticipated for yourself that pure & lasting happiness which is the portion only of the great & good. For this dearest Harriet, from my inmost soul, I thank you." He addressed his wife as "My dearest friend," and ended this letter of July 14, 1814, "Adieu. Bring my sweet babe. I must ever love her for your sake." Ever most affectionately yours, P. B. Shelley."[4]

The following week there was a dosido of ineffectual communications. The first pair in the dance was Harriet Shelley and Percy Bysshe Shelley. They went together to visit William Godwin, but he was not home. Next, Godwin visited Harriet Shelley. He felt betrayed by her husband, his friend, and furious about Shelley's romantic interest in his daughter. Godwin went to see Mrs. Shelley to assure her that he would help her, something beyond his power to do. Next, Godwin saw the offending Shelley. Inside a carriage, during the ride, Godwin commanded him to leave Mary alone and go back to his wife. After this tense conversation, Godwin thought he had succeeded, but Shelley was not in the least resigned to a life without Mary.

Absolutely beside himself, Shelley appeared at Skinner Street and burst into the schoolroom. He had a pistol in his pocket and talked wildly about suicide. Mary screamed and tried to calm him. Eventually he left. The next day, in the middle of the night, Shelley overdosed on laudanum. His life was in danger. The Godwins were informed of the crisis in the middle of the night. Mary's mother, Mary Jane Godwin, tended to Shelley, then a local couple took over the nursing, and finally Mrs. Boinville took care of him, as James Bieri relates.[5]

Cornelia Turner called on William Godwin July 16th; her mother called on him July 18th. On July 28th, Godwin wrote in his diary: "Five in the morning… M and J for Dover."

"Five in the Morning"

Mary and Jane followed through on a plan pre-arranged with Shelley. They both were sixteen, the same age as Harriet Westbrook when she ran away with Shelley without her father's consent. Janet Todd describes what happened that famous dawn:

> Mary woke her stepsister ... Then the pair crept out of 41 Skinner Street. They were dressed in somber silk gowns and carried bundles of their clothes, letters and writings. They walked along the road to the edge of Hatton Garden where Percy Bysshe Shelley, a tall, lanky figure with thick wild hair... and large very blue eyes, had been watching.... Mary was eloping from her father's house.[6]

A coach Shelley had hired was waiting for the sisters. They galloped off to Dartford, where Shelley hired four fresh horses for the dash to the coast.

The Dover packet to Calais was not due to arrive until the next day, too long to wait. Shelley paid two fishermen to take them to France. The men pushed the boat out into the dark water. Mary later wrote about that night. "Suddenly a thunder squall struck the sail and the waves rushed into the boat; even the sailors believed that our situation was perilous."[7] Shelley loved sailing, his favorite pastime. With Mary in his arms and France drawing closer, he felt exhilarated, but Mary, possibly pregnant, felt sick as she huddled next to her lover in the wet hull.

The journey between Dover and Calais, twenty-three nautical miles, took about ten hours. Shelley, Mary, and Jane had boarded the fishing boat at six in the evening, and they did not reach the French coast until dawn.[8] The stormy crossing in a small open boat could easily have killed them.

"Three for the Road"

Hoping to catch the girls before they left the French coast, Mrs. Godwin, frantic and disheveled, appeared in Calais. Shelley refused to allow her to see Mary, but Jane agreed to spend the night with her mother and was almost persuaded to return home with her.⁹ Mrs. Godwin was intent on salvaging her daughter's reputation. The mother of two illegitimate children (Jane and her older brother Charles), she knew "firsthand the cost of toppling from respectability," as Fiona Sampson points out.¹⁰

Encouraged by Shelley, Jane decided, in the end, to ignore her mother's advice. She traveled with her sister and Shelley on to Paris, where they slept in a cheap hotel. Shelley knew they needed money. He had not waited long enough in London to get his share of the proceeds from a post-obituary bond. He wrote the publisher Hookham to ask him to serve as his financial intermediary in London. Hookham refused. Shelley wrote Mrs. Boinville. She refused to lend him more money. Shelley still owed her forty pounds.¹¹ On his twenty-second birthday, August 4, 1814, Shelley pawned his watch and chain and other personal items.

After six days in Paris, Shelley, Mary, and Jane loaded a mule with their belongings. Mary had brought a box containing her writings and letters, including the love letters between her mother and Godwin. In addition to Shakespeare, Tacitus, and Abbe Augustin's *Memoirs Illustrating the History of Jacobinism*, Shelley brought on the trip Mary Wollstonecraft's semi-autobiographical novel *Mary* and her *Letters Written During a Short Residence in Sweden, Norway, and Denmark*.¹² The three dispirited travelers trekked uncomfortably toward Troyes, France, about 120 miles away. They beheld scenes of destruction caused earlier by Napoleon's advancing army. From Troyes, Shelley wrote his wife. He wanted her to join them:

> I write to you from this detestable town. I write to show you that I do not forget you. I write to urge you to come to Switzerland, where you will at least find one firm and constant friend, to whom your interests will always be dear, by whom your feelings will never willfully be injured. From none can you expect this but of me. All else are either unfeeling or selfish, or have beloved friends of their own as Mrs. Boinville to whom their attention and affection is confined.¹³

Shelley sounds hurt. He was. Even Mrs. Boinville did not come to his aid. Not surprisingly, Harriet Shelley declined to join her husband in Switzerland.

Godwin calls Shelley "The Traitor to Me"

Back in London, Godwin seethed. Normally a reserved person, he vented his fury on August 27th to an acquaintance named Taylor, a successful manufacturer in Norwich who had loaned him money:

> You are already acquainted with the name of Shelley, the gentleman who more than twelve months ago undertook by his own assistance to rescue me from pecuniary difficulties... . He lodged at an Inn in Fleet Street and took his meals with me. I had the utmost confidence in him; I knew him susceptible to the noblest sentiments; he was a married man, who had lived happily with his wife for three years... he accompanied Mary and her sister Jane Clairmont to the tomb of Mary's mother, one mile distant from London; and there, it seems, the impious idea first occurred to him, of seducing her, playing the traitor to me and deserting his wife.[14]

Slanderous rumors compounded Godwin's anxiety. The London papers made a terrible accusation: Godwin was so short of money that he was willing to sell Shelley his two daughters! On July 19th Godwin had received 1,280 pounds from Shelley, a portion of money from the sale of the latest post-obituary bond. The girls left Godwin's home with his benefactor on July 28th.

The following month "Wrote to H Boinville" appears in Godwin's diary on August 1rst, August 4th, and August 14th. Godwin remained in close touch with his longtime friend. As Shelley, Mary, and Jane continued on their travels, all of Mrs. Boinville's sympathy lay with those forsaken in London: Harriet Shelley and Mary and Jane's heartsick parents.

"Our Journey's End"

When the three adventurers reached Neufchatel, no money had come from Shelley's solicitor. Dirty, dispirited, and broke they decided to return to England. They could afford the journey only if they traveled by the "water diligence" down the Rhine to a Channel port. This mode of transport was used mostly by local peasants, merchants, and students.[15]

Downstream from Strasbourg, German university students got on board. In her well-researched biography *In Search of Mary Shelley: The Girl Who Wrote Frankenstein,* Sampson suggests that a student named Schwitz could have inspired the German student in Mary's first novel. The riverboat passengers could see in the distance the Rhineland landmark Burg Frankenstein. The Germans may have told the English travelers about the eerie legends associated with this thirteenth-century fort. Later Mary names her protagonist Victor Frankenstein.[16]

From Rotterdam, the craft reached the hook of Holland. In the harbor at Marsluys, Shelley bargained with an English captain to take them across the Channel to Gravesend for three guineas apiece. The crossing took forty-eight hours in heavy swell. Mary waited out the storm down below. Shelley and Jane remained on deck. The travel journal recounts the easterly gale that "nearly kills us, whilst it carries us nearer our journey's end."[17]

At Gravesend on September 13, 1814, Shelley argued with a fellow-passenger against the slave trade. The English captain argued with Shelley. He did not trust him to pay the fare, and sent a sailor to accompany Shelley, Jane, and Mary up the Thames to London.[18]

At his bank, Shelley discovered he had no money in his account. "This was hardly surprising," Holmes observes, considering "the payment of the gift to Godwin, and the personal withdrawals that Harriet [Shelley] had made with Peacock's aid in an attempt to meet twelve months' accumulated bills in London."[19] Next they went to the home of the Voiseys, a family Mary and Jane had known since they were little girls. Mrs. Boinville knew the Voiseys as well. Mrs. Voisey would not let Shelley and the two girls inside.[20]

Desperate, Shelley hired a hackney and hurried to his wife's parents' home on Chapel Street. In *Romantic Outlaws: The Extraordinary Lives of Mary Wollstonecraft & Mary Shelley,* Charlotte Gordon brings to life this extraordinary moment:

When Shelley disappeared into the Westbrooks' house, the sailor and the girls were forced to wait outside for more than two hours, an awkward arrangement that no amount of banter or good cheer could rescue. The girls worried that Shelley would change his mind, that Harriet would talk him into giving their marriage another try, or, worse, that she would decide to join their trio. Neither Mary nor Jane was all that keen on this last idea, but Shelley still nursed the notion of creating a commune of free-minded, loving young people.[21]

John Westbrook obligingly paid the debt. Harriet Westbrook Shelley was in the third trimester of her pregnancy. Shelley's unexpected arrival stunned and pleased his wife and father-in-law. The visit after Shelley's long absence rekindled both their hopes that he would leave Mary.

Three days later, Shelley wrote his wife, "I am deeply solicitous to know the real state of your feelings towards myself and Mary." He also conveyed sad news. "I have heard from Turner. Mrs. Boinville has just received intelligence of her husband's death. She is considerably affected by this circumstance, so that probably some time will elapse before I see her."[22]

Widowed

Harriet Boinville learned that her husband was dead an agonizing seventeen months *after* he died. In September 1814, she began to grapple with the shocking truth: she would never see Jean Baptiste's well-loved face again. The memoir by their grandson describes the last year of her husband's life, when Jean Baptiste

> accompanied Napoleon and la grande armée in the disastrous campaign of 1812. He was then fifty-six years of age. Full of ardour still, and burning with the hope of gaining an independent position, he left Paris with the army, and shared all the hardships and vicissitudes of the famous retreat from Moscow. With hundreds of thousands of his fellow countrymen he fell victim to the cold. In passing the

Beresina [sic] his feet were frozen, and he was carried to the military hospital at Wilna, where, after lingering for a few days, and frequently calling out for his daughter Cornelia, he died as a prisoner of war, on the 7th of February 1813.

Napoleon's Russian campaign was an epic failure, as a book by Sylvain Tesson (translated from the French by Katherine Gregor) makes clear. Tesson wrote about a modern-day motorcycle journey on the same path as Napoleon's retreat: *Berezina: On Three Wheels from Moscow to Paris Chasing Napoleon's Epic Fail.* The Berezina is a river in Belarus and the word bérézina in colloquial French has become synonymous with a disastrous situation.[23]

Before his death Jean Baptiste had served his country as a senior officer in charge of provisioning the army. His title was Directeur des Vivres. Napoleon divided the military's responsibilities into two huge departments: the Ministry of War (responsible for men) and the War Administration (responsible for means). A. Pigeard in "Le service des vivres dans les armées du prémière empire (1804–1815), explains how this important reform improved Napoleon's ability to keep his army supplied.[24] The Russia campaign told a different story, however.

By the time Jean Baptiste left Paris and headed east, Napoleon had gathered together 650,000 troops, the largest army ever assembled. He had conquered Germany and Italy; Poland, Hungary, Austria, and Bavaria; the Netherlands and Switzerland.[25] He believed his massive army would make the Emperor of Russia, Alexander the First, live up to his promises and join the blockade against Britain. Brilliant Russian generals and the weather thwarted those plans. Jean Baptiste and other French officers in charge of feeding, transporting, and sheltering the army could not have prevented the "epic fail."

"No One Could Ever Witness a More Terrible Sight"

Napoleon advanced toward Moscow. He won, although not decisively, the battle of Borodino on September 5-7, 1812, the bloodiest battle of the Napoleonic Wars. Ten days later he entered Moscow. He expected to be greeted by Russian dignitaries ready to offer terms of surrender. Instead he found the city deserted and ablaze.

Winter was coming. Napoleon left Moscow on October 19 with a decimated force of 119,000 soldiers in a column ten miles long. Forty carriages edged West, laden with loot from the Kremlin — gold, silver, and jewels—as well as supplies. Napoleon's engineers raced to complete floating pontoon bridges over the partially frozen Berezina River. On November 27th Napoleon and his Guards crossed the river. Jean Baptiste limped across on frozen feet. In *Russia Against Napoleon*, Dominic Lieven writes that "fewer than 20,000 men survived to serve again in Napoleon's armies." Russian General Aleksei Ermalov described the east bank after the battle:

> Near the bridges, which were partially destroyed, guns and transport wagons had fallen into the river. Crowds of people, including many women, children, and infants, had moved down to the ice-covered river. Nobody could escape from the terrible frost. No one could ever witness a more terrible sight.

As the retreat continued to Vilna, where Jean Baptiste died as a POW, the temperature dipped to minus 37 degrees centigrade.[26]

Widowed at forty, Harriet never remarried. She and Jean Baptiste were married for nineteen years, all of them during wartime except for fourteen months during the short-lived Peace of Amiens. Harriet fell in love with Jean Baptiste in London, eloped with him to Scotland, and sailed with him to St. Vincent. Whenever she could, she crossed the Channel to be with him, risking her life and defying her father. They often were separated during the seemingly endless French Revolutionary and Napoleonic Wars. After Jean Baptiste's death, Harriet found within herself the determination and courage to carry on. For other women in her circle—family members and friends—personal challenges and painful disappointments soon proved to be overwhelming.

Chapter 15

More than a Beauty: Cornelia Collins Newton, 1815–1816

> My Sister never writes—scold her for me if you can. At all times I can ill bear her silence & less well now than ever when I suspect it proceeds from low spirits. Thirty miles cannot separate me from my Friends. That is not the worst evil of absence for those we love we bear about in our hearts but the groundless apprehensio+ns which spring up to alarm us when we might be tranquil are very hard to bear.
> —Harriet Boinville, Letter to Thomas Jefferson Hogg, March 11, 1814.

Cornelia Collins Newton, Harriet's sister, was intelligent, well-read, and musical. Shelley found her charming. In the more than two hundred years since his death, Shelley scholars have written about Cornelia Newton, presenting an incomplete picture. They have stressed her beauty, vegetarian diet, children, and private practice of "air bathing" in the nude.

Cornelia Newton was an important member of the circle that included Hogg, the Godwins, and Shelley and his wife. Sources of information about Cornelia Newton include letters written in 1813 and 1814 by her and about her, letters written long after her death by her niece and namesake Cornelia Turner, and Hogg's posthumous memoir of Shelley published in 1858.

Harriet was very close to her only sister. In the letter of March 11, 1814, quoted in the epigraph, she expresses worry about her sister's morale and impatiently awaits a reply. "Thirty miles" refers to the distance between Harriet's home at Bracknell and London where Cornelia Newton lived on Chester Street with her husband,

John Frank Newton, and their five children, described by Shelley in his notes to *Queen Mab*.[1] (See page 232-235 for the full text of Harriet Boinville's letter to Thomas Jefferson Hogg, March 11, 1814.)

Hogg Writes about Cornelia Newton

In 1813 Mrs. Newton invited Hogg and Shelley to join her and other friends at the popular amusement park called Vauxhall Gardens. Hogg wrote about the occasion in his characteristic prose style: humorous and wordy. In his memoir he devoted several pages to the "pleasant resort" with its fine old elms, twinkling lights, sprightly music, dancing, and Arrack punch, "the nectar of these celestial banquets... . I never drank it at Vauxhall, ... but I have found it a delightful beverage."

Hogg then described Rachel, a pretty Quaker woman who preoccupied his attention at Vauxhall before he focused on Shelley and Mrs. Newton: "Bysshe, for his part, was very entirely taken up, engrossed, captivated, by the charming lady through whose contrivance we had been brought to Vauxhall. A mere mundane critic might have declared that there was a most desperate flirtation between them, a more spiritual observer, a poet and a philosopher like himself, would discern in their union, a close and strong sympathy, and would describe it as such."[2] Most of this passage is amusing fluff, but Shelley did enjoy "a close and strong sympathy" with Harriet's sister. Kenneth Neill Cameron notes that "in spite of Hogg's penchant for caricature—exercised on Mrs. Newton as on all other characters in his [memoir]—we get a picture of Mrs. Newton as a woman of vivacity and wit."[3]

The Newtons' home on Chester Street was not far from Half Moon Street, where the Shelleys lived for a short time. As Hogg explains,

> There was a little projecting window in Half Moon Street, in which Shelley might be seen from the street all day long, book in hand, with lively gestures and bright eyes; so that Mrs. N said, he wanted only a pan of clear water and a fresh turf to look like some young lady's lark, hanging outside for air and song.[4]

This delightful word picture captures Shelley very well—the book in hand, the bright-eyed animation, the closeness to nature, and his bird-like readiness to take flight.

Cornelia Newton Writes about Hogg

A long letter Cornelia Newton wrote Hogg on October 21, 1813, reveals her playful wit and charm. Mrs. Newton assumed for the twenty-year-old Hogg "something of the role of intellectual guide," according to Cameron.[5] A law student, Hogg was also a fledgling novelist, and not a very good one. Mrs. Newton comments in the letter on his first novel, *Leonora*, and on the very popular novel *Sir Charles Grandison* by Samuel Richardson.[6] Mrs. Newton said Richardson's work showed a "true character of genius"; Hogg's novel she did not bother to finish. Like her sister, she was a woman who spoke her mind: "I read the first part of your Leonora & see it is the production of a very young man many parts of which your mature judgment will not confirm. When we meet I will venture to discuss with you its beauties & defects." (For the full text of this 1813 letter, see pages 228-230.)

Mrs. Newton sealed in wax all the letters she wrote, as was the custom. A mother of five, the red wax seal she chose was appropriate: figures gathered around a crouched child. She gave Hogg this sprightly account of her offspring: "Octavia & Camilla I think you will find impro[ved]. Augustus progressing toward scholarship—Chick traveling fast into breeches & Coraly light and nimble as a fairy." She hoped her friend would join the family for Christmas. "I hope you will eat your Christmas dinner with us—whether you continue one of the Holy or not for no change of habits of such a nature can alter the esteem with which I subscribe myself, your very sincere friend Cornelia Newton."[7]

"The Holy" refers to dietary, not spiritual, matters. Apparently, Hogg had given the vegetable diet of the Newton family a try. Knowing his fondness for meat, Mrs. Newton playfully teased him. Come to Christmas dinner, whether you continue "one of the Holy or not."

Hogg Belittles Frances Burney d'Arblay

Because of the high demand for any information about the dead poet in 1858, Hogg had to scavenge in his distant memories for material for his memoir of Shelley. In his sixties he wrote about his friendship with Shelley in their twenties. Sometimes Hogg elaborated on events in which Shelley was not even present. This was the case in his comments about "a personage of some distinction," Frances Burney D'Arblay.

After his flippant and possibly fabricated description of the tête-a-tête between Shelley and Mrs. Newton, Hogg described a meeting that Shelley did not attend with the famous novelist: "It was regretted by some of our party needlessly, I thought, that Shelley had missed the opportunity of seeing the famous Madame D'Arblay and of being seen by her."[8]

Cornelia Newton, however, was pleased to see her. "My sister was delighted with her interview with you," Harriet wrote Frances Burney d'Arblay on March 7, 1814. "She told me you appeared in good health, and your letter confirms the good news." (See page 230 for text of Harriet's letter.)

Although Hogg calls the daughter of Dr. Charles Burney a "gifted authoress," he denigrates her origins: "the daughter of a music-master who got his bread by giving lessons at Court and to the children of the aristocracy." He also faults her conversation: "The favoured novelist had just returned from France, to which country few English went in those days, and from which still fewer returned. Her conversation, therefore, would have been interesting, if she had told us anything to the purpose; but she did not."

Extending his criticisms of Frances Burney D'Arblay, Hogg speculates on what Shelley would have felt about her, writing that she

> could be neither more nor less than what she in fact was, a bundle of conventionalities; and these, however, clever and well arranged, would not have proved attractive to the Divine Poet. Her conversation was not without ability, but it was wholly about herself, and the self not being at all interesting, the conversation could not be so.

Hogg, the English "gentleman," reveals his class prejudices. He found the remarkable novelist to be quite an ordinary person, a "bundle of conventionalities," just what he expected to find considering her lineage. Her father made money giving music lessons to children of the aristocracy. Hogg sniffs at her social class and fantasizes that the aristocratic Shelley would have found her as uninteresting as he did.[9]

Dr. Charles Burney, a music historian and well as music teacher, rose above his station in life through hard work. Egalitarian in outlook, uninfluenced by aristocratical nonsense, Harriet Boinville and her sister Cornelia Newton highly regarded Madam d'Arblay and with good reason.

"Mrs. N is wonderfully recovered"

Cornelia Newton became ill. John Frank Newton urged his wife to rest with her sister at Bracknell, and she appeared to get better. "Mrs. N is wonderfully recovered," Harriet reported to Hogg on April 18, 1814. "Air and exercise, and friendly conversation, are just restoring her good looks." (See page 235 for the full text of this letter).

Sadly, her illness, possibly cancer, progressed. Fresh air and exercise, a healthy diet of fruits and vegetables (as well as visits to the best physicians in London) did not halt her decline. Still hoping for a restoration of his beloved wife's strength, John Frank Newton took her from Bracknell to Hampshire. The mother of five died there on September 2, 1816.

As she had done in 1814, when she learned of Jean Baptiste's death, Harriet pulled over her fingers black leather gloves (a requirement of mourning attire in Britain until the 1820s), and she donned a black dress. To be widowed at forty was hard to bear. And now she grieved for her sister, dead before she ever reached the age of forty.[10]

Harriet Boinville reached out to her Newton nieces and nephews. Letters from the 1840s, exchanged by Godwin's daughters Mary and Claire, reveal she remained in touch with Octavia Newton. Letters written by Cornelia Turner in the 1870s reveal what an exceptional musician her aunt and namesake, Cornelia Newton, was.

"Uncommonly Musical"

In 1874, Cornelia Turner recalled her aunt's connection to the German pianist and composer Jan Ladislav Dussek (1761-1812). He "dedicated one or two of his compositions to Miss Cornelia Collins" before he returned to Germany. Dussek described her as "his most gifted and best pupil" and said she "often passed her evenings playing with two of the first-rate musicians in London," by which he meant himself and Johann Peter Salomon (1745-1815).[11]

Born in Bonn, Salomon was a virtuoso violinist, composer, arranger, and orchestra director. He helped to bring Haydn to England in 1791 and 1794, an accomplishment noted on his tombstone. Salomon's association with Cornelia Newton is confirmed in William Godwin's diary on January 4, 1811: "Tea Newton's w. Salomon." The London social circle of Boinvilles, Newtons, and Godwins included in its impressive sphere the venerable Johann Peter Salomon.

Harriet commented on Salomon's "bewitching musical talent" and her sister's singing in her March 11, 1814, letter to Hogg: "Certain strains sung by my Sister make me so melancholy I cannot bear them, and if anything could make me a convert to her iron Philosophy it would be to hear her sing & think that she has never been happy. I hear at this distance the heartrending complaint of Ariadne and feel that the world is a Desert."[12]

Harriet had worried about her sister, as the letter in the epigraph shows. She could "ill bear" Cornelia's silence," fearing it came from low spirits. Cornelia Newton did not write or talk about her feelings. Despite signs, two years before her death, of a serious illness, Cornelia kept going, aided by her iron will to make the best of things. Decades later, in the face of adversity, Harriet demonstrated a similar tight-lipped stoicism, commented upon by her friends in Paris.

Harriet Boinville, Cornelia Newton, and Cornelia Turner shared an interest in music. "My Aunt married but she never abandoned music as many do after marriage," Cornelia Turner wrote Violet Paget on September 10, 1874. As an elderly woman Turner recalled her childhood visits to her aunt's house:

Her house was the resort of the first musicians of the time in London. They came on the footing of friends and used to enjoy playing their favorite authors for their own pleasure. When quite a little girl I listened evening after evening to Mozart's trios and quartets exquisitely played, besides admixture of Haydn and later of Beethoven. It was a real atmosphere that lulled my childhood.[13]

Harriet had experienced the death of her father, husband, and sister by the time she reached middle age. She had reason to write, "Anxieties, cares, & sorrows crowded fast upon me."[14] Her burden of sorrow increased in 1816 by the sudden deaths of two other people she loved: Fanny Godwin and Harriet Shelley.

Chapter 16

The Deaths of Fanny Godwin and Harriet Shelley, Fall and Winter 1816

> Her voice did quiver as we parted,
> Yet knew I not that heart was broken
> From which it came – and I departed —
> Heeding not the words then spoken.
> Misery—oh misery
> This world is all too wide to thee!
> —Percy Bysshe Shelley about Fanny Godwin[1]

> Be happy all of you. So shall my spirit find rest & forgiveness. God bless you all is the last prayer of the unfortunate.
> —Harriet S., Harriet Shelley's suicide note,
>   December 7, 1816[2]

Five weeks after her sister's death, Harriet was shocked by another death, this time a suicide. Just over a month later a second suicide followed, one Harriet had been asked to help prevent; tragically, she was unable to intervene in time.

Fanny was the illegitimate daughter of the aspiring British writer Mary Wollstonecraft and the American huckster Gilbert Imlay. She was born in Havre, France, on May 13, 1794. Her mother registered her name as "Françoise Imlay." About her week-old daughter, Wollstonecraft wrote: "I feel great pleasure at being a mother—and the constant tenderness of my most affectionate companion makes me regard a fresh tie as a blessing."[3]

Wollstonecraft had met Imlay in 1793 in Paris where she was reporting on the French Revolution. As the streets ran with blood, this brave single woman met the tall and handsome Imlay. He charmed her with his tales of the American West. He called himself "Captain" Imlay, despite minimal participation in the War of Independence. The thirty-four-year-old author of *Vindication of the Rights of Woman* thought Imlay was an honorable man who shared her views, but he was a lying entrepreneur, as Janet Todd explains:

> Sometimes he traded in French royalist silver; sometimes he dealt in frontier property he did not entirely own. Having written a book describing how idyllic (and affluent) life could be on the far side of the Alleghenies, he seduced disillusioned Europeans (and perhaps himself at times) with dreams of places elsewhere—much as he seduced Mary Wollstonecraft. For all his distinction from the geniuses who influenced his daughter's life, Imlay shares with them their talent for peddling non-existent destinations and fictitious utopias.[4]

Mary Wollstonecraft kept hoping, despite growing evidence, that Imlay was a man of integrity. The geniuses who influenced Fanny's life, Godwin and Shelley, differed from Imlay in their lifelong commitment to creating a better world. Imlay's main concern was himself and making money. Godwin and Shelley were celebrated thinkers, but Imlay was merely a glib talker. Wooing Mary he professed to be against slavery, religion, and marriage, which was part of his appeal to her, a free-thinker with unconventional ideas.

"An involuntary sigh whispered to my heart"

The relationship was tumultuous. In the hopes of staying together, Wollstonecraft agreed to undertake a long and dangerous mission to Scandinavia to check on a cargo of silver for Imlay. She took with her baby Fanny and a young French girl named Marguerite. Imlay sweet-talked her into accepting this risky assignment. He told her how much he needed her to safeguard his investment. He promised her they would begin a new life together as a family in America when her mission was completed. In Hamburg, where he had promised to meet her, she realized he had a new lover.

In *Letters Written During a Short Residence in Sweden, Norway, and Denmark,* published by Joseph Johnson in 1796, Mary Wollstonecraft wrote about the journey and "the sorrow that had taken up its abode in my heart." In one village a little girl caught her eye. She was "mounted a straddle on a shaggy horse." Walking alongside was the girl's father with "a child in his arms, who must have come to meet him with tottering steps, the little creature was stretching out its arms to cling around his neck." This family reminded Wollstonecraft of her own painful situation:

> My eyes followed them to the cottage, and an involuntary sigh whispered to my heart, that I envied the mother, much as I dislike cooking, who was preparing their pottage. I was returning to my babe, who may never experience a father's care or tenderness. The bosom that nurtured her, heaved with a pang at the thought which only an unhappy mother could feel.[5]

Imlay abandoned his lover and his child when she was a baby. Fanny's mother died in the summer of 1797 when Fanny was three. The cause was childbirth complications after the birth of Mary Godwin. Fatherless and motherless, the toddler Fanny became deeply attached to her adoptive father, William Godwin, who treated her kindly from the very beginning of his relationship with Wollstonecraft in the spring of 1796. After their marriage and her death, Godwin brought up little Fanny and baby Mary together in his home. The emotional bonds to Godwin, formed when Fanny was little, strengthened as she got older. For many years, Fanny thought Godwin, not Imlay, was her biological father.

In 1801, when Godwin married Mary Jane Clairmont, Fanny became the oldest of four siblings in the blended family: Fanny Imlay, Mary Godwin, Charles Clairmont, and Jane Clairmont. Fanny received little maternal affection or individual attention from her busy stepmother. After the new baby, William, Jr., was born, the father she adored had less time for her.

Fanny tried hard to please her demanding stepmother. She had a more docile and obedient temperament than her sisters, and ended up being given the most chores and other domestic responsibilities. In her youth, Godwin asked her to run errands for him and transcribe documents as his scribe. She even agreed, when Godwin asked, to attend a funeral in his place. Dutiful Fanny represented the Godwin family at the funeral of Mrs. Turner, the mother of Thomas Turner, Godwin's lawyer and Harriet Boinville's son-in-law.

Fanny Godwin and Aaron Burr

Like both her parents, Fanny enjoyed the company of Aaron Burr, a frequent visitor in 1810 and 1812. She was pleased when he asked her to make his tea. She knew just how he liked it. She was delighted when he invited her on a day-long outing to visit the Lancaster School on Borough Road, Southwark. For this special occasion, she carefully prepared a hamper: oysters (a great delicacy), bread and butter, and porter. Burr found the oysters practically inedible, but he did not hurt Fanny's feelings by criticizing the picnic she had lovingly prepared.

Burr admired Mary Wollstonecraft's publications and educational principles. A copy of a Godwin's portrait of Fanny's dead mother was one of Burr's prize possessions. The Lancaster School, a progressive institution founded by Quaker Joseph Lancaster, implemented many of Wollstonecraft's ideas about education. For example, children were motivated to learn without the threat of corporal punishment, a common practice in other schools.

When Burr and Fanny arrived, classes were in session In *Death & the Maidens: Fanny Wollstonecraft and the Shelley Circle*, Janet Todd describes how the school charmed and pleased the two visitors: "The children seemed so happy and cheerful, yet to be learning so much. They were particularly struck by an African boy who had been at the school only five months and had learnt not only the English language but also the rudiments of writing and arithmetic."[6] At that time, few schools admitted pupils of different races and cultures—hence the strong favorable impression made by the African boy.

Fanny's Family Falls Apart

Fanny often saw Shelley in the early days of his relationship with Godwin, when the young man and the philosopher were on the best of terms. On July 7, 1812, Godwin wrote Shelley, "You cannot imagine how much all the females of my family, Mrs. G and three daughters, are interested in your letters and your history." Todd explains the charismatic Shelley's powerful effect; he "excited them all by turns and together, allowing them to live in his exotic realm of noble feelings, high emotions and social possibilities."

Shelley took the time to talk to Fanny, who paid close attention to his winning ways and mesmerizing words. She relished their conversations. Fanny may have viewed him as a rescuing hero. She knew her parents were nearly bankrupt, and Shelley had promised to help her father with his debts.[7]

On July 28, 1814, the sudden departure of her sisters from her home stunned and saddened Fanny. Their European escapade with Shelley made her feel more lonely than ever. The mood at home was glum, her parents always talking about bills they could not pay and the future of Mary and Jane, ruined by their scandalous actions.

Mary wrote letters to Fanny with descriptions of France and Switzerland—places where their revered mother had once traveled. At twenty years of age, Fanny had dreams of her own of visiting a wider world. Home had become a stuffy cage. Surrounded by dirty clothes, dusty books, and discontented parents, she coveted what seemed to be denied to her: love and philosophy and adventure.

In her replies to Mary, Fanny expressed pent up discontent. Mary had caused her "a great deal of pain." Momma said that you said, "I am your laughingstock." Not always truthful, Fanny's stepmother may have put these words in Mary's mouth. One of Fanny's letters was so full of anxiety about Godwin's finances and so pleading in its requests for stories of the great Lord Byron that Mary and Shelley sent Fanny the present of a fine gold watch.[8]

When her sisters and Shelley returned to London in the fall of 1814, Fanny expected to spend time with them. She wanted to be part of their lives, but she saw them rarely and never on Skinner Street. William and Mary Jane Godwin had banned them from the house.

Fanny suffered from depression as had her mother. In his memoir of Wollstonecraft, Godwin described her despair at Imlay's abandonment, and wrote that "she formed a desperate purpose to die."[9]

"She formed a desperate purpose to die"

Fanny hoped for an invitation to join Shelley, Mary, and Jane in Bath. Excluded from Skinner Street and no longer welcome at Bracknell, Shelley described Bath as an "exile's haven" in a letter to his good friend Lord Byron. No invitation came to join her sisters and Shelley. Fanny's despair deepened. On October 8, 1816, she left her father a note, "I depart immediately to the spot from which I hope never to remove."[10] Fanny wrote Shelley as well, saying she would be dead by the time he received her letter. It had a Bristol postmark.

Shelley raced from Bath to Bristol. On October the 9th, Fanny took a fatal dose of laudanum in Swansea, Wales. She died in a room at the Mackworth Arms, a coaching inn on Wind Street. The maid found a note:

> I have long determined that the best thing I could do was to put an end to the existence of a being whose birth was unfortunate, and whose life has only been a series of pain to those persons who have hurt their health in endeavoring to promote her welfare. Perhaps to hear of my death will give you pain, but you will soon have the blessing of forgetting that such a creature ever existed as

That was all. The letter ended abruptly. No name was written. No one claimed the body. Fanny was buried in a pauper's grave.

Todd in *Death & the Maidens* carefully considers the mystery of the missing name. Fanny may have had second thoughts and tore off the name "to spare the Godwins embarrassment, knowing as she did how their lives had been dogged by scandal." A maid or the innkeeper, to avoid publicity, may have removed the name. Or Shelley, acting on instructions from Fanny's father and from Mary Godwin, may have removed the signature, the most likely scenario, according to Todd.[11]

Whatever the truth, Shelley walked into the Mackworth Arms in Swansea, Wales. Filled with dread he entered the shabby rented room, bent over Fanny's cold body, and read her note. On October 13th, Shelley confirmed the tragic outcome in a letter to Fanny's father.[12] In his diary Godwin distilled into one word the tumult of his grief: "Swansea."

Harriet Shelley: "For myself, happiness has fled"

Harriet Shelley, like Fanny Imlay, despaired. She had two children (Ianthe, born in mid-June 1813, and Charles, born on November 30, 1814, a month prematurely). Her husband no longer loved her. In January 1816, she wrote her friend Catherine Nugent, "At nineteen, I could descend a willing victim to the tomb. ... How many there are who shudder at death. I have been so near it that I feel no terrors." The reason she was still alive was her children. "For myself, happiness has fled." To Mrs. Nugent, a kind older woman Harriet had always trusted, she expresses her great pain:

> Mr. Shelley has much to answer for. He has been the cause of great misery to me and mine. I shall never live with him again. 'Tis impossible. I have been so deceived, so cruelly treated, that I can never forget it. Oh no, with all the affections warm, a heart devoted to him, and then to be so cruelly blighted.[13]

Despite her own heavy sorrows, Harriet Shelley in the spring of 1816 was able to express concern for others and their troubles. "It is with the deepest emotions of sorrow that I heard of Mrs. Newton's illness," she wrote John Frank Newton on June 5, 1816:

> That she may still live to enjoy many years of happiness with you and your sweet children is my very fervent wish. If there is anything that I can do for you pray let me know. To the unhappy there is nothing so delightful as being of use to others. If my presence would add in the least to yours or your children's comfort I am very ready to leave Town...; if there is any kind of Fruit I can send you do tell me; at

present there is but little variety owing to our cold spring. If it will fatigue you too much to waste an answer let my favorite Augustus [Newton] give me a line just to say how you are... . Pray don't take any trouble yourself; my sister unites with me in highest regard and best wishes to you all, and I remain,
Your sincere friend,
H. Shelley[14]

The letter to Mr. Newton was addressed to "Burgate House/Near Fordingbridge/Near Hants." This is probably where Cornelia Collins Newton died three months later.[15]

Harriet Shelley's Last Days

The unhappy mother left Ianthe and Charles Shelley in the care of her sister Eliza. With her father's help she moved out of the house on Chapel Street to Elizabeth Street, a short distance away. She was pregnant. She did not register as a tenant under her own name. Her landlord thought her new renter was "Mrs. Smith." Todd offers a plausible explanation for this deception. Harriet Shelley would have been disgraced "if her situation were made public: the whole of London had heard that her husband was living with the two Godwin girls."[16] The name of the father of the child she was carrying has not been conclusively identified, but all agree it was not Shelley.

Harriet's apartment on Elizabeth Street was spacious and she had money from the Westbrooks and from her husband. In April 1816, Shelley had provided for his wife 200 pounds annually. In June 1816 he bequeathed her 6,000 pounds; Ianthe and Charles each were bequeathed 5,000 pounds." This money, however, was no consolation to his distraught wife.[17]

In the late fall and winter of 1816, the personal interactions and geographic movements of Harriet Shelley are hard to trace.[18] It is known, however, that she visited Mrs. Boinville during the summer of 1816, accepting an invitation to Bracknell. Surprisingly, she rested in the same cottage where Mary Jane Godwin had stayed earlier when visiting another friend.[19] At Bracknell, Harriet confided in the white-haired widow about her troubles and also updated her on her legal issues with Shelley concerning custody of Ianthe and Charles.

Mrs. Boinville was one of the few steady supports in the young woman's life. In her final days, Harriet Shelley turned to her. Many scholars have recounted similar versions of what happened, but Edmund Blunden tells the chilling tale most fully and powerfully:

> In Mrs. Boinville's family an account of Harriet's tragedy was handed down until the other day. It is simple and sad. In Shelley's absence Harriet depended a great deal on Mrs. Boinville's understanding and on going for long walks with her. Late in 1816 Harriet wrote a lonely letter, asking for one more walk of the sort and hinting that without it, she would give up. But the country postman failed to deliver the letter punctually. Harriet interpreted Mrs. Boinville's silence with the result that cannot be forgotten.[20]

Although Mrs. Boinville "set out at once" to go to her desperate friend, she was too late.[21]

Meanwhile, Shelley asked Thomas Hookham to try and find out where his wife was living. On December 15, 1816, while in Bath with essayist and poet Leigh Hunt, Shelley received a letter from Hookham saying that he had had the "utmost difficulty" locating Mrs. Shelley. After these preliminaries, Hookham conveyed the terrible news: "information was brought me she was dead—that she had destroyed herself.... I was informed that she was taken from the Serpentine river on Tuesday last, apparently in an advanced state of pregnancy."[22] This news "tore his being to pieces," said Hunt about Shelley who then rushed back to London.

"Found drowned" was the verdict of the jury investigating the death, but *The Times* reported the blunt truth that she took her own life: A "respectable lady with an expensive ring on her finger" and "far advanced in pregnancy" had committed suicide.[23] The Elizabeth Street landlady was interviewed and confirmed the depressed demeanor of her reclusive tenant in "the family way."

Mrs. Boinville Tries to Help Shelley in Custody Battle

Shelley asked Mrs. Boinville to relay to the Westbrooks how much he desired custody of his children. She assumed the delicate role of "go-between" on this fraught issue. On December 18, 1816, just a few days after his wife drowned, Shelley wrote Eliza Westbrook:

> Dear Eliza,
> Before you receive this letter, Mrs. Boinville will probably have informed you of my resolution with respect to Ianthe. My feelings of duty as well as affection, as a father, incite me to consider every moment of absence & estrangement from these beloved & unfortunate children, as an evil, the sense of which has been increased to agony by the terrible Catastrophe which is the occasion of this address.... . there is no earthly consideration which would induce me to forego the exclusive & entire charge of my child....

Shelley ends the letter, "I may as well say—tho' I dare say Mrs. B has told you as much—that my applying to my attorney on this occasion was founded entirely on error."[24] Determined to have Charles as well as Ianthe with him, Shelley fudges in this letter. Long before his wife's suicide, he had been pursuing legal action to win custody of them.

Mary Godwin also wanted to raise Ianthe and Charles. "How very happy I shall be to possess those darling treasures that are yours.—I do not exactly understand what Chancery has to do," she wrote Shelley on December 17, 1816, the day before Shelley wrote Eliza. "My heart says bring them instantly here." The vision of a larger family pleased Mary. "[N]ow I long more than ever that our house should be quickly ready for the reception of those dear children whom I love so tenderly [and] then there will be a sweet brother and sister for William who will lose his pre-eminence as eldest and be helped third at table—as his Aunt Claire is continually reminding him."

Neither Shelley's letter to Eliza Westbrook, nor Mrs. Boinville's mediation with the Westbrook family, succeeded in advancing Shelley's and Mary's desire to keep Ianthe and Charles. Litigation over the children's custody continued for years. A suicide note, discovered eighty years after Harriet Shelley's death, specified her final wishes for her children.

"Oh I must me be quick"

Before Harriet Shelley placed rocks inside the pockets of her dress and slowly made her way, deeper and deeper, into the Serpentine River, she wrote her sister a letter with trembling hand. This suicide note addressed to Eliza Westbrook was not discovered until eighty years later.

"Do not regret the loss of one who could never be anything but a source of vexation & misery to you all belonging to me," the distraught young woman wrote. She mentions her husband and her last request: "Bysshe," and her last request: "to let Ianthe remain with you always dear lovely child, with you she will enjoy much happiness with him none." To persuade Shelley, she mentions what they once had: "my dear Bysshe let me conjure you with my remembrance of our days of happiness—to grant my last wish." Her sister has watched over Ianthe "with unceasing care." She begs Bysshe not to refuse her last request and states, "I never could refuse you & if you had never left me I might have lived but as it is, I freely forgive you & may you enjoy that happiness which you have deprived me of." She mentions their son Charles: "There is your beautiful boy oh! be careful of him & his love may prove one day a rich reward. As you form his infant mind so you will reap the fruits hereafter now comes the sad task of saying farewell—oh I must be quick."

Harriet Shelley ends her letter with a poignant farewell:

God bless and watch over you all. You dear Bysshe. And you dear Eliza. May all happiness attend ye both is the last wish of her who loved ye more than all others. My children I dare not trust myself there. They are too young to regret me & ye will be kind to them for their own sakes more than for mine. My parents do not regret me. I was unworthy of your love & care. Be happy all of you. So shall my spirit find rest & forgiveness. God bless you all is the last prayer of the unfortunate Harriet S[25]

On July 25, 1818, the disposition of the custody case was resolved, and not in the way the children's mother had wanted. Ianthe and Charles were put into the care of a foster parent, Dr. Thomas Hume. The Westbrooks and Shelley were given once-a-month visiting rights.[26]

A few weeks after Harriet Shelley drowned, Mary Godwin and Percy Bysshe Shelley married at St. Mildred's Church in London. William and Mary Jane Godwin witnessed the union and welcomed the couple, now husband and wife, back at 41 Skinner Street for a meal.

Harriet Shelley's suicide devastated Mrs. Boinville. If only her friend's plea for help had not been delayed in the post. If only, if only. The tragedy also ended forever Mrs. Boinville's friendship with Shelley. She never saw him again.

After Shelley died, Mrs. Boinville wrote his widow. These letters, never published before, express in intimate detail her feelings about Shelley and about Godwin. As future chapters explain, Mrs. Boinville's friendship with Mary Shelley, severed in 1816, resumed and blossomed in subsequent decades.

Chapter 17

Mary's *Frankenstein*, Byron's "Love" Child, and Harriet's Son, 1817–1818

> I saw with shut eyes the pale student of unhallowed arts kneeling beside the thing he had put together. I saw the hideous phantasm of a man stretched out, and then, on the workings of some powerful engine, show signs of life, and stir with an uneasy, half vital motion. Frightful must it be; for supremely frightful would be the effect of any human endeavor to mock the stupendous mechanism of the Creator of the World.
> —Mary Godwin Shelley's Introduction to *Frankenstein*[1]

> Maidens, like moths, are ever caught by glare.
> —Lord Byron, "Childe Harold's Pilgrimage"[2]

In the eventful period of 1817 to 1818, Claire Clairmont gave birth to Lord Byron's daughter; Mary Shelley's Gothic classic *Frankenstein, or The Modern Prometheus* appeared in print; and Harriet Boinville had something important to celebrate: the marriage of Alfred, her youngest child and only son to Harriet Lambe, the daughter of the renowned London doctor and pioneering vegetarian William Lambe. After so many deaths—her sister, her husband, and her friends (Harriet Shelley and Fanny Godwin)—she basked in the happy moment.

Mrs. Boinville had watched Claire and Mary, playmates of her daughter Cornelia, grow up on Skinner Street, but now she was not in close touch with either them. The sisters' running away to Europe with Shelley, the husband of her friend, had angered her. In her journal on October 11, 1814, Mary noted receipt of a cold and sarcastic letter from Mrs. Boinville. Claire called the letter "very sneering."[3] This important letter, unfortunately, has been lost, but decades later the friendship was restored. Mrs. Boinville reached out to Mary and to Claire. Her Paris letters to Mary repaired hard feelings of the past, and she repeatedly welcomed Claire in her home on the rue de Clichy. The sisters' riveting letters to each other about Mrs. Boinville shed new light on her character and reveal her importance in both their lives.

Because news spread in London that Claire accompanied Mary and Shelley to Europe when she was sixteen and returned with them to Europe two years later when they visited Lord Byron, the bad boy of the era, she lost a secure place in polite society. Her youthful choices had long-term consequences.

Claire Clairmont's Uphill Road

Claire's steep path in life began in 1798, when she was born, to use the old-fashioned term, "out of wedlock." Claire's mother is well described by Fiona Sampson as a "canny survivor" and "practical woman, who, despite contemporary handicaps of gender, makes things happen." Claire's father was Sir John Lethbridge, a member of the Somerset gentry. He quickly became bored with Claire's mother and "tried hard to avoid supporting her and his child. "He told his solicitor, "I had no business to have anything to do with her."[4] All her life, Claire mistakenly thought that she had the same father as her older brother Charles.[5]

In her late teens and twenties, Claire sometimes lived in short-term lodgings with Mary and Shelley, an arrangement Mary increasingly disliked. Scholars have long debated whether Claire and Shelley slept together and speculated on when they might have become lovers. There is no doubt that for Shelley, the vivacious and impetuous Claire held a certain wild appeal. In his poem "Epipsychidion,"' Mary was the moon and Claire, a comet: "O Comet beautiful and fierce/ Who drew the heart of this frail Universe/Towards thine own."[6] Until his death Shelley remained her friend, demonstrating in that relationship an uncharacteristic steadiness. In Claire's tumultuous life, no other person maintained as genuine an interest in her welfare, according to Marion Kingston Stocking, the editor of Claire's letters.

"Pardon my writing to you again"

As a letter writer, Claire Clairmont was extraordinary. Her words to Lord Byron—"Pardon my writing to you again"—highlight her epistolary zeal. When she was seventeen, she made up her mind to meet the dark and dashing aristocrat, a veritable media celebrity. To achieve her goal, she peppered him with letters, twenty in number, in March and April 1816. Here is a representative sample:

> An utter stranger takes the liberty of addressing you. It is earnestly requested that for one moment you pardon the intrusion, & laying aside every remembrance & what you are, listen with a friendly ear. ...
>
> Lord Byron is requested to state whether 7 o'clock this Evening will be convenient.
>
> I have called twice on you, but your Servants declare you to be out of town.
>
> Pardon my writing to you again.
>
> There is little in your lordship's stern silence to embolden me.
>
> Will you be so kind as to admit me Sunday evening at 7 alone?
>
> Since you disappointed me last evening, will you see me tonight? If you do not entirely hate me, pray do.
>
> You bid me write short to you & I have much to say...time shall show you that I love gently and with affection.
>
> ...I have decided my fate in my own mind.
>
> I steal a moment to write to you.... tomorrow will inform me whether I will be able to offer you that which it has been the passionate wish of my heart to offer you.[7]

In one of his rare replies to Claire's letters, Lord Byron called her a "little fiend," so fierce was her epistolary onslaught.[8] He eventually agreed to meet her in private. The result was predictable. For Byron, Claire quickly became a forgettable sexual partner, but Claire was in love with all her young and tender heart.

Stocking suggests that the rumors circulating in London about the breakup of Byron's marriage might have influenced Claire. The naïve teen may have thought she could win Byron's love and become his wife. Her family had no money to help her and provided at this time no guidance and encouragement. Claire faced an "increasingly urgent problem of what to do with herself in the world."[9]

Based on her knowledge of Shelley, Claire made wrong assumptions about Byron, assuming the poems she so admired reflected something beautiful and good in the man. But Byron was cynical, jaded, and fickle. He did not resemble Shelley, who for all his faults had firm principles.

Mary's *Frankenstein*

Mary conceived of the idea for *Frankenstein* in May 1816 in Lord Byron's Swiss villa. She and Shelley had been introduced to Byron back in London. This European trip was Mary, Shelley, and Claire's second escapade—the one that had so disheartened their sister Fanny, left at home.

The Shelleys and Claire stayed near Byron's Villa Diadoti on Lake Geneva. One night, as the rain fell in the darkness outside, Mary, Shelley, Claire, and other guests gathered around Lord Byron's blazing fire. Their host, "who was in the habit of staying up until three in the morning, suggested they should amuse themselves by reading a French translation of some German fantasy tales."[10] Tales, many macabre in nature, were read and told. Byron then issued a challenge: Write a ghostly story of your own. Although others tried their hand at writing a story, eighteen-year-old Mary was the member of the house party who persevered.

In a flurry of amazing productivity, she finished her story on May 14, 1817, and in September gave birth to her second child, Clara Everina Shelley. *History of a Six Weeks' Tour Through a Part of France, Switzerland, Germany, and Holland* was published in Novem-

ber and *Frankenstein, or The Modern Prometheus*, in January 1818.
Mary dedicated her novel to her father:

To
WILLIAM GODWIN
Author of *Political Justice*, Caleb Williams, &c.
THESE VOLUMES
Are respectfully inscribed
BY
THE AUTHOR

Her sister praised the book, "a most wonderful performance & the fiction is of so continued and extraordinary a kind as no one would imagine...could have been written by so young a person."[11] Shelley sent Sir Walter Scott a copy, and he commented on the unknown author's "original genius and happy power of expression." Many readers thought Shelley, who wrote the unsigned Preface, was the author. As Charlotte Gordon points out, Mary lived "during a time when middle-class women were supposed to be wives and mothers, not famous authors."[12]

Frankenstein in 1818 became an "immediate bestseller" and Mary's identity as the author became known. After the second edition, published in 1823, *Blackwood's Edinburgh Magazine* exclaimed: "For a man it was excellent, but for a woman it was wonderful," revealing the startling gender disparities of the day.[13] In *Mary Shelley: A Very Short Introduction* (2022), Gordon calls attention to the persistence of gender disparities concerning the author of *Frankenstein*. Gordon uses the name Mary Shelley, even though she was born Mary Godwin, "to rectify the past practice of referring to her husband as Shelley, and Mary by her first name, a diminishment of her status as an author."[14]

Mary Shelley's Gothic tale has remained enduringly popular because it lends itself to multiple interpretations. Interpretation as a birth myth is particularly compelling. A year before Mary began to write her story, she gave birth prematurely to a daughter who lived only two hours. Mary wrote in her journal about the infant, "Dream that my little baby came to life again; that it had only been cold, and that we rubbed it before the fire and it lived."[15] The subtitle Mary chose is fitting. Prometheus stole fire from Zeus to save the human race. In her dream Mary imagined saving her baby by warming it by the fire. How she longed for the still, cold form to move once more.

In Claire's Own Words

Pregnant with Lord Byron's child, conceived back in London, Claire wrote him a letter in May 1816 that expressed her love, her loneliness—and her way with words: "I know not how to address you; I cannot call you friend for though I love you yet you do not feel even interest for me; fate has ordained that the slightest accident that should befall you should be agony to me; but were I to float by your window drowned all you would say would be Ah voila!" [16]

Claire awaited the birth secluded in Bath. The Godwins had no idea she was pregnant. Claire, Mary, and Shelley had kept them in the dark. As her condition became more obvious to neighbors, Claire called herself Mrs. Clairmont, just as Mary Jane Clairmont had done before the births of her two illegitimate children, Charles and Claire (named Clara Mary Jane).

In her third trimester, Claire begged Byron, "Write me a nice letter beginning not with those scanty words "dear Clare" but "<u>My</u> dearest Claire," and tell me that you <u>like</u> me that you will be very pleased to have a little baby of which you will take great care" (emphasis Claire's).[17] Aware of Claire's isolation and anxiety, Shelley wrote to Byron, asking him to write to Claire, but he refused.

On January 12, 1817, Claire and Byron's daughter was born. She called her Alba or Albé, a name with a sound associated with Lord Byron's initials, L.B. In the coming months, Byron made known his wishes. He chose a different name, Allegra, and he decided that he should be in charge of Allegra's future. Plans were made for Claire to relinquish her beloved daughter into his care in Switzerland at some future date. She felt it was in Allegra's best interest, if not her own. Compared to the immensely rich Byron, what had she to offer her precious child? Anticipating the coming separation from her daughter, Claire wrote Byron on their daughter's first birthday:

How I envy you. You will have a little darling to crawl to your knees and pull you till you take her up; then she will sit in the crook of your arm and you will give her a raisin off your own plate and a tiny drop of wine from your own glass and she will think herself a little Queen of Creation. …

Her pen raced across the page. The more she wrote, the more anxious she became: "I so fear she will be unhappy, poor little Angel! In your great house, left perhaps to servants while you are drowning sense & striving all you can to ruin the natural goodness of your nature who will be there to watch her."[18] Claire feared for her daughter, "all my treasure."

Rumors had spread that Shelley was Alba's father. After the sojourn in Bath, Claire and her baby had moved into the Shelleys' home, Albion House, in Marlow. Chancery's recent decision to deny Shelley custody of Ianthe and Charles made Shelley and Mary anxious about the future of their son William and baby Clara. With this latest scandal in the press, could these children be taken away by the courts? England began to feel colder and more inhospitable than ever before.

"The sun shines bright"

In the early spring of 1818, plans to move to Italy were set in motion. Allegra was to be handed over to Byron in Geneva. Like Shelley, Mary and Claire were ready to leave their native country and try and begin a new life abroad. The day before they left, the Godwins called. Mary was tired from packing and the Godwins' visit was short. "Our adieus" was all Mary wrote that night. If Godwin's daughter "cried a little at the thought of leaving behind the father she loved and worried for so much, she was not going to admit it to her diary," Miranda Seymour writes.[19]

On March 11, 1818, Shelley, Mary, and Claire left Dover at dawn. A large party, encumbered with possessions, headed toward Calais: three parents (Mary, Shelley, and Claire); three babies (William Shelley, born on January 24, 1816; Clara Shelley; and Allegra); and two nursemaids (a Swiss nurse Elise and an English nurse Milly). Mrs. Boinville did not come to say goodbye.

From Lyons, they traveled toward Switzerland, and then south. Mary wrote to their close friends Leigh and Marianne Hunt: "The sun shines bright and it is a kind of Paradise we have arrived at..." Mary and Shelley eagerly anticipated a fresh start but their destination, Italy, would soon feel more lonely than heavenly. Shelley thought about his former friend, Mrs. Boinville, as his numerous future letters reveal.

Alfred Boinville Weds Harriet Lambe

Unlike most of the principal unions of young people described so far in this biography (Harriet and Jean Baptiste, Harriet Westbrook and Shelley, Mary Godwin and Shelley, Claire Clairmont and Lord Byron), the union of Harriet Lambe and Alfred Boinville pleased both families. It was a good match, everyone agreed.

The bride was the intelligent and likable eldest daughter of Dr. William Lambe; the groom, a well-educated, well-mannered gentleman of twenty-one. They had become well-acquainted before the wedding. Godwin's diary records the frequent interactions of the Godwin, Boinville, Lambe, and Newton families. They called on each other and dined in each other's homes.

The date in 1818 and the details of the marriage ceremony and festivities are not known, but the beverages surely included distilled water and plentiful fruits and vegetables were served. The bride and groom's families were vegetarians, and one of the guests was the widower John Frank Newton whose advocacy of a vegetable diet in *Return to Nature* reflected the scientific research of Dr. Lambe.

In recorded history, Alfred's sister Cornelia Turner has left a long trail that winds through fascinating terrain. We will continue to follow it until her death in 1875. Alfred Boinville, however, has left hardly a trace. What little is known about him comes primarily from one source, the memoir published in 1880 by his son Charles.

Like his mother, Alfred was born in the Caribbean. He spent less than a year in St. Vincent, where he was born in 1797. As a young boy he lived in his grandfather's London house on Berners Street with his mother and sister, before probably being sent away to school.

Chapter 17

Alfred did not see his father often during the French Revolutionary and Napoleonic Wars. Despite the danger, illegality, and opposition of her father, John Collins, Harriet repeatedly crossed the Channel to be with her husband. In the early 1800s, she took her young children with her when she could. Records of Frances Burney d'Arblay from the period 1810 to 1812 confirm that Jean Baptiste's primary residence in those years was Paris. Alfred was then in his early teens. He was sixteen when Jean Baptiste died on the retreat from Moscow.

The memoir is silent about Alfred's feelings about his distinguished father. When little Alfred heard the oft-told story of Jean Baptiste escorting Marie Antoinette's carriage away from Versailles, did he roll his eyes or ask to hear the story again? Did his father's close relationship with the revered General Lafayette fill him with pride? Perhaps he shared his mother's love of France, or maybe not, considering his father's terrible death in the service of Napoleon.

The memoir, on the other hand, relays a great deal of information about Alfred's distinguished father-in-law, William Lambe, and the close relationship he had with his daughter until his death in 1847. William Lambe became a member of a literary set that has dazzled through the ages: Robert Southey, Samuel Taylor Coleridge, Charles Lamb, Charles Dickens, and Robert Browning. Harriet Lambe described her father "as a man of great classical and mathematical attainments." The literary lion Samuel Johnson (quoting Dr. Parr) called him "a man of learning, of science, of genius, and of distinguished integrity and honour." The writer Walter Savage Landor said he was "the wisest and best man it has ever been my happiness to know."[20]

It speaks well of the young groom that he was considered a worthy choice by William Lambe and his wife. Happy well-wishers in both the Lambe and Boinville families surrounded the couple on their wedding day. The following year there was another reason to rejoice: the birth of a baby, Charles Alfred, named after his grandfather. Charles's memoir will have a lot to say about the Paris years, when Harriet reached out to Mary and Claire. She did not reach out to Shelley, however. As the next chapter will explain, Shelley called Mrs. Boinville "a lost friend."

Chapter 18

"Tell them, especially Mrs. Boinville, I have not forgotten them," 1819–1826

> *I most devoutly wish that I were living near London.... All that I see in Italy ... is nothing—it dwindles to smoke in the mind, when I think of some familiar forms of scenery, little perhaps in themselves, over which old remembrances have thrown a delightful colour.*
> —Percy Bysshe Shelley, Letter to Thomas Love Peacock
>   August 24, 1819

Magnificent Italian landscapes aroused in Shelley memories of home, and he wished he was back in London. The English landscapes he pictured in his mind's eye were delightfully transformed by "old remembrances" of friends.

In Italy Shelley's lifestyle continued to be peripatetic. Mary bore the responsibility for managing the constantly uprooted household. They moved from Milan to Livorno, Este, Venice, Naples, Rome, back to Livorno, Florence, and Pisa in pursuit of better company, or better weather, or better lodgings, or better morale. Shelley kept running, and to Peacock he makes a shocking admission: "The ghosts of dead associations rise and haunt us, in revenge for our having let them starve and abandoned them to perish." He had not forgotten the dead: Harriet Shelley, left in London; Fanny Godwin, left in Wales; and his year-old daughter Clara, who died on September 24, 1818, left near Venice.

He had insisted that Mary and the children join him, Lord Byron and Claire in Venice. Mary reluctantly began to pack up and began the ill-advised journey. Their baby Clara, weakened by dysentery, grew sicker and sicker. The long carriage ride in the heat proved to be fatal. Like Harriet Shelley and Fanny Godwin, Clara Shelley became another ghost that haunted Percy Bysshe Shelley. His daughter, like his first wife and his friend Fanny, was dead and abandoned, "buried on the lonely beach of the Lido, as desolate as the sea which stretched beyond it. No tablet marked her grave."[1]

Nine months later Shelley and Mary's son William died of a fever at the age of three. He was buried in the Protestant Cemetery in Rome. Malaria was the probable cause of death. Maria Gisborne (formerly Reveley), a longtime friend of the family living in Italy, took Mary under her wing and tried to comfort her. She had consoled and cared for Mary Godwin as a newborn baby in 1797 following the death of her mother, Mary Wollstonecraft Godwin. Mary was inconsolable. Two weeks after William's death, Mary wrote Marianne Hunt: "May you my dear Marianne never know what it is to lose two only & lovely children in one year—to watch their dying moments—& then at last to be left childless & for ever miserable."[2]

Figure 18.1. Shelley appears lost in his thoughts in this painting by Alfred Clint, completed in 1819. Source: Public Domain.

London Dinner Parties and the Boinville Circle

In Italy, Shelley and Mary paid close attention to what was happening in the lives of their London friends. Hogg and Peacock, who once strolled the night streets of London with Shelley, talking about books and women and what they were writing, now sat at desks—Hogg as a lawyer and Peacock as a businessman with the East India Office. Shelley learned that Peacock met monthly with his old friends. "You don't tell me if you see the Boinvilles, nor are they included in the list of the *conviti* at the monthly symposium. I will attend it in imagination."[3] Shelley's imagination was a needed place of retreat. In their grief, Shelley and Mary felt very unhappy and lonely in their marriage. The smallness of their social circle in Italy increased their sense of isolation. Eagerly they awaited mail and replied to every morsel of news.

In the spring of 1819 two dinner parties in London peaked the couple's interest. Letters went back and forth, relaying information about the dinners: those who were invited, those who attended; and how the Londoners and the exiles in Italy felt about the gatherings. This gossipy correspondence is significant for what it reveals about those present and those absent. Thomas and Cornelia Turner, perhaps at the encouragement of her mother, hosted the first dinner. The Turners had moved from Binfield, near Bracknell, into town. Tom Turner personally called on Peacock to invite him. Peacock accepted. Hogg was also invited and attended the dinner as well.

Peacock enjoyed himself, as he had so many times at Mrs. Boinville's country house. He wanted to reciprocate the Turners' hospitality and invited them and Hogg to dinner. He also wanted to include Leigh and Marianne Hunt, very close friends of the Shelleys. Peacock felt anxious about whether the Hunts would come, and so he wrote to ask. Peacock's uneasiness stemmed from what had happened at Bracknell in 1814. Shelley's passionate attachment to Cornelia had raised alarms within the Boinville family and caused her husband to whisk her away.

In the end Hunt agreed to spend an evening with Tom and Cornelia Turner. On March 9, 1819, he wrote Mary:

Peacock has told you, I suppose, that Mr. Turner called on him the other day, and invited him & Hogg to dinner with his wife & Marianne at Kensington. Peacock asked me if I had any objection to meet them at his lodgings to dinner. I said I had, because as I was not an old acquaintance of theirs, I could avoid their company, and *would never meet a person who would not meet Shelley* [emphasis added]; but Hogg says they are now very desirous of seeing him, and so my grandeur relented.[4]

Five years after the drama at Bracknell (the hasty exit by Shelley and Mrs. Boinville's "ungentle mood"), the Turners wanted to renew their acquaintance with Hogg, Peacock, and Shelley. If Shelley came to London, they were "very desirous of seeing him."

In her reply to Hunt, Mary made a few sharp comments of her own: "We must thank you also for your delicasy [sic] about meeting the Turners—These people are very strange." Without elaborating, she calls Thomas Turner, a bad man, slanderous and envious. Turner was Godwin's trusted lawyer and financial adviser. In Mary's opinion, Turner misrepresented the financial interests of both her father and her husband. More to the point, Mary disliked the Turners because, before she met Shelley, Shelley had been infatuated with Cornelia.

"If we saw [the Turners] we should at least keep a kind of barrier in the way of intimacy," Mary tells Hunt. Then she spears Mrs. Boinville, calling her "a very delightful woman, but someone who has the unhappy knack of either forgetting or appearing to forget her friends as soon as they turn their backs."[5] At the time she eloped with Shelley and Shelley left his wife, Mary had felt the sting of Mrs. Boinville's disapproval. Now, in 1819, she imagined Mrs. Boinville still disapproved of her. After all, she had not written to Mary or her husband one word since they left Italy.

After Harriet Shelley took her own life in 1816, Mrs. Boinville did not halt all dealings Percy Bysshe Shelley. When he asked her to mediate with the Westbrooks about the future of his children, Ianthe and Charles Shelley, she agreed. Mary and Shelley both had wanted to assume responsibility for the motherless children. Not surprisingly, the Westbrooks refused to give their grandchildren to the man who had ruined their daughter's life.

"So you know the Boinvilles"

On the same day, April 6, 1819, that Mary criticized Mrs. Boinville in the letter to Hunt, Shelley wrote Peacock praising her:

> So you know the Boinvilles? I could not help considering Mrs. B., when I knew her, as the most admirable specimen of human being I had ever seen. Nothing earthly ever appeared to be more perfect than her character & manners. It is improbable that I shall ever meet again this person whom I once so much esteemed & still admire. I wish however you would tell her that I have not forgotten her, or any of the amiable circle once assembled round her.[6]

Shelley's glowing praise of Mrs. Boinville affirms her importance in his life. How he missed her and those happier times! "When I knew her" gives the first hint that Shelley feels forgotten by his lost friend. Silence had replaced their warm rapport at Bracknell when he lived in her home for two months and they conversed on "a thousand different subjects" (See March 11, 1814, 232.)

Shelley follows his praise of Mrs. Boinville and her "amiable circle" with this comment to Peacock: "I wish however that when you see her you would tell her that I desire such remembrances to her as an exile & a *Pariah* may be permitted to address to an acknowledged member of the community of mankind." He capitalized and emphasized *"Pariah."* To be viewed as a pariah by Mrs. Boinville, who once thought so highly of him, hurt. He had put her on a pedestal: "nothing earthly ever appeared to be more perfect than her character and manners." He idealized her and found her fascinating:

> Cornelia, though so young when I saw her, gave indications of her mother's excellencies, & certainly less fascinating, is, I doubt not, equally amiable & more sincere. It was hardly possible for a person of the extreme subtlety & delicacy of Mrs. Boinville's understanding and affections to be quite sincere & constant."[7]

It is surprising that Shelley, considering his marital infidelity and impetuous and unpredictable nature, faults Mrs. Boinville for inconstancy. He feels abandoned, not only by the dead but also by the living. Shelley views Cornelia—"so young when I saw her"—as just as amiable as her mother but "more sincere." Shelley's memories of the young Cornelia can be compared to her memories of the young Shelley. In 1873, the year before her death, Cornelia wrote about Shelley to her friend Violet Paget (later famous as the writer Vernon Lee), as will be explained in Chapter 26.

Cruel Losses

On August 4, 1819, Shelley's twenty-seventh birthday, Mary was in the third trimester of another pregnancy—and suffering:

> I begin my journal on Shelley's birthday—We have now lived five years together & if all the events of the five years were blotted out I might be happy—but to have won and cruelly have lost the associations of four years is not an accident to which the human mind can bend without much suffering.[8]

The birth in Florence of Percy Florence Shelley on November 12, 1819, did not remove the dark shadow on the Shelleys' marriage cast by deaths, especially the deaths of their small children: Clara on September 24, 1818, and William on June 17, 1819.

Claire Clairmont was also without her child. She had agreed that Allegra would go to Lord Byron, but the manner in which Allegra was taken away stunned her. Byron sent a messenger, an English shopkeeper working in Venice, to collect his daughter. Two days before the wrenching parting, Claire wrote Lord Byron. "I assure you I have wept so much to night that now my eyes seem to drop hot & burning blood."[9]

Her weeping continued. On March 1, 1821, against Claire's wishes, Lord Byron placed four-year-old Allegra in a convent school twelve miles from Ravenna. In defending his action to British friends, he said his servants could not control Allegra, and he was not the person to "attend to a nursery." The "air was good" in that area, he said in his defense, and then added an amazing comment about morality, amazing because Lord Byron did not appear to have moral scruples, or at least some of his past actions do not reflect them. He said Allegra's learning and morals would be advanced in the convent. Roman Catholicism was "the best religion, as it is assuredly the oldest of the various branches of Christianity."

Claire's suggestion that Allegra go to a boarding school in England where she could be visited by friends, he dismissed, adding that "he would never give a natural child an English education, since "with the disadvantages of her birth her after settlement would be doubly difficult." Immensely wealthy, he was thinking about money and the financial consequences of Allegra's birth out of wedlock. He anticipated her marriage. A dowry of five or six thousand pounds "would allow her to marry very comfortably abroad."[10] That the little girl was far from her mother and friends did not matter to him. Allegra, Claire's treasure, died a year later on April 19, 1822, at the convent at Bagnacavallo from a fever, probably typhus. Claire never got over her death, never forgave Lord Byron, and never had any more children.

"Our Lost Friend"

Maria Gisborne and her husband visited the Shelleys in Leghorn, Switzerland, and in Pisa. In Livorno on July 25, 1819, Shelley wrote Hogg about Mrs. Gisborne. He described her as "a very amiable and accomplished woman about forty-five who resembles Mrs. Boinville in her acquirements, her freedom from certain prejudices and the gentleness of her manners, though she does not approach our lost friend in the elegance and delicate sensibility of her mind."[11] Shelley scholar J. L. Bradley has described Maria Gisborne as a liberally minded and kind woman with intellectual inclinations.[12]

In 1820, Mary took a trip to London with Percy Florence for a few months. When she returned to Italy, she and Shelley resumed their life together. In 1821 Edward Williams and his partner Jane became part of the Shelleys' small circle. Edward had been at Eton with Shelley and shared his passion for sailing. Wistfully, Shelley wrote his English friends back home, "I wonder none … stray to this Elysian climate, and, like the sailors of Ulysses, eat the lotus and remain as I have done."[13]

Shelley and Lord Byron, and a new English acquaintance, Edward John Trelawny, lived and breathed sailing. Shelley and Lord Byron ordered two sailboats custom made to their specifications by Genoan boatbuilders. Byron named his craft *Bolivar*. Shelley's yacht, *Don Juan*, was a veritable nautical nightmare.[14]

Shelley wrote Hogg, "Do you see the Boinvilles now? Or Newton? If so, tell them, especially Mrs. Boinville, that I have not forgotten them."[15] The following month, the *Don Juan* arrived from Genoa, "the perfect plaything for the summer." Shelley loved taking her out on the Gulf of Spezia, even though the weather could be unpredictable and he did not know how to swim. On July 8, 1822, Shelley, Edward Williams, and Charles Vivian, a young deckhand, left the coast in the *Don Juan*. They had planned for Trelawny to accompany them in a separate boat, but he did not show up.

Hours passed. The sailors did not return. Mary and Jane Williams became frantic and a search was mounted. Trelawny discovered Shelley's wet corpse in the sand on a beach near where the women waited. Later a funeral pyre was built on the sand and Shelley laid upon it. Mary did not watch as flames consumed her husband's body. Once the fire died down, Trelawny removed Shelley's heart from the pyre. Mary kept it, wrapped in fabric in her writing desk, as a relic of their love for decades afterwards.

Mary Shelley remained in Italy, staying with Leigh Hunt and his wife, who had moved to Genoa. In the months after Shelley's death, Mary often saw Byron and Trelawny and Claire. Trelawny had an affair with Claire. He sent her flowers and proposed marriage, but Claire said no.

In 1823, Mary and Percy Florence returned to London. Mary had become famous as the author of *Frankenstein*. Mrs. Boinville, silent for years, the former friend who never wrote, began to correspond with Mary. The two widows would visit each other and collaborate on the literary legacy of Percy Bysshe Shelley, the great poet, drowned at twenty-nine. (See pages 235, 243, 246, 248 for Harriet's letters to Mary Shelley, October 16, 1829; June 11, 1836; December 18, 1837; and January 26, 1839.)

PART III
Life in Paris

Chapter 19

Leaving London and Reconciling with Mary Shelley, 1827–1829

> My intimacy with Shelley ought not to have ended as it did. I say this with self-reproach & I still feel that sharpened pang added to all my other feelings on his life.
> —Harriet de Boinville, Letter to Mary Shelley, October 16, 1829[1]

About six years after Percy Bysshe Shelley's death, Harriet left London and began a new life in Paris. The exact timing and reasons for the move are not clear, but by 1828 both of her children—Cornelia (thirty-three) and Alfred (thirty-one)—had serious personal problems. Alfred had become mentally ill and incapable of caring for his five children. Cornelia had separated from her husband, Thomas Turner.

Harriet may have moved to Paris to find better treatment for her son or to give her daughter a home in a country with rules of propriety that were less rigid than in England. In early nineteenth-century Britain, a married mother with children who was not living with her husband was viewed as scandalous. British wives could not divorce their husbands, and British law bound wife to husband as property. Children legally belonged to their fathers.[2]

In 1828, Cornelia Turner had been married sixteen years and had three children: Oswald, fourteen; Alfred, eleven; and Pauline, only two.[3] Many years earlier, on July 4, 1803, Turner had reached out for help to William Godwin, whom he considered a wise and compassionate man. At the time Turner was tormented by confusion over homosexual encounters. Cornelia and Tom Turner's decision to separate may have been mutual. He left their home in Kensington, moved to Leghorn (the English name for the Italian city of Livorno), and became a banker. In the years ahead, he periodically visited his wife and three children.

Harriet Bids the Godwins Farewell

Before she moved to Paris, Harriet visited William and Mary Jane Godwin in their humble quarters, 44 Gower Place, London. William Godwin had been forced to declare bankruptcy in 1825, but the consequences proved surprising, as Peter Marshall has explained: "By enormous industry, by underhand jobbery, by plain doggedness, he had managed to postpone the inevitable for twenty years. But when it came, he was pleasantly surprised: his bankruptcy proved to be a liberation."[4] Godwin enjoyed the company of his daughter and his grandson when they visited, and he kept writing. His morale was high, but Mary's morale worried him. He wrote her on October 9, 1826:

> How differently are you and I organized! In my seventy-second year I am all cheerfulness, and never anticipate the evil day with distressing feelings til to do so is absolutely unavoidable. Would to God you were my daughter in all but poverty! But I am afraid you are a Wollstonecraft.[5]

Godwin feared for Mary, believing she suffered from depression as had her mother (Mary Wollstonecraft) and her half-sister (Fanny Wollstonecraft Godwin).

In January 1827, Harriet repeatedly went to see the aged philosopher. She visited him on the 16th and again on the 17th, when they spoke with Thomas Holcroft, a playwright whose stance in favor of parliamentary reform had led to his trial for treason in 1794. Godwin's eloquent defense had saved Holcroft's life. Harriet went back to Gower Place on the 26th and 27th, the last of seventy-three mentions of her in Godwin's diary. On that cold wintery day the two old friends solemnly parted.

Harriet's Fresh Start at Fifty-Five

When Harriet moved to Paris she was fifty-five. She not only changed countries. She made a radical change in her lifestyle. After living alone, with her adult children living separately from her with their spouses, she became the matriarch of a multigenerational household of five. Harriet and her daughter and three grandchildren lived at 74 Rue de Clichy in the ninth arrondissement. One can imagine the teenage boys Oswald and Alfred devouring the food at their grandmother's table and two-year-old Pauline running through the halls of the house.

Harriet's youthful flexibility and adventuresome spirit are revealed in her letters to her grandson Charles de Boinville and in his letters to her. She was an active participant in his life and in the lives of his children: William, Alexander, Cornelia, and Frank.

By the time she moved to Paris, Harriet had already weathered considerable adversity and sorrow, including the deaths of her husband and sister. More heartbreak lay ahead—namely, her son Alfred's mental illness. In 1818, Alfred's life had looked full of promise when he married Harriet Lambe, the eldest daughter of the renowned London physician William Lambe. The couple had five children, but by the time Charles, the eldest, was eight, their father had to relinquish to his wife responsibility for their care. He was too ill to take care of them. This sad truth is revealed in the *Memoir of the Reverend Charles A. Chastel de Boinville*, published in 1880. Charles apparently considered his father's mental illness a private matter. He says practically nothing about it. Thomas Constable, who wrote the memoir based on the journals and letters Charles gave him, wrote only this:

> Of Charles's early years there is scant record, but we know that, although *by the serious and disabling illness of their beloved and admirable father* [emphasis added], he and the other children were thrown, when he was not above eight years old, on their mother's sole care; it was in repeating the Lord's Prayer along with his father, and by his side, that the earliest religious impression was made and left upon his mind.[6]

Charles carefully skirts the taboo subject of mental illness. He conveys respect for his father and early memories of praying with him. Nothing is said about the circumstances or behaviors that led to Alfred's institutionalization in Ivry, France, in the late 1820s. Harriet's grandson Frank de Boinville, as well as Alfred, would die in the same hospital, a tragedy mentioned decades later in correspondence between Mary Shelley and her sister Claire Clairmont.[7]

Mary Shelley's Literary Career

By 1829, the year Harriet (Collins) de Boinville reconnected with Mary Shelley, Mary had written five publications: a travel book and four novels. *History of a Six Weeks' Tour through a Part of France, Switzerland, Germany and Holland* (1817) and *Frankenstein; or, The Modern Prometheus* (1818) were published anonymously. *Valperga; or, The Life and Adventures of Castruccio, Prince of Lucca* (1823) and *The Last Man* (1826) were published under her own name. She never sought a publisher for her novel *Mathilda*, written in 1819 and 1820, because her father advised against it and she put the manuscript aside. Its themes of incest and suicide shocked William Godwin, and he worried about her public reputation.

Mary's books were not lucrative enough to free her from financial dependence on Sir Timothy Shelley, who did not like her, never deigned to meet her, and warned her that he would not tolerate any more negative press coverage associated with the Shelley name. Mary had to be extremely careful what she said or wrote about her late husband. Interest in the dead poet was high, and the public was eager for tidbits. Former friends and acquaintances of Shelley were eager to cash in on their knowledge of him—something Harriet de Boinville, to her credit, never did. Mary lived a quiet life. She was careful to appear the epitome of respectability and not risk her father-in-law's ire.

"My dear Mrs. Shelley"

On October 16, 1829, Harriet replied to a "kind letter" from Mary Shelley that she received "with almost equal pleasure & surprise."

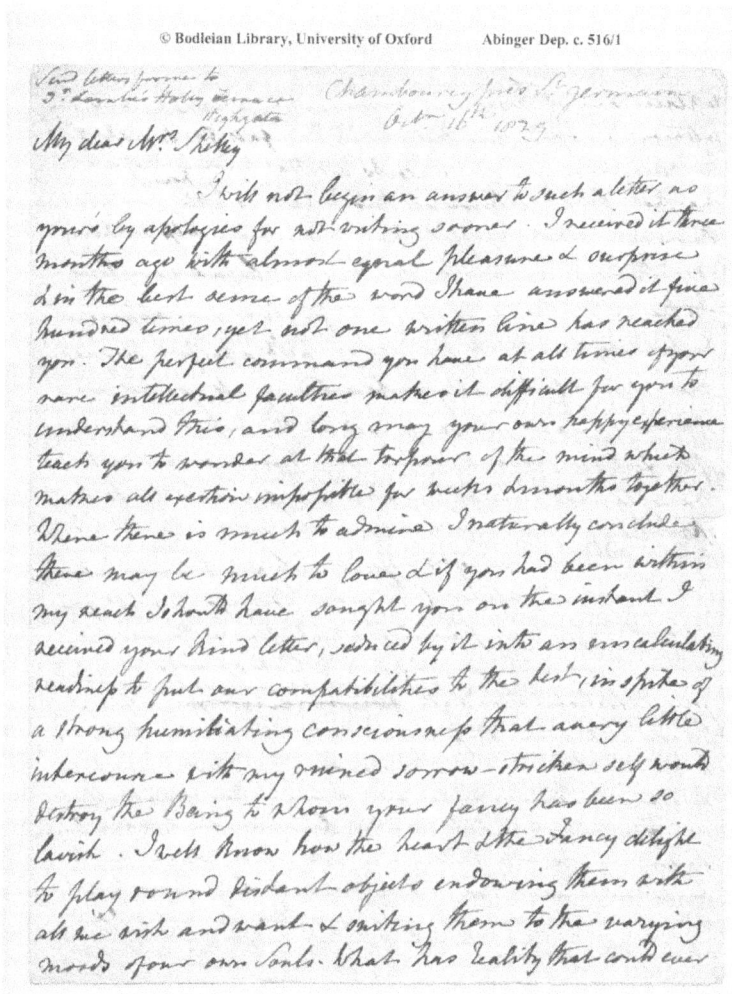

Figure 19.1. Harriet de Boinville's letter to Mary Shelley, Oct. 16, 1829. Source: Bodleian Library, University of Oxford, Abinger Dep. c. 516/1

Mary's letter is lost. We have only Harriet's answer. There is a ten-year gap between 1829, when Mary wrote kindly, and April 6, 1819, when Mary wrote critically about Mrs. de Boinville to Leigh Hunt, calling her a woman with "the unhappy knack of either forgetting or appearing to forget her friends as soon as they turn their backs."[8]

Something happened that restored their rapport and prompted Mary to confide in her. Mary visited Paris in mid-April 1828, and perhaps the two widows saw each other then. Mrs. de Boinville knew Mary well when she was growing up on Skinner Street, but Mary's elopement with Shelley, a married man, when she was sixteen ended their cordial relations until 1829.

Harriet did not reply to Mary's letter for three months, and the reason she gives for the delay is surprising:

> The perfect command you have at all times of your rare intellectual faculties makes it difficult for you to understand this, and long may your own happy experience teach you to wonder at that torpor of the mind which makes all exertion impossible for weeks & months together.

"My ruined sorrow-stricken self"

If you lived nearby, she tells Mary, I would have rushed right over to see you with "an uncalculating readiness to put our compatibilities to the test, in spite of a strong humiliating consciousness that a very little intercourse with my ruined sorrow-stricken self would destroy the Being to whom your fancy has been so lavish." The Being you imagined I was when you wrote your letter, with its lavish compliments, is very different than the person I am now, dramatically altered by sorrow.

Harriet imagines Mary "at the moment of writing me that letter." She thinks of the pleasure of Mary's "own conceits" as she put pen to paper:

> I well know how the heart & Fancy delight to play round distant objects endowing them with all we wish and want & suiting them to the varying moods of our own Souls. What has Reality that could ever replace one of these our own creations? What could my intercourse afford you that would not fall far short of the pleasure of your own conceits at the moment of writing me that letter?

Harriet's explanation for not writing Mary sooner may be honest but it is certainly awkward. I did not write because a letter from me would have destroyed the favorable impression you had of me. Harriet is troubled by "a strong humiliating consciousness" that her real self does not resemble Mary's idea of her. She is different now, and later in the letter she will describe more specifically how she has changed.

Mary: "An Exotic Transplanted in Unsuitable Soil"

By the fall of 1829 Mary had left Italy and was living at 33 Somerset Street, Portman Square, London. Percy Florence was ten. In response to Mary's confidences, Harriet refers to specific problems. For example, "I am not surprised at the dissatisfaction you often feel in those around you. You are an exotic transplanted into an unsuitable soil." Harriet considers Mary, with her "rare intellectual faculties," to be an exceptional person. She values her as a deep-feeling and deep-thinking woman, not likely to be satisfied by mundane talk about mundane topics.

A social circle well suited to Mary would have to be polished and refined: "Your early and intimate intercourse with the most refined of human beings has left you a standard for comparison which few in the most polished circles could bear & from which springs (by necessity) your dissatisfaction with your present society." Harriet's reference to "the most refined of human beings" may mean Godwin and Shelley or just Shelley, but the gist of her remark is clear. She understands why Mary is dissatisfied with her present society. Mary necessarily has a high standard for friendship.

Shelley: "That Ethereal Being"

In terms of literary history, what Harriet says about Percy Bysshe Shelley ("that ethereal Being") is perhaps the most significant part of the letter. "Accidental circumstances" and "some discordant views" had rudely parted her and Shelley. What was discordant was Harriet's opposition to Shelley's desertion of his wife, Harriet Westbrook Shelley, to run away to Europe with Mary and her sister. When contacted by Shelley for a loan of forty pounds,

Mrs. de Boinville refused.[9] After Shelley, Mary, and Claire returned to London, she did not take their part but sided with the Godwins and with Mrs. Shelley.

Harriet admits to strong feelings of remorse about how she behaved toward Shelley after he moved to Italy:

> Need I tell you with what deep regret my mind often returns to all the endearing circumstances of my intimacy with that ethereal Being who did not belong to the gross & palpable world over which we still wander bearing about vain longings & warm regrets. My intimacy with Shelley ought not to have ended as it did. I say this with self reproach & I still feel the sharpened pang which this thought added to all my other feelings on his life.

Just as Shelley continued to think about his "lost friend," she continued to have "tender recollections" of him. Shelley had written in 1819 about ghosts of the dead that pursued him in Italy (Harriet Shelley, Fanny Godwin, Clara Shelley). Mrs. de Boinville refers to a ghost, but one associated with happy memories of Shelley:

> —some ghost of former pleasures flitting before me would bid me write—yet I did not & for the very reason perhaps why I should have written—because I felt though suddenly & rudely parted by accidental circumstances & some discordant views & feelings—there still remained for us some sympathies which nothing could kill & which would sooner or later bring us together again.

She had thought more time remained for them because she shared with Shelley "sympathies" that nothing could kill. His sudden death changed everything. She is left with self-reproach and pangs of regret. Her remorse is genuine. What she writes next in her self-defense is lengthy and labored:

> I felt that he in some measure belonged to me & I did not write because I knew that a line springing warm from my heart would at any time bring that wayward Child of Fancy

from the world's end with uncalculating haste to see me & I would not have had him risk the incalculable ills of such a visit to a country where there was so much to annoy him. So I try to excuse myself to myself—but I am not satisfied for he is gone.... . He's gone and I think in vain of the warm greeting, the interchange of glowing thoughts—and affectionate looks on which I used to reckon with blind forgetfulness of the instability of all things.

With stunning certitude, Harriet asserts that one line "springing warm from my heart" would have brought Shelley back to England to see her with "uncalculating haste." Fearing the consequences for him ("incalculable ills"), she did not write. The press, still outraged at his lifestyle, would have hounded him. He would have been annoyed by a visit to his country, controlled by conservative persons with views so alien to his radical principles. Perhaps this is what she is trying to say to Mary—weak excuses for her silence and she knows it. "So I try to excuse myself to myself—but I am not satisfied."

Harriet: "write to me again"

"I cannot help wishing that something may bring you to Paris before very long," Harriet tells Mary. "In the meantime if you can forgive my apparent neglect do, & write to me again with a perfect persuasion that I shall feel really interested in all you tell me of yourself."

Fortunately, Mary's plans did bring her to Paris, and the two women deepened their friendship. Harriet collaborated with Mary in the 1830s to promote Shelley's literary legacy. Toward the end of the long letter of October 16, 1829, Harriet inquires about Hogg, Peacock, and other members of her former circle. "Tell me much of W. Godwin to whom I beg to be remembered in the kindest manner," she writes.

Adieu my dear Mrs. Shelley.
Cornelia sends you her love &

I am faithfully & affectionately yours,
H de Boinville.

I am glad to hear so grand an account of Percy.
Cornelia's Oswald is to me a bosom friend.

After decades in England where she signed her letters Harriet Boinville, she added "de," possibly reflecting her position in Paris as the widow of a French nobleman. In France she started over. Fresh hardships arose, particularly concerning her grandson Oswald Turner.

Harriet also confronted a major health challenge: deteriorating vision: "You see my dear Mrs. Shelley that if I have not written sooner tis not that I could find nothing in my heart to say to you. I am almost blind & absorbed in a most melancholy way for weeks & months together so that I undergo the almost insufferable privation of reading & writing & my mind is forced to look inward & feed upon itself."

Remarkably, considering her physical and mental condition, Harriet advanced rather than retreated in the years that remained to her. In Paris she established a welcoming home for Cornelia, Oswald, Alfred, and Pauline Turner. In the 1830s and 1840s, she will invite to this home many relatives, friends, and strangers. The popular host of Bracknell in her forties becomes—in her fifties, sixties, and seventies—the popular salonnière of the Rue de Clichy.

Chapter 20

Godwin's Death and Significance, "The Extinction of a Mastermind" 1830–1836

> The extinction of a master mind gives a shock to the feelings for which mine were ill prepared… Everything is interesting which relates to such a man, one of the gifted few under whose moral influences society is now vibrating.
> —Harriet de Boinville to Mary Shelley, June 11, 1836, about the death of her father.[1]

The "ruined sorrow-stricken self" Harriet described to Mary Shelley in 1829 is nowhere in evidence in the letter she wrote Mary in 1836. Harriet reveals a vibrant interest in life, in her relatives and friends, and in politics—particularly the revolution in the Italian states.

Harriet relocated to Paris two years before Lafayette (the general revered by her father, her husband, and herself) returned to the center stage of French politics. A three-day coup (July 27, 28, and 29, 1830) toppled the conservative Bourbon ruler Charles the X. Louis Philippe I, the cousin of Louis XVI, ascended the French throne. From the steps of the Hotel de Ville in Paris, Lafayette proclaimed the new king "the best of republicans." The people interpreted Lafayette's endorsement as a guarantor of reforms to come. French novelist Stendahl called Lafayette "the anchor of our liberties."[2]

Harriet viewed with pleasure the tricolor flag floating above the Tuileries Palace, but the new king soon disappointed liberals because he did not fulfill his promises of sweeping reforms. In the 1830s, Stendahl lived near Rome and lamented what was happening in Italy where "abject despotism, Bourbon, Hapsburg, or Papal, still prevailed."[3] By 1836, Italy occupied a great deal of Harriet's attention. Early in the decade, however, she enjoyed introducing her grandchildren to Paris and its glorious monuments.

"A very lively time"

In 1833 on the Rue de Clichy, more young people arrived in Harriet's home. Fifteen-year-old Charles de Boinville and his younger brothers visited. Brought up in the English countryside near the border with Wales, Charles found Paris thrilling. The boys, as well as their tutor, Monsieur Gollet, who accompanied them, arrived on Sunday, May 12th for what the memoir described as "a very lively time." A fun-loving grandmother, Harriet appears to have believed "the more, the merrier"—the more grandchildren and the more sights to see the better. The fun in Paris began on the very first evening. Charles

> saw with great admiration the fireworks at Tivoli, the following day visited Notre Dame and the Tuileries, and on the next the Jardin des Plantes, and went again to Tivoli at night. In short, what with theatres, museums, bathing, lessons in dancing, and the caressing attentions of kind relatives and friends, in Paris and elsewhere on their homeward route, they had not leisure to mark the flight of time, until on Sunday, the eleventh of August, they found themselves once more at home in Hereford.[4]

Harriet orchestrated the whole vacation, mindful that her son Alfred could not play an active part in his children's lives.

In his teen years, Charles began to confide in his attentive grandmother. Despite the allure of Paris, he decided he wanted to become a farmer and told her about his decision. "This has been an important year in your life," she wrote him in 1834; "you are growing fast into a man—a good and valuable one I am assured you will be; you have decided an important question, that of your occupation for life. I have no doubt you will pursue it with steadiness."

To encourage Charles, she mentioned that the famous Lafayette relished farming:

M. de Lafayette, in the midst of the great interests that have busied him, thinks with delight of his farm, is eager to improve his breed of merinos, and to regulate his crops in the best manner. The brother of the poet Burns says, "I can say, from my own experience, that there is no sort of farm labour inconsistent with the most refined and pleasurable state of mind, threshing excepted—glory be to the threshing machine!" You, my dear Charles, will ally the cultivation of the ground to the cultivation of your mind, and out of this will spring pure pleasures and sound health, I trust.[5]

In this letter to her grandson, Harriet shows her warm and loving nature. She chooses her words carefully to encourage him as he begins his chosen "occupation for life."

Figure 20.1. Horse-powered threshing machine. Source: Unknown author (*Dictionnaire d'arts industriels*). Public domain.

"Your dear good mother"

Charles began as a farming apprentice in Dilwyn. In order to supervise his studies, his remarkable mother left their home in Hereford with her four other children. Harriet admired Harriet Lambe de Boinville. She told Charles, "The removal of your dear good mother to Dilwyn is an important thing for you, as it will enable you to spend your leisure hours most profitably and pleasantly."[6] After long days in the fields, he spent evenings at home under his mother's loving and watchful eye.

Charles benefitted from his grandmother's assurances that she believed in him. Her 1834 letter shows something of the intelligence, kindness, and wisdom that made Percy Bysshe Shelley admire her so much. Charles was fortunate in his mother and grandmother. The circle of brave women in the 1830s included Mary Shelley.

"Dark night shadows the world"

As she approached her thirty-sixth birthday, the age her mother had died, Mary Shelley was feeling depressed. In August of 1833, reflecting her mood, she wrote, "dark night shadows the world."[7] Influenza had twice laid Mary low. She and Percy Florence had both fallen ill in April 1833, and Mary suffered a relapse the following month.[8] The year before, Mary's half brother succumbed quickly from influenza. William Godwin, Jr. was only twenty-nine.

Peter Marshall, in his biography of William Godwin senior, notes the father's fondness for his son. He never left his bedside during the young man's fatal illness. William and Mary Jane Godwin buried their son in the Church of St. John the Evangelist, in the Waterloo Road near their house.[9]

Mary kept writing steadily to help pay the bills and she also spent time with her father. In his late seventies, Godwin remained mentally vigorous, but his body had weakened. In 1834 he was named "Office Keeper and Yeoman Usher in the Receipt of the Exchequer" with an annual salary of 220 pounds and a rent-free apartment at 13 New Palace Yard. His daughter called it his "tiny, shabby place under Government."[10] He wrote Mary that summer about aging: "I am now well—now nervous—now old—now young."[11]

On April 7, 1836, soon after his eightieth birthday, Godwin died. According to a letter Mary wrote to a friend, he had "a catarrhal fever, which his great age did not permit him to combat... His last moment was very sudden—Mrs. Godwin & I were both present. He was dosing [sic] tranquilly, when a slight rattle called us to his side, his heart ceased to beat, & all was over."[12]

Godwin's will, written in 1827, directed William Jr. and Mary to choose from his library a book or set of books as a memorial of his affection. He left to Mary John Opie's 1797 portrait of Mary Wollstonecraft, the one hung in his study and admired by Aaron Burr.[13] The will asked Mary to review manuscripts "in my own handwriting and decide which of them are fit to be printed, consigning the rest to the flames." With regard to his letters, "judge if any ... be found proper to accompany my worthier papers." A tireless letter writer and prolific author, he left his daughter a mountain of work.[14]

"One of the gifted few"

On June 11, 1836, a month after Godwin's death, Harriet wrote Mary Shelley about her father. She considered his death "the extinction of a mastermind" and said "everything is interesting which relates to such a man, one of the gifted few under whose moral influences society is now vibrating." Harriet repeats the word "moral" a striking number of times in this letter (see the full text on pages 243-246). She understood that a moral purpose underpinned the masterpiece she greatly admired, *An Enquiry Concerning Political Justice and Its Influence on General Virtue and Happiness* (1793). A decade earlier, in 1784, Godwin's friend James Marshall had sailed out to St. Vincent to ask Harriet's father to fund their writings. Harriet first learned of Godwin when she was eleven during Marshall's visit. John Collins did not agree to a publishing venture with Marshall and Godwin, but his relations with them remained positive. As an adult, Harriet saw a great deal of Godwin in London between 1809 and 1827, as his diary entries show.

Harriet refers in the 1836 letter to her private feelings about the death of her longtime good friend and contrasts those feelings to the loss felt by the British public: "If I had never known Mr. Godwin I should have felt the general loss, have been saddened by the gloom of another light put out, but accident had created for me a whole set of private feelings & associations connected with your father which have been revived by his loss & which drew me toward you with a strong sympathy." She asks Mary to write "such details as you can bear to give of the melancholy event. I am anxious to hear he did not suffer much physically, whether he was aware of his approaching end, by what disease we have been robbed of him & where he is interred."

Harriet mentions "another loss which came still nearer to my heart," the death of Percy Bysshe Shelley. That death of Mary's husband "we must unceasingly lament," she says, and "will never let us become strangers to each other." Perhaps referring to her failure to answer letters or to answer them promptly, Harriet then states: "Communication may be suspended but circumstances will be perpetually springing up to revive it for it is the peculiar property of intellectual ties that they are not to be broken by the accidents which destroy more material ones."

Percy Bysshe Shelley scholars rarely fail to mention Harriet's beauty when he met her in 1813, but it was not Harriet's appearance but her evident intelligence that most captivated him. Harriet felt connected to Mary by "intellectual ties" as well. Those strong bonds would not let them become strangers to each other, although they had been out of in touch: "It is so long since I heard from you, I do not even know where you live, & must send you circuitously this letter which I hope you answer soon for I want to know something of the present state of your mind on certain points." Those points were Mary's feelings about Italy.

"The present affecting state of Italy"

Mary had told Harriet about her happy memories of Italy, and Harriet wondered if her feelings had changed. "An interval of several years with all its various incidents strangely modifies our thoughts & feelings, so that a letter addressed to the feelings which ruled you ten years ago may find little hold on those which possess you today." After this lead, Harriet gets to the point:

> When I last saw you were looking with a tearful eye to Italy — as the land of your happiest recollections. Italian nature was to you beautiful nature and your regrets and longings were really touching; but the rust of absence has had time to form. Has it so eaten into your love that you take no great interest in the present affecting state of Italy? Even if it were

so which I should be sorry for, I think you will find in the little book of Poems which I send you enough of strength & originality & deep feeling to make them interesting to you.

Harriet hoped to kindle Mary's interest in the Risorgimento, the movement for the independence and unification of the states in the Italian peninsula. The movement was not going well. Many rebels had been wounded or killed. Harriet sympathized with brave survivors who had taken refuge in Paris. She praised the Italians she knew, men "distinguished morally & intellectually."

Harriet lived the comfortable life of a wealthy woman in Paris, but she did not seclude herself in a cocoon of privilege. The Italian patriots she knew lived

in honourable privation uncrushed morally by the numerous ills of exiles & devoted heart & soul to intellectual labours for the benefit of their country and of humanity. I say humanity for we are…arrived at the point where the true interests of particular nations merge in the true interest of all.

In that day, women tended to focus on their own domestic concerns. Some took an interest in national politics, but Harriet's global perspective is quite extraordinary. Harriet also reveals some of her views about marriage in this letter. This topic arises when Harriet brings up their mutual friend Frances Wright.

The Social Reformer and Abolitionist Frances Wright

Born in Scotland in 1795, Frances Wright moved to New York City in her twenties. In 1827 she had invited Mary Shelley to join her in Tennessee at the Nashoba commune where slaves received an education and worked on the 2000-acres of woodland to earn their freedom. Harriet admired this work. Her childhood in St. Vincent, where Africans were enslaved on her father's sugar plantation, influenced her egalitarian views. A great admirer of Mary Wollstonecraft, Wright had hoped Mary would accept the invitation to come to America, but this did not happen.

William Godwin's good friend Robert Owen, a Quaker social reformer, had been influential in the creation of the utopian community at Nashoba. Earlier, Owen had founded a socialist village in New Harmony, Indiana. He had a sweeping utopian vision: the creation of a "New Moral World" characterized by enlightenment and prosperity based on education, science, and communal living. Owen's son Dale courted Mary in the 1820s; they became friends, but she rejected his romantic advances.[15]

Frances Wright had once been Lafayette's mistress. She married another Frenchman, Monsieur Darusmont. According to Mary Shelley's biographer Miranda Seymour, Madame Darusmont was "an emancipated and courageous philanthropist."[16] Harriet describes her as "a delightful creature—not only endowed with a strong intellect & great reasoning powers but with a quick sensibility & capability of loving which make her quite irresistible."

Harriet considered the Darusmonts "a rare couple" because their marriage was a partnership of equals. Of interest to Harriet was not whether the wife was worthy of the husband but whether the husband was worthy of the wife, and Mr. Darusmont was, in Harriet's opinion. Frances Wright is now "most happily married to a man quite worthy of her morally—partaking her own enthusiastic views & hopes for improvements—with a very active mind well stored with scientific acquirements." Harriet valued knowledge derived from science and believed scientific advances were essential to the improvement of humankind.

The Darusmonts were "tenderly united & enjoying a degree of happiness which is awful—for the Gods you know are jealous of such happiness." Harriet writes "you know" because Mary also had been shocked by the news that her husband was dead. Both women had been suddenly widowed. Jean Baptiste froze outside Moscow; Shelley drowned in Italy.

As Mary read Harriet's enthusiastic praise of the Darusmonts' happy marriage, she may have felt a twinge of envy. She had had several suitors. Dale Owens had not been the only one. At least twice she had hoped to receive a proposal of marriage, only to be rejected for another woman. When they were young Mary and Harriet had defied their fathers to run off with the men they loved. Mary was sixteen at the time; Harriet, twenty. The news of Madame

Darusmont's marital happiness genuinely pleased Harriet, but Mary may have reacted wistfully. She was thirty-nine and lonely.

"Adieu, my dear Mrs. Shelley"

"The lengths & subjects of this letter will prove to you how much pleasure I should have in meeting you again," Harriet concludes. "Are you ever attempted to pass a short time in Paris?" They did reunite several times in Paris. Referring to her daughter, Harriet adds, "Accept from Cornelia the love of an old companion and friend & believe me very affectionately yours, H de Boinville."

In a postscript Harriet inquires about members of her former circle back in London:

> Tell me what has become of Mr. Hogg and Mr. Peacock & if Mr. Peacock's little girl has grown up all that his fondness could hope—remember me kindly to him. I pray say for me to Mrs. Godwin all that her melancholy loss can dictate.

Harriet is interested in William Godwin's literary legacy: "I suppose you will give us the memoir of Mr. Godwin," she writes and adds that if Mary needs help, she has someone (not named in the letter) in mind.

One of the most striking aspects of the 1836 letter is Harriet's preoccupation with "the present affecting state of Italy." She sends Mary poems and two articles from an Italian review. "I wish you would give me your opinion of both." Harriet recommends these writings to Mary "to sow seed which may come up & in time produce a plentiful harvest." At the age of sixty-three, Harriet is looking eagerly to the future, promoting the work "of great minds belonging not to one country but to Europe."

Chapter 21

Harriet Rescues Shelley's *Queen Mab* for Posterity, 1837–1841

> *I seize an opportunity offered by a very obliging friend on whom I can depend to lend you my copy of* Queen Mab. *I value highly this copy ... a relic of genius, of friendship, of past happy days which it would really grieve me to lose.*
> —Harriet de Boinville, Letter to Mary Shelley, January 26, 1839[1]

Harriet de Boinville's decision to loan Mary Shelley her own prized copy of *Queen Mab* had long-lasting consequences. Lending this copy, with the poet's original wording, promoted Percy Bysshe Shelley's reputation in the years ahead as a radical thinker and doer. As Harriet's letters to Mary attest, she also cared a great deal about the literary legacy of William Godwin.

Mary Shelley and William Godwin's Will

As instructed in her father's will, Mary dutifully began to sort through Godwin's voluminous papers. She knew posthumous fame "had been a matter of great concern to the old man; his will laid on her the burden of securing it," Miranda Seymour correctly notes.[2] Mary's apparent intention was to create a collection of Godwin's correspondence with biographical notes and a separate history of his life that ended with the death of her mother, Mary Wollstonecraft, in 1797.[3] She wanted to steer clear of personal information about Shelley: his relationship with her before and after their marriage in 1816 and his relationship with her father. The collection she envisioned would honor her father *and* avoid enraging her difficult, publicity-shy father-in-law.

Sir Timothy Shelley had given Mary a mandate: do nothing, say nothing, write nothing that would lead to more publicity about his son's life. Mary also saw a danger in calling attention to Shelley's radical lifestyle and principles. Bad publicity could jeopardize her son Percy Florence's education and entire future as a respectable English gentleman.

Efforts to comply with Godwin's will exhausted Mary. Claire Clairmont worried about the toll on her sister's health, and Mary had reason to worry about the effects of a memoir on her father's reputation. She knew all too well the disastrous consequences of William Godwin's memoir about her mother, *A Memoir of the Author of* A Vindication of the Rights of Woman (1797). Godwin had intended the memoir to be a tribute to his talented wife, a powerful writer and a bold champion for women's rights, but reviewers did not focus on Wollstonecraft's important writings or progressive ideas but on intimate details of her personal life. Many in the press viewed Wollstonecraft as an outrageously immoral woman.

In addition, the memoir increased public scrutiny of her daughters, Fanny and Mary. With its references to Wollstonecraft's despair and suicide attempts, the memoir may have contributed to her daughters' later struggles with depression (fatal in Fanny's case). The book certainly intensified Mary's wariness of the press and irrevocably damaged her father's reputation.

"A lover of his fame… and the memory of a great name"

Harriet expected Mary to write about her father, and she mentioned in the June 11, 1836, letter that she had a capable friend who could help her. The following year, on December 18, 1837, she refers to "My friend Dr. Constancio," someone "about to furnish a short memoir of Mr. Godwin to a reputable biographical publication."

Francisco Solano Constancio, a Portuguese diplomat and man of letters, was "well-pleased" to write the article. She assures Mary that Constancio has "a due appreciation of your distinguished father." Harriet then tells Mary that Constancio needs "the best materials"

—for these we naturally apply to you and entreat you to send me some of the most striking circumstances of his life—with a correct list of his works—and the exact place & time of his birth with other such particulars as you may think best calculated for a limited Memoir. Some one will certainly write this article & we desire it should come from the pen of a lover of his fame & just appreciator of his doctrines. Whatever materials you may furnish will be valuable & we hope you will be disposed to aid this tribute to the memory of a great name. ...

Harriet, sixty-four years of age, presumes quite a lot of her much younger friend: "For the trouble it may give you [to send the materials] I will make no apology, but entreat you to send me a speedy answer. Your pen I know flies like the wind so this will cost you less than it would any other person." Whether she got a speedy answer is not known.

Harriet then returns to the subject broached in 1836, a subject Mary may have wished she would drop: "We are looking with impatience for your own important memoir of Mr. Godwin." It was not Harriet's long personal relationship with Godwin that made her so insistent, but rather her belief in Godwin's ideas. Like Constancio, Harriet was a "lover of his fame & just appreciator of his doctrines."

Quill pen in hand, she thinks about the essence of his teachings. "Science has realized some of the dreams of political justice, & many of the seeds scattered thro' his works are springing up here & there & making promise of future harvest." She uses the word "science" in a broad sense, as Godwin and Shelley might have used it, to include the pursuit of knowledge and the Enlightenment emphasis on reason.

Mary Wollstonecraft once called thinking a "fierce exercise." She challenged women to cultivate their minds.[4] In this letter to Wollstonecraft's daughter Mary, Harriet demonstrates the ferocity of her convictions. In 1813, William Love Peacock had commented on the "earnest discussion" and "fervour" with which Harriet and her guests at Bracknell debated Godwin's masterpiece on political justice.[5] Two decades later her enthusiasm had not waned. Godwin's hopes for a more just world remained her hopes.

As instructed in her father's will, Mary Shelley reviewed Godwin's letters and papers, but she never wrote about his life. Seymour considers the possible reasons why and concludes: "It is tempting to suppose that, having sacrificed so much of her life to her father's needs, Mary simply abdicated from a task which threatened to consume the remainder. And who could blame her? She had already done more than enough."[6]

Helping Constancio with his biographical article about her father may have interested Mary as little as writing about him herself. She had other demands on her time—caring for her teenage son and pursuing her own literary projects. Mary considered her finest novel her last novel, *Falkner*, completed in 1837 when she was forty. She wrote in total eight books after she finished *Frankenstein* and more than fifty short stories and essays. In her discussion of *Falkner*, Charlotte Gordon notes the author's interest in politics, philosophy, and human rights. Gordon says Mary "judged her books, and all books for that matter, on their ethical standards. If one adheres to these criteria, then Mary Shelley is right; *Falkner* is her best work, as it is in this novel that she gives full voice to many of her most radical ideas and the female characters enjoy their greatest triumphs."[7]

Original Publication of *Queen Mab*

In 1838, Mary Shelley agreed to a publisher's request for a collection of her husband's work. She realized she did not have the *original* version of *Queen Mab, A Philosophical Poem: With Notes*, which went to press in April or May 1813.

Queen Mab pulsed and throbbed with radical views. Percy Bysshe Shelley feared arrest and had reason to be afraid. He limited the first printing to 250 copies. He did not want *Mab* to get into the hands of the London authorities. Whenever he made a gift of the poem, he removed the title page, which identified him as the author. He listed the address of his father-in-law, John Westbrook, on Chapel Street as the printer's address. His intent was to prevent the police from tracking him down in his own dwelling. He also removed the dedication to his wife in the gift copies he distributed.

That spring of 1813 his friendship with Mrs. Boinville flourished. She recognized in the young poet a hint of his latent genius.

Her friendly encouragement as a person and as a writer helped him find his literary stride. Around the time of the birth of his daughter Ianthe Shelley in June 1813, Shelley gave "Mrs. B" a copy of *Queen Mab* as a present.

"I have not partiality to irreligion"

Twenty-five years after the original publication of *Mab*, Mary Shelley had a problem. She did not have a copy of the first printing, and she was not sure if all of the radical passages from the original version should appear in the collection she was working on. On December 11, 1838, she wrote Thomas Jefferson Hogg. He was then living with Jane Williams, whose partner Edward had drowned with Shelley in 1822.

> Dear Jeff — Jane has told you I suppose that I am about to publish an Edition of Shelley's Poems—She says you have not a Queen Mab… Did not Shelley give one to you—one of the first printed. If you will lend it me I shall be so very much obliged & will return it safely when the book is printed. The Bookseller (Moxon) has suggested leaving out the sixth & seventh parts as too shocking & atheistical. What do you say? I don't like mutilations — & would not leave out a word in favor of liberty. But I have not partiality to irreligion & much doubt the benefit of disputing the existence of the Creator —give me your opinion.[8]

Hogg did not have *Queen Mab*, but Harriet did. Therefore, P. B. Shelley's first major work appeared in Mary Shelley's collection as originally written, without "mutilations" and with all the incendiary passages. This utopian epic is aflame with the twenty-year-old poet's radical ideas. Shelley attacks the monarchy, the church, commercial greed, and war. The seventeen notes are essays on topics such as free love, republicanism, atheism, and vegetarianism. Shelley refers in one note to the vegetable-fed children of Harriet's sister and brother-in-law, Cornelia and John Frank Newton.[9]

"A relic of genius, of friendship, of past happy days"

Harriet reluctantly agreed to Mary's request for an original copy of *Mab*: "I confess that I lend it with reluctance & to no one but yourself would I confide it. I commit it to your care & rely confidently on your promise to return it to me as soon as you have made the use you wish of it." She used a trusted friend as a courier to get the thick, bound copy safely from Paris into Mary's hands in London. She values highly Shelley's gift to her, "a relic of genius, of friendship, of past happy days which it would really grieve me to lose." (For the full text of Harriet's letter of January 26, 1839, see page 248.)

By parting with her cherished copy, Harriet made an important contribution to literary history. She quite literally saved the poem so it could be enjoyed and studied in its entirety. Without Harriet's reluctant generosity, *Mab* might have been read through the centuries in its abridged and bastardized form.

During the winter and spring of 1839, *The Poetical Works of Percy Bysshe Shelley* was published in four volumes, edited by Mary Shelley with her preface and notes. Of the 250 original copies of *Queen Mab,* only 70 were distributed in England, Ireland, and America.[10] The poem influenced working-class protests in England. Chartists, who were advocating for democratic reforms in northeastern Britain, published an edition of *Queen Mab* in 1839, and "Shelley's name was assured currency in the working movement for the next twenty years."[11]

Percy Bysshe Shelley became the bright star of the Chartists for three reasons:

> The first was their estimation of Shelley's political philosophy as more intrinsically radical than the mainstream of British radicalism, as exemplified by Godwin. Second, Shelley's stands on the questions of religion, inheritance and political reform proved to be appealing to the Chartists. Third, and most important of all, to the Chartists Shelley was a political poet—and poetry they saw as a principal means of moving the people.[12]

Figure 21.1. Portrait of Mary Shelley by Richard Rothwell, 1840.
Source: Public domain.

Peter Marshall once wrote, "The political for Godwin is the personal."[13] The same might be said of Harriet de Boinville. Letters to Mary Shelley in 1829, 1836, 1837, and 1839 reveal her passionate side. She raved about the Italian patriots exiled in Paris and the path-breaking social reformer Frances Wright. She shared Wright's and Godwin's interest in utopian communities in America. Godwin and Shelley were two of the most famous and most radical writers in Britain in the eighteenth and nineteenth centuries. Harriet greatly admired them. Like Godwin and Shelley, she favored reform of the aristocracy's tight hold on British government and British education. She held unconventional, egalitarian views about social class. As to her views on religion, it is hard to say. Godwin and Shelley were professed atheists; references to God in Harriet's letters (to Hogg and to her grandson Charles) suggest that she was not.

"Tell me all you can of yourself"

The 1839 letter reveals the warmth of Harriet's character as well as some of her ideas. She wants Mary to be happy and understands something of her widowed friend's loneliness: "When you write pray tell me all you can of yourself. It would give me pleasure to hear that you are as happy as a thinking Being can be & that you have the society of a few friends that suit you; many you cannot expect to have for you naturally require more than is easily found." She refers to their previous correspondence, "Percy you tell me contributes largely to your satisfaction. I rejoice at that & hope one day to know him."

Harriet looked forward to introducing Mary to her grandson Oswald. "Mr. Godwin and Shelley I am sure would have valued him." The letter concludes:

> I wish that instead of sending you this letter I could throw on my cloak & have an hour's chat with you. Speak of your health when you write & think of me sometimes as of an old friend who is very affectionately yours,
> H. de Boinville.

In 1840, Mary made two stops in Paris. To her empathetic friend, Mary later wrote: "I should so like to see you all again—I passed happy hours among you in Paris."[14]

Chapter 22

"A Noble Nature and a Loyal, Loving Heart," 1842

I felt a strong desire to preach the gospel in France, the land of my fathers.
—The Reverend Charles A. Chastel de Boinville, Memoir, published in 1880

In 1842 Harriet's grandson Charles moved to Lille, a town in northern France near the border with Belgium, and began to serve with Methodists. He visited from house to house and preached from place to place. Under the Charter of 1814, Louis XVIII allowed Protestants to continue to practice their religion in France, as they had under Napoleon, but Catholicism was the state religion and discrimination against the Protestant minority continued. It was a hard life Charles chose. His grandmother continued to write to him letters of encouragement.[1]

Charles's spiritual odyssey began many years earlier, when he was eighteen and began his farming apprenticeship in Dilwyn, England. His mother, Harriet Lambe de Boinville, influenced his education at that time when he lived with her and his siblings in Dilwyn. Before going to work in the fields, he studied Latin. In the evening he returned home;

> after one or two chapters of the Bible, our mother read aloud to us the novels of Sir Walter Scott; we much preferred the novels, but after a time I grew weary of them, and used often to leave the room, that I might read in private books of the more serious kind, or natural history or narratives of travel. On Sunday, after morning service, my mother would

assemble us around the table for a time, that we might read the Bible together by turn. After this, we were at liberty during the remainder of the day to read or play, and in the evening we had a game of cards; but our mother always taught us to respect those persons whose views were stricter than our own.

Harriet Lambe de Boinville's five children were baptized in the Church of England. This was the church that controlled admittance to Oxford and Cambridge universities and to the British government. It was the church of the upper class, his class. Although his mother taught her children to be tolerant of the stricter beliefs of dissenters, she felt "no special favour for dissent in general" the memoir states, "and certainly none for that body with which Charles elected to connect himself," the Primitive Methodist Society.

Charles had a transforming experience, described in detail in the memoir, one day in Dilwyn, when he rested next to the threshing machine and opened his pocket Bible. The third chapter of the book of Romans deeply affected him: "it was as the dawn of heaven to my soul; the burden of my sin seemed lifted off, with all my sorrow. That day I thought was the only happy one I had ever known."

The days that followed, however, were not all happy. He became troubled "inwardly by waning interest and a temptation to spiritual pride, outwardly by the openly expressed distress of a mother whom he fondly loved." She feared lest "the change in my religious views should weigh down my spirits and make me fit for nothing." His grandmother invited him to Paris, where he enjoyed the "warm affection" of his relatives: grandmother, his Aunt Cornelia, and his cousins, Oswald, Alfred, and Pauline Turner. Then, he left for Lille, "the way the Lord hath led me."

"These days have been hard to get over"

Pauline Turner wrote to Charles after he left the Rue de Clichy. She said the house felt sad without him. Everyone was away. Only her mother, the maid, and Monsieur Robecchi, a friend of the family, were at home. Pauline brought up their talks about religion. She had many questions. "You tell me that you understand all that you read in the Bible and yet some say there are passages that no one can understand. How can that be?"

On January 6, 1842, Harriet wrote to Charles with the news that Pauline had died. Pauline's death from consumption at the age of sixteen shook the family. Pauline had lived with her grandmother on the Rue de Clichy since she was two:

> Our poor little girl gone forever! and some little circumstance perpetually starting up to bring her suddenly and painfully before us. These days have been hard to get over; and now, what will '42 bring? Let us not think of that but hide our faces thankfully in the obscurity of the future... .

Harriet responded to the awful tragedy as stoically as she could. The rest of the letter conveys concern for her grandson. She tells Charles that she had been thinking of him all day. She worries about him, "not comfortable in any way" and "without any circumstance to cheer" him in this sad time. "A dear friend of mine used to say that a loving unsullied soul carried everywhere a paradise within itself. *Is* that true? *You*, dear fellow, can tell."

Harriet writes Charles that she had received a letter from "R." He was someone Charles had helped. The memoir relates the story. R went to Charles's boarding house and asked to borrow 500 francs to feed his family. With 600 francs to his name, Charles gave away 500. Within the month R came back and said he could not repay the debt but invited the impoverished minister to live in his home. Charles moved in with R and his many children. In her letter Harriet writes:

> *Do* tell me if you have plenty of firing, a warm room, and all-sufficient covering at night; these little things are most important to your old anxious granny... . Tell me too about your money; a great part of it, I dare say, has found its way into pockets more empty than your own. I wish you had some watchful loving sister to examine your hoard, and make a calculation for you... . Yesterday's post brought a few lines from R--, despairing over the want of money to go to the end of the month. I fear by this time you repent hav-

ing gone to live with them, for I suspect their roof affords no quiet of any kind.... . God bless you, dear boy, and preserve you from the dangers of your best qualities... .

Harriet was right. There was no quiet under R's roof. The memoir describes shrieks and moans. The children whimpered. R broke furniture and tried to strangle his wife. The wife threatened to poison herself. Charles stayed in the home despite the domestic abuse, at one point selling his overcoat for money for food. Years later R's wife visited Cornelia Turner in Paris to express her gratitude for all Charles de Boinville had done to help her family.

After referring in the 1842 letter to the "best qualities" of her grandson, she adds: "Nul ne peut sortir de la région intellectuelle qui lui est assigné, et les qualités sont encore plus indomptables que les défauts." A rough translation is as follows: No one can leave the intellectual region assigned to him, and innate good qualities are even less easily changed, than defects. Then she closes with "Write, write, write—tutto, *tutto*, TUTTO!"

Educational Pressures and "Smart Bonnets"

Charles was pressured by relatives (with the single exception of his Parisian grandmother) to leave France and complete his studies at Oxford or Cambridge. "Such a course would have been more comfortable," he admitted. He said "a snug English parish" tempted him, but in the end he went to the Academy of Lausanne.

Charles Wesley (1707-1788), the itinerant preacher on horseback who addressed laborers in their fields, sparked the Methodist movement in Britain. In France, the law prohibited open air preaching, much to the disappointment of Harriet's grandson Charles. In Batignolles, a district outside Paris, he became friends with laborers, known as *chiffoniers*, who picked rags. Some pawed through common garbage; the more fortunate sorted trash from the houses of the rich. "On considering the state of the French people, I am appalled at the difficulties that lie in the way of doing extensive good," Charles wrote in the memoir. "The laws forbid field-preaching, and if they did not, it would be difficult to bring people together. The greater part of those who call themselves Christians manifest little personal zeal in works of active charity; the few churches where pure gospel is preached are crowded with smart bonnets; it is not preached to the poor."

Harriet de Boinville's Red Sash

Charles praises his grandmother at the beginning of his memoir. He greatly admired how she lived her life. He faulted her, however, on one point, her appreciation of the principles of the Enlightenment with its emphasis on reason not faith. Harriet was sixteen when the French Revolution began in 1789. Writing nearly one hundred years later, Charles associates his grandmother's beliefs with her core identification with the revolution, manifest in the red sash she wore then and for years to come. She

> had early imbibed the political principles of her father, which she carried indeed still further. Round her slight figure she wore the badge of republicanism, a wide red band, and I have often heard her call herself *une enfant de la revolution*. With this she had also unfortunately accepted the principles of the false philosophy of the age, but her general conduct, unbounded generosity, devotedness of character and unfeigned modesty of nature, might well have put many professing Christians to the blush, for in the refinement and elevation of her sentiments she surpassed almost any woman I have ever known.

It is interesting that Charles comments on Harriet's British father, John Collins, a man who welcomed French exiles in his home, raised money to help free Lafayette imprisoned by the Austrians, and influenced her republicanism. Collins bought slaves in St. Vincent in 1785; he sold them before 1806, when his will was officiated. His book on the medical treatment and management of slaves is titled *Practical Rules*, but it contains much philosophy. It discusses the immorality of cruel masters and affirms that slaves have souls and should not be treated like animals.

After Pauline Turner's death in 1842, Harriet grieved for Cornelia, another granddaughter who died at the age of sixteen from tuberculosis. John Keats, in "Ode to a Nightingale," describes the terrible illness, "the weariness, the fever, and the fret" when "youth grows pale, and specter-thin, and dies." Keats died of tuberculosis, caught while nursing his consumptive brother. Keats was twenty-one. Pauline and Cornelia were vibrant girls cut down too soon.

Fortunately, a few months after Cornelia de Boinville's death on June 7, 1843, there was a new arrival in Paris, Mary Shelley's sister, Claire Clairmont. Claire was a needed distraction from grief, someone to befriend. Claire wrote Mary many letters about Madame de Boinville and the writers, artists, musicians, and Italian refugees she gathered into her circle.

Chapter 23

Claire Clairmont Joins Harriet's Circle in Paris, 1842–1845

> There is something in her society and conversation that animates and pleases me.
> —Mary Shelley, Letter to Claire Clairmont
>   September 20, 1843[1]

On May 11, 1842, Claire Clairmont moved to No. 3 Rue North Clichy. She frequently visited the bustling de Boinville-Turner household down the street and wrote her sister Mary Shelley riveting letters about what was going on. One can imagine the white-haired salonnière of No. 74 Rue de Clichy speaking her flawless French, gesturing and smiling in the way that had won her French husband's heart. Thomas Jefferson Hogg noted her "Frenchness" in his memoir of Percy Bysshe Shelley, calling her "an amiable and accomplished old lady, and tolerably agreeable, but too much of the French school to be quite so." Hogg—the British gentleman and heir to Norton House—was most definitely of the English school.

Claire and Mary's correspondence shed light on a feature of Harriet's life that she rarely showed as she graciously greeted a steady stream of guests in her home. Stoical by nature, she hid her sorrow over the mental illness in her family. So-called "madness" affected not only her brother and her son but also her grandson Oswald Turner.

In 1842, Claire was forty-five. A look back at her youth, and the many years she spent as a governess, is necessary to understand the woman she became in middle age. The young Claire marched forward, chin up, down a twisting and difficult path in life. It is easy to cheer for her.

Claire the Governess

In *Thoughts on the Education of Daughters* (1787), Mary Wollstonecraft, described "the unfortunate situation of females fashionably educated and left without a fortune."[2] This was Mary Wollstonecraft's situation, and it was Claire Clairmont's as well. They faced a similar challenge: the absolute necessity of earning a living when few respectable occupations were open to well-educated women with little money.

Born in 1759 into a large family where she experienced poverty and abuse, Wollstonecraft started a school for girls with her two sisters. When it was forced to close, she traveled alone to Ireland to become a live-in governess in the castle of Lord and Lady Kingsborough, members of Ireland's Protestant aristocracy. For forty pounds a year, Wollstonecraft taught three of their five daughters. Fourteen-year-old Margaret, the eldest, was her favorite. Although Wollstonecraft taught Margaret for only one year, her influence changed Margaret's life. The pampered and privileged teen became an independent and accomplished woman. In adulthood, Margaret adopted republican principles and "gloried in having had so clever an instructress, who had freed her mind from all superstitions."[3] She went on to write four books for children and studied medicine, accomplishments that would have made her mentor proud.

Remarkably, Margaret became Claire's mentor years later. Claire, Mary, and Shelley met her in Italy in the early 1820s. She had left her second husband, Lord Mount Cashell, and eloped with an Irishman named George Tighe. The couple lived under the fictitious names of Mr. and Mrs. Mason.

After the tragic death in April 1822 of her five-year-old daughter Allegra, Claire went to live with the kindly Masons for a month. Then she steeled herself for a new life. Claire traveled alone to Vienna where her brother Charles Clairmont lived. Immediately upon arrival in Biber Bastei, on September 24, 1822, Claire wrote Mrs. Mason (Lady Cashell):

> I tried the whole journey to follow your advice and admire the scenery—dearest Lady it was all in vain—I saw not mountains or vallies, woods or rushing streams... . I saw

only my lost darling… I am not in need of money, all the expenses of my journey paid, I have over ten pounds still in my purse, and my brother says that he will soon find me a situation as governess, as English governesses are very much in request in Vienna.[4]

After two years as a governess in Vienna, Claire bravely moved on into cold and unknown territory: Russia. There her progressive, one could say Wollstonecraftian, ideas about how her female pupils should be taught clashed mightily with the ideas of their parents:

I may safely say that the Russians and I are always at cross purposes—they pull one way and I another—they educate a child making the external work upon the internal, which is, in fact, nothing but an education fit for monkies, and it is a mere system of imitation—I want the internal to work upon the external; that is to say, that my pupil should be left at liberty as much as possible, and that her own reason should be the prompter of her actions.[5]

The Godwins had raised Claire, and her sisters Mary and Fanny, to think for themselves. They encouraged independent reading and learning, not monkey-like imitation. Claire also objected to how boys and girls were treated differently. The daughters of Russian aristocrats were expected to comport themselves at all times with lady-like self-control, and the results were disastrous in Claire's opinion:

[A] tutor is ten thousand times happier than a governess, because boys may jump and play, but girls must always be in a perpetual state of etiquette, which constraint spoils their disposition, by forcing it from its natural channel into a narrow space—the superfluity of gaiety which belongs to childhood is forced to escape, or rather evaporate (for to escape would make too great a noise) in ill humour and fretfulness, and the child becomes as hateful and troublesome as the parent.[6]

Claire believed that gaiety and exercise were essential for a child's well-being. She wondered if Allegra been given enough time to run and play. Teaching other people's children, Claire never forgot her beloved daughter, who died in the convent where she had been placed by Lord Byron.

For many years Claire toiled as a governess. In 1841, she returned to Italy to see Mary Wollstonecraft's former pupil, her own motherly mentor. Claire visited her after the death of her own mother, Mary Jane (Clairmont) Godwin. Just as Wollstonecraft had influenced young Margaret's politics and republicanism, so the grown-up Margaret (Lady Cashell, a.k.a. Mrs. Mason) influenced Claire's liberal views.

As a governess, Claire had to watch what she said to avoid being fired. Closely monitored by her employers, she felt constrained. Once she moved to Paris, she relished free speech. Eagerly she voiced her ideas, as she explained in one letter to her sister Mary Shelley:

> At Madame de Boinville's the people are clever and I go there and I like the conversation, but I am never allowed to speak myself ... after fifteen years being silent, I want to talk a good deal ... to clear out my mind of all the ideas that have been accumulating and literally rotting there for so many years—but they won't allow me this in Rue Clichy—the instant I speak, the whole coterie fall upon my words and pick them to pieces ... seize upon my argument (so dear to me)... . They are liberals but of such opposite characters.... . I beg it to be understood that I am the most liberal, I am proud to say, not one of them can keep pace with me in liberality I leave them all five hundred miles behind me.[7]

Bravo for Claire, barreling down the highway. At Madame de Boinville's, crowded with people just as opinionated as she was—republicans, egalitarians, and former Italian revolutionaries—she felt she could not get a word in edgewise.

Claire, Harriet's Neighbor

Claire was something of a busybody. She closely observed the extended de Boinville family and reported to Mary what was happening. Harriet's niece Octavia Newton, now the wife of Leon Gatayes, a Parisian musician, had gone to the country with Cornelia and Oswald Turner. Oswald was looking "painfully languid and weak." Claire was not surprised, "when one considers the life he leads—no amusement, nothing except Mathematics and Chemistry; fatiguing his brain for hours, days and months, and the only passe temps a walk with his Mama and Grand Mama."[8]

Claire believed Oswald had "an intellect of the highest order." She might have been right that walks with his mother and grandmother were insufficient relaxation for a thirty-year-old man. Oswald studied obsessively, but his mother and grandmother were not the reason. Oswald's fatigue was the result of own compulsions.

Oswald's younger brother, Alfred Turner, had "scientific and literary ambitions," and Claire thought he was too serious, "not enjoying anything in life except mathematics—in all other things he finds the most dreadful faults, or rather subjects of reproofs and discontent." Claire wanted young men to be happy. She was a believer in enjoying life.

Mary Takes a Stand

Mary planned a visit in December 1844 to see her sister. Mary did not want Claire to be so bossy and critical of her neighbors at No. 74: "When last with you, no one was in Paris, I was averse to society, & you were so aigue [sharp] with your neighbors of Rue Clichy—that I saw no one & did nothing & was very content—I could not do this again." Mary warns Claire not to monopolize her time, stating emphatically "I like the society of Mme de B and it is privation to me not to see her when in Paris."

Apparently, Claire had criticized Madame de Boinville's stoical response to family problems. "She may be deceitful ce m'est égal, Mary writes, but "I do not seek her for friendship & sympathy—but because there is something—there is something in her conversation and society that animates and pleases me—and I find this so seldom among my fellow creatures—and finding it enjoy it so seldom, that it is a privation not to get it when I can."⁹

Mary Shelley found Madame de Boinville's company animating and pleasurable, as had Mary's husband and father. She dismisses Claire's criticism with "ce m'est égal." You might be right, she is saying, but it's all the same to me. The family problems in 1844 centered around Harriet's grandson Oswald Turner, who got in trouble in Switzerland.

"Very disagreeable rumours are afloat"

"Very disagreeable rumours are afloat—so disagreeable that I do not wish to be the medium of communicating them," Claire wrote Mary, but communicate them she did:

> Madme de Boinville fell ill the day before yesterday and was bled yesterday—Mrs. Turner told me that she never got over the shock of the news she received from Switzerland. Something much more serious occurred there than they gave out.¹⁰

Exactly what the drama in Switzerland was all about is not clear, but Claire had several theories. One was that Oswald angered "uncivilized Mountaineers" who saw him dressed in "a short cambrier or cotton blouse with pantaloons of the same—no hat—no gloves and a ribbon tied round his neck to keep his locks in order like a girl." These men "evidently annoyed him, looking on him probably as mad—& so made him worse."¹¹ Some confrontation, never explained, ensued, and Oswald returned to Paris, where he began to rant in public. He spoke wildly about his cousin Octavia Newton, and about the de Boinville's friend Giulio Robecchi, "and many other people and he wore a costume so pretty and fanciful that he excited attention in the streets and so they could not keep him at home any longer."

Claire sympathized with Oswald. In December 1844, she wrote Mary about Oswald's institutionalization in Paris—and his breath-taking escapes:

He has done some wonderful things since his confinement: guarded in the strictest way he managed to escape three times—he climbed a high wall immensely high where there was not a place of a hair's breadth to put his foot on and jumped into the street and walked quietly into his grandmother's and asked for some tea.[12]

Claire wrote Mary that she had seen Oswald one day on the Pont de la Concorde: "he took my hand and looking gravely and most friendly at me he said—All you see and hear interpret by a contrary—I asked what he meant—but he said I can't stay now to explain but remember what I have said, and walked off.'[13] Oswald, the crazy person on the street, may have been speaking words of wisdom like Shakespeare's fool.

"Is he mad or not?"

On June 24, 1845, Claire wrote Mary about Oswald's chemistry experiments: "Struck by Frankenstein and the idea of creating human Beings, he endeavored to prove its truth." Night and day he worked on his experiments. "Magnetism I have no doubt would cure him; but how to get his mother or Grandmother to let magnetism be tried on him....Is he mad or not?"[14]

And the answer is hard to know. Claire's opinions vary from letter to letter. Sometimes she thinks Oswald is a confirmed lunatic and speculates about "homicidal tendencies." At other times she describes her young friend as a poor victim. Certainly, Oswald's circumstances were tragic, for him, his mother, and his grandmother. He went to live with his grandmother when he was fifteen. Fifteen years later he was still with her. In her home, she served him tea, took him for walks, observed his chemistry experiments, and worried and worried.

Only a few thousand persons were institutionalized for "lunacy" in England in 1800, but by 1900, that number had grown to 100,000. In response to the disturbing increase in institutionalization, some argued that "overburdened families and sinister medical professionals were manufacturing madness." Asylums housed social misfits and embarrassing relatives, "a convenient place to get rid of inconvenient people."[15] Harriet de Boinville and Cornelia Turner may have been wrong in their decision to institutionalize Oswald, but they were not indifferent to his suffering.

By December 25, 1845, Oswald was in a truly a pitiful condition. Claire recognizes his suffering—and his loving grandmother's agony:

> Poor Oswald is very bad—very gloomy—his relations visit him but he is very sullen with them—no wonder—he won't eat—they are obliged to force him. All this is terrible... Frank de Boinville is in a mad-house and I am most grieved to hear that they fear very much another of the Sons is going the same way—which is dreadful for poor Harriet de Boinville who is a most amiable person and most attached mother. Poor Woman Poor Woman—they say she frets very much and will not be consoled.[16]

Frank de Boinville was Harriet's grandson. Frank, like his father Alfred, had a "debilitating illness." The memoir by Frank's brother Charles says nothing about the symptoms or behaviors of his father and brother. It is silent on the taboo subject of mental illness.

Like Claire, Mary felt sorry for the matriarch of the family. "Poor Mrs. Boinville," she wrote her sister, "what a fate is hers—Madness being in the family, of course she has long feared this—& they must all have suffered distress enough."[17]

Harriet's grandson Charles suffered greatly, as did all the family, when his wife died. Claire wrote Mary about it. The minister's wife died "in her confinement after a year and a half's marriage... this just happened under their eyes for the young couple lived in Paris. You know how calm the whole family are in appearance—and how sweet tempered and gentle.... they force their manners to gentleness and circumspection, not to remind people of their misfortunes."[18]

Faced with calamities, Harriet de Boinville and Cornelia Turner carried on, presenting an appearance of gentleness and calm that seemed unnatural to Claire, whose emotions flowed as freely as her views. In 1845 and 1846 Claire wrote Mary impassioned letters about refugees she met in Harriet's home—pianists, painters, and Italian exiles.

Chapter 24

Welcoming Refugees in her Final Years 1845–1846

They are ready to make any sacrifices (I mean the De Boinvilles) for Italians.... it prevents them from feeling domestic sorrows.
—Claire Clairemont, Letter to Mary Shelley[1]

Despite family tragedies, Harriet welcomed into her home refugees from around the world. For example, she befriended the Russian pianist Vera de Kologrivoff, the Italian painter Luigi Rubio, and a former Genoan insurgent named Giovanni Ruffini who would become her daughter's partner and a highly regarded Victorian novelist.

These exiles felt at ease with Harriet for several reasons. She was fluent in French and Italian. She had traveled widely. Like many of her guests, she had experienced warfare and danger. Although a wealthy and cultured woman, she was no stranger to rugged living. Long before the arrival of steamships in the 1840s, she had sailed 5,000 miles to St. Vincent with her baby daughter, slept in a wildly swinging hammock, and scrambled across slippery ship decks. Once during the war with France, she capsized in the Channel, lost all her bank notes, and clung to a sailor's back to reach shore. The welcoming host on the Rue de Clichy was not a pampered fine lady of the British aristocracy, but a brave woman able to empathize with the refugees who had endured many hardships.

"Une grande favourite de Madame de Boinville"

The Russian pianist Vera de Kologrivoff was "une grande favourite de Madame de Boinville." Giovani Ruffini thus described her in a letter he wrote to Violet Paget (famous today as the writer Vernon Lee) in the 1870s.

Vera de Kologrivoff had been a child prodigy, giving her first public concert at the age of eight. In Paris she studied under the Polish composer Frédéric Chopin from 1842 to 1846. By the time Chopin died in 1849, many of his pupils had become de Kologrivoff's students. Despite her exceptional musical talent, the pianist could not make ends meet. "How many times have I seen her under the cold shadow of St. Germain, cutting her slice of bread, her dinner, with no butter visible," Ruffini recalled. "Without Madame Turner and her mother Madame de Boinville, I do not know what she would have done."[2]

Claire Clairmont became acquainted with Vera de Kologrivoff and kindly offered her a place to live in her own apartment. Soon Claire regretted that she had been so hospitable. The Russian woman was "a most desperate character," she wrote Mary and called her "a spy paid by the Russian government." Claire accused the woman of reading her mail and opening her bureau.[3] Claire tended to be suspicious. Ruffini, perhaps a more reliable judge of character, said Vera de Kologrivoff "has good in her, she is capable of affection, but she is not Russian for nothing, and dreams, like her native land, of universal conquest."[4]

Others thought the pianist "lacked amiability," but Harriet remained her friend. She introduced Vera de Kolgrivoff to Luigi Rubio, the Italian painter. Born in Rome, Rubio painted in Geneva, Turkey, and in Russia. One painting of Rubio's won a gold medal at a French exhibition, and his work was included in the Museum of Versailles opened by King Louis Philippe I. Harriet and her daughter tried to convince the French government to commission a painting by Rubio, a campaign Claire thought had little chance of success:

> Madame de Boinville and Mrs. Turner were very busy in getting deputies to sign a paper to the Chambers to buy a certain picture of Rubio's. It will most likely not succeed because the French only encourage their own artists of which they have a clamorous multitude. And then Rubio is not a painter of first rate talent, and has no right to expect such

a favour. Only Ingrez [sic] or Vernet, or Paul de la Roche may pretend such a distinction; but they are ready to make any sacrifices (I mean the De Boinvilles) for Italians....it prevents them from feeling domestic sorrows.[5]

Harriet's matchmaking, if not her attempt to influence the deputies, succeeded. The Italian artist and the Russian pianist married in 1846. Harriet arranged a wedding feast in her house. To help the newlyweds furnish their home, she gave them some of her own mahogany pieces.[6]

Giovanni Ruffini

Giovanni Ruffini and Giulio Robecchi became very important people in Harriet's life. Robecchi was not only her friend but her physician; Claire and Oswald Turner were also his patients. On January 24, 1846, Harriet met Giovanni Ruffini at the bedside of his dying compatriot. A few days later Robecchi was buried in the de Boinville family's plot at Montmartre Cemetery.

When she went to visit her dying friend, Harriet was accompanied by her daughter and grandson Alfred Turner. A deathbed is an unlikely setting for a new beginning, but that was where Harriet's friendship with Ruffini began and where Ruffini met Cornelia Turner, the future love of his life.

Giovanni Ruffini was born in Genoa, then part of the First French Empire, on September 20, 1807. In his youth, he fought alongside the rebel leader Giuseppe Mazzini, "surely among the most charismatic personalities of the century," according to Allan Conrad Christensen, the author of *A European Version of Victorian Fiction: The Novels of Giovanni Ruffini.*[7]

In Genoa, Ruffini's mother encouraged her three sons to rebel against the Austrians. Because of his insurgent activities, Jacopo Ruffini was thrown into prison and died there at the age of twenty-eight, "either because he believed his friends had betrayed him to the tyrannical authorities or because he feared that under torture he might betray his friends." Mazzini then used Jacopo's suicide to build support for the movement known as the Risorgimento. Mazzini claimed that after Jacopo cut his neck, he wrote in blood on the wall of his cell: "I bequeath the vendetta for my brothers."[8]

Sentenced to death, Mazzini, Giovanni, and Giovanni's surviving brother Agostino fled Genoa. Before their departure, Donna Ruffini gave her son Giovanni bread and wine and devoted him to Mazzini's glorious cause. She was known in the rebel movement as "La Madre Santa," the holy mother. Her blessing did not have the galvanizing effect she desired. Giovanni Ruffini would turn away from Mazzini's extremism, preferring the Piedmontese formula for Italian unity that favored a constitutional monarchy.[9]

Hunted by the Austrians, Ruffini left Genoa and arrived in London in 1833. He devoted himself to the study of English literature, especially Shakespeare, and developed his own masterful prose style. Ruffini also read Dickens, Thackeray, Scott, Sterne, Defoe, Fielding, Smollett, Mrs. Radcliffe, Thomas Hope, Macaulay and Ruskin. Scottish novelist Margaret Oliphant, who spent one winter in Paris with Ruffini, wrote that "his written English was beautiful, but he spoke it badly and with difficulty."[10]

In 1841, Ruffini left London for Paris and quickly made a name for himself as a librettist for the Italian composer Gaetano Donizetti. He wrote the libretto for Donizetti's opera *Don Pasquale*. Because the composer changed so much of the original working in the libretto, Ruffini refused credit in the program when the opera premiered on January 3, 1843, at the Théâtre-Italien in Paris. He did, however, accept payment, 500 badly needed francs.[11]

By 1846, when he met Harriet de Boinville and Cornelia Turner at Robecchi's bedside, Giovanni Ruffini had been living in exile for thirteen years, enduring the "daily insecurities of a life of grinding poverty."[12] Meeting Harriet and Cornelia marked a turning point in his life, and his relationship with them developed quickly over the next year.

Chapter 25

Harriet Dies and Giovanni Ruffini Comforts Her Family, 1847–1848

I am fulfilling a sad duty for your aunt Cornelia, broken by sorrow and fatigue. Alas, my dear Charles, our sweet and well-loved grandmother is no more. This morning at six she took her last breath.
—Giovanni Ruffini, Letter to Charles de Boinville
   March 1, 1847[1]

Harriet died in Paris on March 1, 1847, at the age of seventy-three or seventy-four. Her birthday in 1773 is not known, nor the name of her mother. Not one word about this possibly bi-racial woman appears in the family memoir. During Harriet's final hours, Cornelia Turner and Giovanni Ruffini kept watch. The same day she died, Ruffini wrote her grandson Charles, serving in Lisieux, France: "Notre douce et bien-aimée Bonnemaman-à-tous n'est plus." Our sweet and well-loved grandmother is no more.

Ruffini scholar Allan Conrad Christensen describes Harriet as "an exquisitely sensitive and intelligent woman who inspired Ruffini's devotion until her death." Beatrice Corrigan explains one of the reasons for his devotion: "With their customary benevolence, Mme de Boinville and her daughter persuaded Ruffini to leave his miserable room, and installed him more comfortably in an apartment above their own on the Rue de Clichy."[2]

Harriet's daughter-in-law, Harriet Lambe de Boinville, received the news of the matriarch's death from her son Charles:

I do not know whether you have received the sad intelligence from the Rue de Clichy. The enclosed from Mr. Ruffini will tell you all. I received it this afternoon. Though this event was not unexpected, my grief is very great. I always met with such love and kindness from her. The mother, grand-mother, and great-grandmother of us all is gone. I wrote to Aunt Cornelia as comforting a letter as tears would allow.[3]

Charles remembered his grandmother's unwavering loyalty. She took him sightseeing in Paris when he was a boy. She supported his decision to become a farmer when he was a teen. She supported his later decision to become a minister instead. She alone stood by him when he refused to attend Oxford or Cambridge to complete his studies. She understood that he did not want to serve in what he called a "snug English parish" but rather in France among the poor. Charles remembered her letters, always expressing concern: "Do tell me if you have plenty of firing, a warm room, and all-sufficient covering at night; these little things are most important to your old anxious granny."[4] Holding Ruffini's letter in his hand, Charles bowed his head and cried. How long and tenderly she had loved him.

Burial of the Matriarch

Harriet was laid to rest in Montmartre Cemetery. Today a grand white obelisk marks her grave at 20 Avenue Rachel, division 19.[5] Carved at the top of the tall stone memorial is her name, though not as one might have expected to find it:

Henriette Chastel de Boinville, née Collins,
b. St. Kitts 1773, d. Paris 1847

"Henriette" appears on her tomb and it appeared on the red wax seal she used to fasten her letters. Perhaps her mother liked the name "Henriette" and suggested it to her husband for their first-born child. On the stone memorial one can read other names, including "Giulio Robecchi," the good doctor with the soul of a poet who died in 1846.[6]

Harriet influenced some of the greatest writers of her age. The novelist Frances Burney, whom she met in 1793. William Godwin, whose *Enquiry Concerning Political Justice* sparked many a debate in her home at Bracknell. Percy Bysshe Shelley, the wild young man she met in 1813, the year he finished his first major work, *Queen Mab*. "Through Mrs. Boinville and the circle centered around her, Shelley made his first living contact with the traditions of the French Revolution," Kenneth Neill Cameron wrote. "There can be no doubt that the Boinville circle opened a whole new world to Shelley."[7]

Harriet also influenced her friend Mary Shelley, an important writer, the author of *Frankenstein* and six other novels. Harriet recognized Mary's "rare intellectual faculties" and felt connected to her by "intellectual ties." Their losses also connected them, what Harriet called "sympathies" that would never let them become strangers. Harriet corresponded with Mary about the literary legacies of Percy Bysshe Shelley and William Godwin. They confided in each other about their problems as well, such as Mary's dissatisfaction with her social circle and Harriet's worsening eyesight.

Figure 25.1. Harriet de Boinville in old age. Source: The de Boinville family.

Harriet attempted to arouse Mary's interest in Italian politics and introduced her to several of the Italian exiles she had befriended.[8]

The Writer Giovanni Ruffini

Giovanni Ruffini completed seven novels in English between 1853 and 1870. Charles Dickens admired his work. For his periodical *All the Year Round,* Dickens asked the assistant editor to seek contributions from Frances Trollope, Anthony Trollope, George Eliot, Elizabeth Gaskell, and Ruffini. That he was included among such celebrated Victorian authors is testimony to Ruffini's literary stature in Britain during the years of the Italian *Risorgimento*.[9]

Harriet met Ruffini in 1846, many years before he became a novelist. In 1847 Giuseppe Mazzini wanted to help Ruffini and managed to obtain for him a position teaching English in Brighton. Ruffini turned down this job that would have assured him financial security. Cornelia, he wrote, was the reason:

> Can I kick away the only element of happiness that consoles me in life? Heaven has offered me this port, should I venture to leave it? I feel unfortunately that the future is dark, dark for me with respect to material existence, but to assure this last should I sacrifice the life of my soul? I feel that in Brighton, even if I became rich, I would be miserable.[10]

Ruffini never became rich, but at Cornelia's side he would experience more than two decades of happiness.

In 1848 Ruffini was recalled from exile and elected deputy to the Parliament in Turin. He nearly refused to go, but Cornelia insisted that it was his duty. After the discouraging defeat of the Piedmontese in the March 1949 battle of Novara, Ruffini turned away from politics and channeled his energies into his writing.[11]

The Revolutions of 1848

In January 1848, fighting broke out across Western Europe and on the streets of Paris. On the Rue de Clichy Cornelia Turner nervously awaited the arrival of Scottish guests, Henrietta Jenkin and her two children, Fleeming and Anna Jenkin. What happened during their visit is described in a memoir Robert Louis Stevenson wrote thirty-two years later, *Memoir of Fleeming Jenkin* (1880).

Stevenson was the son of an engineer and, for a time, studied engineering to please his father. Fleeming Jenkin became a distinguished engineer and professor at the University of Edinburgh. In 1848, however, he was a boy. In the following passage from his memoir, Stevenson quotes Mrs. Jenkin:

> As we reached the Rue de Clichy, the report of the cannon sounded close to our ears and made our hearts sick, I assure you. The fighting was at the barrier Rochechouart, a few streets off. All Saturday and Sunday we were a prey to great alarm, there came so many reports that the insurgents were getting the upper hand. From the upper windows we could see discharge from the Bastille—I mean the smoke rising—and also the flames and smoke from the Boulevard la Chapelle.[12]

The Paris revolution forced King Louis Philippe of France to abdicate, and on February 25, 1848, a Second Republic was declared.

Cornelia's nephew Charles de Boinville witnessed the rioting in Lisieux in 1848 and "the great discontent among the lower orders." The revolution in Paris "came like a thunderbolt in the provinces," he wrote in his memoir. "The Republic was proclaimed, the greatest excitement prevailed; the bread and flour stealers of the preceding year were released, and a golden age was proclaimed."[13] The golden age did not arrive that year. Napoleon III, elected president of France in 1848, did not live up to his promise to institute far-reaching reforms, disappointing many liberals.

On the Italian peninsula, changes to the old order at first seemed imminent. Pope Pius IX fled Rome just before Giuseppe Garibaldi and his forces arrived and established a Roman republic. Mazzini became chief minister of the republic, and a new constitution was written that specified freedom of religion and free public education. By the following year, however, French and Austrian forces had returned power to the princes and to the Pope. Once more, Garibaldi and Mazzini fled into exile.

Henrietta Camilla Jenkin (1807-1885) and Cornelia Turner became close friends. During 1848, a period of political volatility internationally, Cornelia Turner and Giovanni Ruffini experienced domestic contentment. She was fifty-three, and he was forty-one when they began to live together. "Our friendship has all the entirety and intensity of what is called love but without the storms," Ruffini once said of their union.[14]

By 1848 Cornelia had lived separately from her husband, Thomas Turner, for almost two decades. She lived with Ruffini "in nearly perfect harmony from year to year, ever more wholly devoted, loyal, and indispensable to each other," Christensen writes. Their extra-marital cohabitation scandalized some observers. Scottish novelist Margaret Oliphant visited the couple in the winter of 1864-1865. She noted how the pair grew old gracefully "with what seemed to me a delightful innocence and naturalness." Referring to the couple's holidays in Switzerland, she wrote: "They made their *villeggiatura*, these two together, sometimes in a couple of chalets on a Swiss mountain, as if there had not been such a thing as an evil tongue in the world." Ruffini stayed with his incomparable companion" until her death in 1874.[15]

Engraved on Cornelia Turner's tomb are the words "A daughter worthy of her mother." As the next chapter will explain, those words are just right.

Chapter 26

Cornelia Turner and Vernon Lee Continue the Literary Life, 1848–1874

"Life here has a patriarchal stamp."
—Cornelia Turner, from her novel *Charity: A Tale* (1862) about the town of Monforte in Sardinia.[1]

In her fifties, sixties, and seventies, Cornelia Turner demonstrated that she was a daughter worthy of her mother. Percy Bysshe Shelley scholars have focused on the teenage Cornelia at Bracknell in 1813 and 1814. Shelley was tormented by her beauty and enraptured by her sweet smile. Her loveliness and gentle manners inspired poetry and drove him wild with desire. There is more to say, however, about this intelligent and talented woman, as her two novels, collaboration with other novelists, and letters attest.

Cornelia embodied many of her mother's best qualities. She was brave, kind, and unpretentious. She did not base her associations with other people on their social class, and she shared her mother's republican ideals. In her two novels, published anonymously in 1860 and 1862, Cornelia's interest in the unification and independence of the Italian states is evident. The narrative action in *Angelo Sanmartino: A Tale of Lombardy in 1859* begins in the early 1830s. Lucy Morestead, a British girl, goes abroad with her parents and falls in love with an Italian whom she later marries. He dies during the Risorgimento. When the young widow returns home, British ladies in her village reveal their xenophobic perspective:

> "What a comfort it must be to you," sighed out Mrs. L—, "to be once more in quiet England! As for me, I make it a rule never to read of those horrid broils abroad."

"You should not look at the papers, dear Mrs. Sanmartino: pray do not," observed Mrs. B —, persuadingly."[2]

Cornelia Turner, like Harriet de Boinville, did not "leave politics to gentlemen" but followed closely what was happening in the world. She did not read the papers to learn about fashions or sensational trials. Unlike Mrs. L in her first novel, Cornelia did not dismiss the "horrid broils abroad" but learned about them from Giovanni Ruffini and the other Italian exiles she knew in Paris.

Cornelia's fictional portrait of Lucy's brother, a conservative British aristocrat, is masterful:

> John Morestead was a favourable specimen of an English country gentlemen, a kind husband and father, a fair landlord, a good agriculturalist...a friendly neighbour and a proper dispenser of beef and blankets, and a supporter of schools for the poor. He was regularly sent up to Parliament at every election. In politics he was a Conservative and a Tory. He had a natural and invincible aversion and jealousy towards France. As for other nations, he very seldom gave them a thought, or if his mind glanced at them at all, it was to wonder for a moment why any countries had been created but England and her dependencies. Then he would turn away from the subject as from some inscrutable dispensation of Providence and comforted himself in the contemplation of the superior greatness, power, wisdom, and virtues of England and Englishmen.[3]

The novelist deftly mocks the self-assured John Morestead, a pompous aristocrat who can see only a slit of the world. His narrow perspective contrasts sharply with Harriet de Boinville's global perspective, expressed in the June 11, 1836, letter to Mary Shelley: "We are... arrived at the point where the true interests of particular nations merge in the true interest of all."

In *Charity: A Tale*, Cornelia creates a character who resembles her mother. The widow Mrs. Leslie lived at Grove House, an old-fashioned country home in England (not unlike the house at Bracknell) surrounded by a "gleeful progeny of grandchildren."

Her granddaughter Mary, small and slight of stature, was affectionately called Queen Mab. The setting of the novel begins in England and shifts to Italy. The town of Monforte was "divided into two parties, the liberal and the retrograde; the first, friendly to the free institutions of 1847 and consequent progress; the second, on the contrary, are bitter enemies to both, who not only sigh over the good old times, but form a watchful phalanx, ever covertly at work to bring back despotism both monarchical and clerical."

Charity: A Tale denounces despots as well as "cowardly desertion of principle and honor." It affirms moderation and tolerance in matters of church and state. The author creates a character (Mrs. Leslie's son Oliver) who is a Protestant. He states:

> Truly the grand principles of Protestantism are: the right and duty to examine the Scriptures according to the light which god vouchsafes to each, and liberty of conscience for all within the limits of the Christian faith. Just remind me of that if I slide into intolerance. I would fain not be illiberal, especially in the eyes of Catholics.[4]

Cornelia Turner's affirmation of religious tolerance in this novel occurs in the real-world context of prevalent antagonism between Catholics and Protestants.

She was a woman who said and did what she thought was right. She acted on the courage of her convictions. By deciding to live with Ruffini in 1848, she did not heed the clucking tongues and wagging fingers of those who were scandalized by her extramarital relationship with a much younger man, an Italian exile no less. She followed her conscience, acting independently, no mean feat for a British woman in the nineteenth century.

Giovanni Ruffini's Muse

Ruffini scholar Allan Conrad Christensen portrays Cornelia Turner as Ruffini's literary muse. She closely collaborated on Ruffini's novels and on the novels of their mutual friend Henrietta Jenkin.[5] Ruffini was never very interested in publishing his novels in Italy. The Italian language "presented an even greater spectacle of disunity than the political scene" in the years before the unification of Italy in 1870.⁶

As Christensen and Patricia Cove explain, Ruffini's linguistic process was remarkable. He sketched out his first novel, *Lorenzo Benoni*, in English and partly completed it in French; then Cornelia translated what he had written into English. He wrote his second novel, *Doctor Antonio*, in English with occasional French words and then corrected the draft assisted by Cornelia. His humorous third novel, *The Paragreens*, published by Thomas Constable, benefitted from Cornelia's ear for comedy. This novel reflected a particularly happy collaboration: "As soon as Ruffini sketches out the episode, Cornelia develops it and connects it to something else; they are like two fresh rivulets of humour that flow freely into convergence in a work of literature."⁷

Ruffini wrote no novels before his life with Cornelia began. Then he found his stride and kept moving forward. Their home became a place of vibrant creativity.

Violet Paget's Mentor

Cornelia Turner befriended Violet Paget, later famous as the prolific writer Vernon Lee (1856-1935). When they met, Cornelia was seventy-five; Violet, fourteen. Violet became an extraordinary woman of letters, completing novels, short stories, travel essays, studies of Italian art and music, as well as works on psychological esthetics, polemics, and other subjects.

Violet's half brother, Eugene Lee-Hamilton, introduced her to Cornelia and Ruffini. Eugene had met the couple in the summer of 1868 in Thun, Switzerland. A member of the staff of the British embassy, Lee-Hamilton was transferred to Paris in 1870 and on June 16th he took his sister to the rue de Vintimille, where Cornelia and Ruffini then lived. "Mrs. Turner was oh so kind!" Violet wrote her father the next day and enthusiastically described the visit:

> We went last evening, after their dinner and before ours. They live at six Rue de Vintimille, beyond the Rue Saint Lazare, in a very unfashionable neighborhood. The house is very nice but the staircase (they live on second) narrow

and dark. We found Mrs. Turner sitting on one side of the table, and Mr. Ruffini on the other, both reading. They have the funniest little drawing room conceivable, full of sketches, sepias, photos, daguerrotyphs [sic] and etchings of the different people they know. They have a copy of two of the angels on guilt grounds of Fra Domenica de Fiesole's celebrated picture in the Uffizi at Florence. Then there is a kind of small machine with shelves, on which the books are kept. I never saw anything so kind and friendly.[8]

The charming furnishings and the friendliness of her hosts transformed the apartment at the end of a dark hall into a rosy place that glowed brightly in the girl's mind.

Cornelia Remembers Percy Bysshe Shelley

Violet Paget was a coin collector. Her first story was an ingenious tale about an ancient coin that travels through time, passing from the hands of a Roman gladiator into the hands, at long last, of a modern numismatist. Violet told her father that Mrs. Turner had agreed to read her story. Cuts an editor made in *Les aventures d'une pièce de monnaie,* upset Violet, and Cornelia tried to console her:

> "Nevermind," as poor Shelley the poet used to say when he was vexed, there is enough there to do you great credit, and the subject as well as the treatment suffices to place you at once out of the category of what my friend Shelley used to name with horror "young ladies." You have taken on superior standing to this offending class.[9]

Fortunately, in her old age, Cornelia Turner remembered many long-ago conversations with the young poet. She wrote Violet about Shelley's mood after he completed *Queen Mab* in 1813. Shelley "had lamented his dryness and felt he would never write again." Cornelia mentioned Shelley's writer's block to encourage her protégé to keep writing.[10]

Like his partner, Ruffini was closely involved in young Violet's literary progress. He urged her to read what the poet-dramatist-librettist Pietro Metastasio had written. Violet followed Ruffini's advice. In 1871 she read what the renowned musicologist Dr. Charles Burney, Frances Burney d'Arblay's father, had written long ago about Metastasio.

Cornelia learned that Violet had become discouraged while doing research about Metastasio. Although Violet began with her usual energy and determination, the ambitious project became overwhelming. The more Violet read about eighteenth-century Italian music, the more she realized she did not know. Feeling inadequate, she confided in Mrs. Turner in February 1873 and her kindly mentor replied. Cornelia told Violet about her own struggles related to music when she was a young girl. She had wanted to master classical music because her aunt (and namesake), Cornelia Collins Newton, was an accomplished musician.

Cornelia Turner related to Violet advice she once gave Shelley when he was blocked, unable to finish what he was trying to write:

> a poet's mind is like a China rose. It is covered with a first crop of roses. Then the blossoms fall and the mere green leaves all forlorn remain, but after a while a fresh set of buds come forth and blossom, and thus crop succeeds crop of beautiful flowers through the years.[11]

These comments about a poet's mind and about Shelley's struggles as a writer helped Violet persevere. In 1878 she completed *Studies of the Eighteenth-Century in Italy*. "Mrs. Turner corresponded regularly with Violet," Beatrice Corrigan explains, "encouraging her to use her talent, discussing books and music, and reassuring her when she deplored the decline in modern literature."[12]

In 1875 Violet began to use the pseudonym H.P. Vernon Lee. She explained her choice to Mrs. Turner on April 6th: "The name I have chosen as containing part of my brother's [Eugene Lee-Hamilton] and my father's [Henry Paget] and my own initials is H. P. Vernon Lee. Vineta Colby notes that "the use of a masculine pseudonym was hardly unusual in the nineteenth century, although by the last quarter of the century many women were publishing under their own name. But it was a necessity for an unknown young woman who chose to write on weighty subjects."[13]

Like his sister Violet, the diplomat Eugene Lee-Hamilton had literary ambitions. Cornelia Turner helped him find English publishers for his poems and essays.[14] Grateful for her efforts on his behalf, Lee-Hamilton went out of his way to return the kindness. During the Franco-Prussian war, he traveled to the asylum in Ivry, France, to visit Cornelia's relatives. The astonishing truth is that her brother (Alfred de Boinville), her son (Oswald Turner), and her nephew (Frank de Boinville) were all considered at one time to be "mad" and institutionalized.

In her final days Cornelia was surrounded by loved ones, Ruffini wrote Charles de Boinville, to comfort him: "We vied with each other as to who should make the most of her and not a day passed without her saying 'What have I done to be loved and petted as I am?' Alas! those loving eyes are now closed for ever, silent forever, is the sweet voice." Cornelia Turner died on October 25, 1874.

"A Daughter Worthy of Her Mother"

Visitors to Paris can find Cornelia's grave in Montmartre Cemetery. They can read on the same towering obelisk, Cornelia's name and the names of her mother, her sons, Oswald and Alfred, and the family's beloved physician Giulio Robecchi. (Cornelia's partner, Giovanni Ruffini, was buried in Genoa, where he died in 1881.)

> Henriette Chastel de Boinville, née Collins,
> b. St. Kitts 1773, d. Paris 1847
>
> Cornelia Turner, 1795-1874
> Digne fille de sa mère
> "I have glorified thy name on earth.
> I have finished the work thou gavest me to do."
>
> Oswald Turner, 1814-1876
>
> Alfred Turner, 1817-1893
>
> Giulio Robecchi, 1806-1846

Figure 26.1. Inscription on tombstone memorializing Henriette Collins Chastel de Boinville and her daughter, Cornelia Pauline Eugénia Turner née Chastel de Boinville, Cemetery Montmartre division 43.

Memoir of the Reverend Charles A. Chastel de Boinville Compiled from his Journals and His Letters, published in 1880 and written by Thomas Constable, has been digitized. The memoir stands as a long-lasting tribute to Harriet de Boinville and her family. In the first sentence of Chapter 1, Charles describes Jean Baptiste as a man of ability and high connections; "the part he took in politics and in some of the principal events of the French Revolution, would probably have brought him into greater notice had he been more fortunate in the declining years of his life." Then the author expresses his hope "that our children and grandchildren will be glad to know something of their forefathers whose lot was cast in troublous times." Fortunately, future generations will also be inspired by the valiant foremothers who played a role in Charles de Boinville's life (Harriet Collins de Boinville, Harriet Lambe de Boinville, and Cornelia Turner). It is the hope of this author that their lives will also inspire men and women through the ages.

Before her death Cornelia Turner told Giovanni Ruffini that she wanted Violet Paget to have an heirloom, her mother's gold watch. Like the ancient coin in Violet's first story, this watch traveled through time from hand to hand. It was passed from Dr. Charles Burney, to Frances Burney d'Arblay, to Harriet de Boinville, to Cornelia Turner, to Giovanni Ruffini, to Violet Paget. On June 28, 1875, Ruffini sent the watch with this accompanying note:

A vous enfant précoce, revenant de droit le souvenir de cette autre enfant précoce, qui fut Madame D'Arblay.
To you, a precocious child, rightly belongs this memento of the precocious child that was Madame D'Arblay. [15]

And so the gold watch ended in Violet Paget's grateful hands.

Afterword

Mark Twain and the Boinville Circle

Samuel Clemens, the American writer known as Mark Twain, blamed Percy Bysshe Shelley and the Boinville circle for the break-up of Shelley's first marriage in 1814. Eighty years later, he blasted Mr. Shelley and the "Boinville circle," "the Boinville menagerie," and "the sty at Bracknell" in *The North American Review* (1894) in a piece entitled "In Defense of Harriet Shelley." Twain was prompted to defend Shelley's wronged wife after reading Edward Dowden's popular biography *The Life of Percy Bysshe Shelley* (1886).

Dowden's book incensed Twain. On page one Twain writes with biting satire:

> I was not aware that Shelley's first wife was unfaithful to him and that was why he deserted her and wiped the stain from his sensitive honor by entering into soiled relations with Godwin's young daughter. This was all new to me when I heard it lately, and was told that the proofs of it were in this book and that this verdict is accepted in the girls' colleges of America and its view taught in their literary classes.[1]

Twain makes many derogatory comments about Mr. Shelley in his book that are correct, but tarring Harriet de Boinville and her daughter and sister with the same brush is unjustified. It is because Dowden mentions Harriet de Boinville, Cornelia Turner, and Cornelia Newton that Twain takes aim at them. Twain twists Dowden's words to suit his own comic purposes.

Twain and the Cake Walk

Everything about Dowden's book infuriated Twain, not only what he said but how he said it. Twain likens Dowden's literary style to a cake-walk. "Our negroes in America have several ways of entertaining themselves," Twain writes, revealing his racial prejudice. He then describes how the contestants compete to win the prize of a cake:

> One at a time the contestants enter, clothed regardless of expense, in what each one considers the perfection of style and taste, and walk down the central space and back again.... All that the competitor knows of fine airs and graces he throws into his carriage, all that he knows of seductive expression he throws into his countenance. He may use all the helps he can devise: watch-chain to twirl with his fingers, cane to do graceful things with, snowy handkerchief to flourish and get artful effects out of...and the colored lady may have a fan to work up *her* effects and smile over and blush behind and she may add other helps according to her judgment.

Twain's purpose is to equate Dowden's biography with gimmickry. He discounts Dowden's book as mere show. He wants his readers to think that this book is as light and insubstantial as a cake.

The "prairie-dogs' nest" at Bracknell

In the first passage about Harriet de Boinville, Twain layers in quotes from posthumous biographies of Shelley by Dowden and by Thomas Jefferson Hogg: "Shelley had made the acquaintance of a charming gray-haired, young-hearted Mrs. Boinville, whose face 'retained a certain youthful beauty'." Her young daughter, Cornelia Turner, "was equipped with many fascinations. Apparently, these people were sufficiently sentimental." Twain cannot resist repeating Hogg's caricature of his host at Bracknell:

> Hogg says of Mrs. Boinville: "The greater part of her associates were odious. I generally found there two or three senti-

mental young butchers, an eminently philosophical tinker, and several very unsophisticated medical practitioners, or medical students, all of low origin and vulgar and offensive manners. They sighed, turned up their eyes, retailed philosophy, such as it was," etc.

Shelley moved to Bracknell, July 27th (this is still 1813) purposely to be near this prairie-dogs' nest. This fabulist says, "It was an entrance into a world more amiable and exquisite than he had yet known."

Twain notes Mrs. Boinville's beauty, age, and hair color. He repeats Hogg's description of her guests as odious folks of low origin. He mocks Mrs. Boinville for discussing Godwin's ideas about political justice by repeating Hogg's reference to butchers ("sentimental" and "young"), a tinker ("eminently philosophical"), and medical practitioners and medical students ("unsophisticated"). All her guests had "vulgar and offensive manners" and dared to talk about philosophy, something way beyond their understanding. Unlike her critics, Mrs. Boinville was an egalitarian, not a bigoted snob.

Twain brings up Mary Shelley's first novel. He wants his readers to associate Dowden's book with horror and to see it as a monstrosity. Dowden's *Life of Percy Bysshe Shelley* is "the strangest book that has seen the light since *Frankenstein*. Indeed it is itself a Frankenstein, a Frankenstein with the original infirmity supplemented by a new one; a Frankenstein with the reasoning faculty wanting."

Twain finds the much-discussed Italian lessons at Bracknell irresistible material. Again he splices Dowden quotes into his own comments:

Shelley's Latin instructions to his wife had ceased. "From a teacher he had now become a pupil." Mrs. Boinville and her young married daughter Cornelia were teaching him Italian poetry.... Up to this time we have submitted to having Mrs. Boinville pushed upon us as ostensibly concerned in these Italian lessons.... Cornelia "perhaps" is sole teacher.... Then the author of the book interlards a most stately and fine compliment to Cornelia, furnished by a man of approved judgment who knew her well "in later years."

Edward Dowden did know Cornelia Turner. He liked her and praised her. Twain continues: "It is a very good compliment indeed, and she no doubt deserved it in her 'later years', when she had for generations ceased to be sentimental and lackadaisical, and was no longer engaged in enchanting young husbands and sowing sorrow for young wives."

Harriet de Boinville wrote Hogg on March 11, 1814, about Shelley: "Seriously, his mind and body want rest." Twisting her words, Twain writes, "Yet he has been resting both for a month, with Italian and tea, and manna of sentiment and late hours, and every restful thing a young husband could need for the refreshment of weary limbs and a sore conscience, and a nagging sense of shabbiness and treachery." Shelley had reason to have a sore conscience for the sorrow he brought his wife, but his marital unhappiness, which began before he met Cornelia Turner, was not the fault of Harriet or her daughter.

Harriet de Boinville's married sister, Cornelia Newton, does not elude the spear of Twain's pen. Twain includes her in his gender stereotypes: "part of Shelley's plan, as he wrote Hogg, was to spend his London evenings with the Newtons—part of the Boinville Hysterical Society." Twain mocks the women in the Boinville circle as hysterical, or sentimental, or enchantresses interested in luring men astray.

Twain calls Dowden "the fabulist counsel for Shelley and prosecutor of his young wife." The fabulist "knows how to detect what does not exist, he knows how to see what is not seeable; it is his gift." Twain, like the cake-walk contestants, has the gift of gimmickry. Not interested in facts, he is interested in appearances and puts on a marvelous show.

Closing the Circle

We now will close the circle and consider Harriet de Boinville's friends and how their lives unfolded after her death in 1847.

Thomas Jefferson Hogg

Hogg died in 1862. He was seventy. He and Jane Williams, whose husband drowned with Shelley, had children together but never married. Mary Shelley became the godmother of one of the children. For many years, Hogg practiced law in London.

Percy Florence Shelley gave Hogg personal papers to write a posthumous biography of his father. Hogg was fifty-six when his reminiscences of P. B. Shelley were published in two volumes. He had intended to write a third, but the Shelley family thought two were more than enough. They disliked what he had written and insisted that Hogg return the documents they had given him. According to Edward Dowden in 1906, "it was not unjust nor indiscreet that the material should have been withdrawn from his hands."

A new edition of Dowden's biography of Shelley came out in 1906. Dowden admitted that Hogg committed "grave" offenses as a biographer. "It is impossible to commend Hogg as a biographer for discretion, good taste, or good workmanship." Hogg's late-in-life memories of Harriet de Boinville were full of hyperbole and bias, but they provide a glimpse into her life at her country home. Hogg noted Shelley's "kind friends" at Bracknell who "asserted that they were wise in their generation... that a dinner of herbs, a vegetable dinner, is better than roast beef and love and friendship therewith." Hogg suffered from gout in his later years, perhaps because of his dietary preferences.

Thomas Love Peacock

Peacock was a "cold scholar," according to Cornelia Newton. She did not think much of his amateurish first novel *Leonora*. Peacock retired from the East India Company after thirty years of service. In retirement he completed his posthumous memoir of Shelley. Harriet de Boinville, his host at Bracknell, is portrayed as overly talkative and not very serious. She went on and on about William Godwin's masterpiece, *An Enquiry Concerning Political Justice and Its Influence on Morals and Happiness* (1793). Peacock portrayed himself and Mrs. Harriet Shelley as skeptical observers of the heated discussions about politics. In Peacock's cool opinion, Harriet de

Boinville and her guests did not know what they were talking about. Peacock died in 1866 at the age of eighty, after trying to save the books in his library from a fire.

Mary Shelley

On January 23, 1851, Mary fell into a coma in her London house in Chester Square. She died on February 1, 1851, at the age of fifty-three from a brain tumor. After her death, her daughter-in-law, Jane Shelley, destroyed many of Mary's letters, including those referring to Harriet Shelley and Mary's feelings of remorse about the tragic end of Shelley's first wife. Jane Shelley was kind to her mother-in-law while she lived, but she took appalling liberties after Mary died, as Miranda Seymour explains in her biography of Mary Shelley.

Mary was buried, in accord with her wishes, in the churchyard of St. Pancras, where her parents were interred and where, in the shadow of the willows, she and Shelley first made love. Mary's body was later dug up, as were the bodies of her mother, Mary Wollstonecraft, and her father, William Godwin. Mary's daughter-in-law, Jane Shelley, did not approve of St. Pancras as a final resting place. The old church was crumbling; the grounds were neglected. She ordered the reinterment of Mary Shelley, Mary Wollstonecraft, and William Godwin. She wanted them reburied at St. Peter's, Bournemouth, near her home at Boscombe Manor. This church, in a posh neighborhood, was a more suitable final resting place, in her opinion.

When Jane Shelley spoke to the vicar of St. Peter's about moving the bodies, he objected. He did not want three radicals buried at his church, but Lady Shelley took matters into her own hands. She directed the removal of the remains and had the coffins of Mary Wollstonecraft, William Godwin, and Mary Shelley placed in her private carriage. Then she drove the carriage right up to the church gates. The vicar witnessed the arrival. Not wanting a scene, he let the carriage drive through but insisted that the burial take place in the cover of night.[2]

William Godwin's second wife, Mary Jane Godwin, was left behind at St. Pancras. This infuriated her daughter Claire Clairmont.

The Shelleys had acted as though her mother was not part of the family. And so Mary Jane Godwin remained behind in the weedy plot where she had been buried in 1841. Also left behind was Mary Wollstonecraft's original gravestone, upon which Mary Godwin had learned to write by tracing her mother's letters.

Mary's new epitaph at St. Peter's read: "Mary Wollstonecraft Shelley, Daughter of William and Mary Wollstonecraft Godwin, and Widow of the Late Percy Bysshe Shelley." Visitors who came to pay their respects would be reminded of Mary as a daughter, a wife, and a mother—not as an author. Not a word is said about the first of her seven novels, *Frankenstein*, although Godwin's memorial cites *Political Justice* and Wollstonecraft's memorial cites *A Vindication of the Rights of Woman*. As Charlotte Gordon insightfully notes, Jane Shelley "wanted her daughter-in-law to be seen as a noble grieving widow, not as a rebellious stepdaughter or the author of a disgraceful novel."[3] Mary would have been pleased at the mention of her mother on the plaque, if not in the decision to dig her up and move her. Mary once wrote: "The memory of my Mother has always been the pride and delight of my life."[4]

In the drawing room of their home at Boscombe Manor, Sir Percy Florence Shelley and Lady Jane Shelley erected a shrine to the dead. Glass cases displayed Mary Shelley's hand mirror, Mary Wollstonecraft's amethyst ring, hair bracelets, and love letters. In 1852, the year after his mother's death, Percy Florence made the upsetting discovery of his father's desiccated heart, wrapped in velvet, in his mother's desk, next to her journal and her treasured copy of Shelley's *Adonais*.

In her creative and readable *In Search of Mary Shelley*, Fiona Sampson describes what St. Peter's, Bournemouth looks like. The church no longer is in a fashionable neighborhood. In 2017, a department store and a chain pub called the Mary Shelley welcomed customers not far from Mary's grave. "We can imagine her own wry, half-smiling reaction at such an end to her story. But of course it is not the end," Sampson writes. "Adaptation is the mark of a survivor's intelligence, and she was a great survivor. Out of material we would most of us find overwhelming she created an astonishing life. Despite being born a girl and motherless in her particular time and place, and despite being almost crushed by the 'great men' around her, she produced, while still only a teenager, the novel that uniquely sums up the restless, experimental spirit of her Romantic times."[5]

Claire Clairmont

Claire Clairmont died on March 19, 1879, at the age of ninety-one. She spent her last years living with her niece Paulina Clairmont in Florence, Italy. Three years before her death she wrote a friend, "I find great consolation in how many distinguished and excellent and virtuous friends I have had.... And in this way I banish from old age that stupid Melancholy which generally accompanies that stage of life." Claire's relationship with Mary Shelley frayed in the 1840s. Once reason was Claire's mistaken idea that her sister had inherited a lot of money. In her journal Paulina Clairmont wrote: "This morning my Aunt died about ten, calmly, without agony, without consciousness—as she had predicted herself, she went out like a candle... she was buried as she desired, with Shelley's little shawl at the Cemetery of the Antella."[6]

In October 1852, Claire wrote to Cornelia Turner about what she remembered of their youth. Cornelia replied, "I can clearly state that I was acquainted with you when we were both girls... . I distinctly remember your being present at a dance on the day I completed my fifteenth year in 1810, and you were then to the best of my knowledge twelve years of age." (See the Appendix, page 250, for the full text of Cornelia Turner's letter to Claire Clairmont.)

Harriet de Boinville lived a full life at the center of a wide circle of family and friends. She influenced writers Frances Burney d'Arblay, William Godwin, Percy Bysshe Shelley, Mary Shelley, and Giovanni Ruffini. In the Caribbean, London, and Paris, she acted upon her egalitarian ideas and political convictions. Brave, independent, and outspoken, she was a revolutionary woman in revolutionary times. Perhaps most importantly, she was a kind and loving human being.

Appendix-Letters

Jean Baptiste Boinville to Alexandre d'Arblay
September 24, 1793
Source: Original signed letter in French. The Henry W. and Albert A. Berg Collection of English and American Literature, The New York Public Library, Astor, Lenox and Tilden Foundations.

Clyst St George, prés de Topsham, Devonshire, Angleterre
24 Septembre 1793
répondu

Mon cher ami,
    Ton billet en date du 2 du mois dernier n'est parvenue six semaines aprés. Je l'ai reçu avec grande joie, comme bien tu penses. Je te fais mon compliment bien sincere sur ton heureux mariage. Je ne doute plus de ta felicité avenir; puisque elle est etabilie sur l'amabilité et les qualité d'une femme charmante. L'établissment champetre que te projettes te procureras tout espece d'agréments. Je suis bien content d'apprendre tout cela, tu me promets des details; adresses les moi le plutôt possible.
    J'ai quitté Londres le 7 de Julliet ; pour venir habiter dans cette province, La Provence de l'angleterre une jolie chaumière prés de la mer et entourée d'un campagne delicieuse. Je passe un temps enchanté avec un etre que, j'adore et qui reunit tout ce qui est aimable et bon. Pendant le court séjour que j'ai fais à Londres. J'ai été te chercher chez Mr Lock: mais cela fait en vain. J'aurais pu te répondre quelques jours plutot; mais le désir que j'en ai eu a été contrairié par une maladie grave, de la quelle j'ai été sauvé par l-à-propos d'un vesicatoire sur la poitrine. J'attends de tes nouvelles avec impatience mon cher ami. En response je te donnerai aussi des details sur ma position. Nous pouvons nous vander toi et moi de n'etre pas les émigrés les plus à plaindre.

Adieu mon cher bon et ancien ami. Comptes bien à jamais sur moi,
Boinville

Tu ne me donnes pas ton adresse. Je crains de la mal imaginer.
L'adresse de nos camarades d'infortune est
At Mr. Heming's.
Old ford, near Bow
Middlesex

English Translation

Clyst St George, near Topsham in Devonshire, England
24 September 1793
a reply

My dear friend,
    Your letter of the 2nd of last month did not arrive until six weeks later. I received it with great pleasure. I sincerely congratulate you on your happy marriage. I no longer doubt your future happiness; it is established on the amiableness and qualities of a charming woman. The rural establishment that you will get will give you plenty of space for pleasure. I am very pleased to have learned all of this. You promise me details. Send them as soon as possible.
    I left London on the 7th of July to come stay in this area, the south of England, in a pretty thatched cottage near the sea and surrounded by delightful countryside. I spent an enchanting time with someone I adore and who embodies all that is amiable and good. During the short stay I made in London, I went to look for you at the home of Mr. Lock: but that was in vain. I would have replied to your letter several days earlier, but my intention was thwarted by a serious illness, from which I have been rescued by the application to my chest of a blistering plaster. I await your news with impatience my dear friend. In response I will give you news of my situation. We can boast that you and I are not the emigrants most to be pitied. Goodbye my dear and old friend. You can always count on me,
Boinville

You did not give me your address. I am afraid to guess.
The address of our comrades in misfortune is
At Mr. Heming's.
Old ford, near Bow
Middlesex

Harriet Boinville to Frances Burney d'Arblay
February 19, 1802
Source: Original letter. The Henry W. and Albert A. Berg Collection of English and American Literature, The New York Public Library, Astor, Lenox, and Tilden Foundations.

Not many of those who are happy enough to be personally & intimately acquainted with you Madam, can have taken a deeper interest, or greater share in all the painful feelings that have lately agitated you; the impertinence of unavailing condolence on a Mind full of such feelings, is, however so obvious that I should not certainly have presumed to address you at this moment, my dear Madam, had not M^r d'Arblay encouraged me by an assurance that he had very kindly pre-disposed you to receive with indulgence these few lines, which are indeed a very imperfect expression of my sentiments and of my earnest wish that you would before long indulge me with an opportunity of assuring you in person how truly I participate in your regret and anxieties—that their duration may be very short & that they may be succeeded by all the happiness your own heart can desire is the ardent hope of
Dear Madam

Your devoted humble servant
H Boinville
Watford
February 19th, 1802

Cornelia Newton to Thomas Jefferson Hogg
October 21, 1813
Source: The Carl H. Pforzheimer Library, *Shelley and His Circle*, 1773-1822, ed. Kenneth Neill Cameron (Cambridge, Mass.: Harvard University Press; London: Oxford University Press, 1970), SC 251, 3: 252-254. A few paragraph breaks and minor editorial changes have been made to improve readability.

Chester Street, Octr 21st

After allowing your elegant & friendly letter to remain so long unanswered you will perhaps suspect that I am incapable of making a due estimate of its merit; but the truth is I am a reluctant writer unless stimulated to the use of my pen by painful emotions. This peculiarity of my nature will I trust at least acquit me of not deriving <u>pleasure</u> from your ready compliance with my request— for I do not forget that Clementina's woes were introduced to your acquaintance at my suggestion & and that I likewise urged you to favor me with your opinion of this celebrated composition to which the Episode is incomparably the most interesting part. In your estimate of the character of Grandison you must keep in view that Richardson designed to paint a perfect <u>civilized</u> being whose passions are always obedient to his reason—she never for one moment quits the <u>Helm</u>—a disgusting object enough I will confess contrasted with the wild & beautiful starts of passion so conspicuous in his fair mistress. But the fidelity & consistency with which his Hero is delineated & supported throughout the work proves indeed what has never been denied to Richardson the true character of Genius. In reading this voluminous novel we never confound one object with another & the images remain indelibly impressed on the mind. This at least was the judgment of it I formed years ago, for it is long since I wept over the artificial woes of Clementina, whose madness is the most touching picture of the kind I believe in the literature of any country. At least we have the authority of an excellent scholar on this subject Dr. Warton who concludes his encomium on this masterly performance by saying that he questions whether it would not be pedantry to prefer the madness of Orestes to Clementina's or whether even Lear's has so many strokes of genuine passion. The author who does not yield the palm to Euripides or Shakespear has surely the strongest claim to our admiration and respect.

From this subject I turn to one I am persuaded not less interesting to you your friends the Shelleys who were all well when we parted. Since their arrival in the North where I imagine necessity will fix them for some time. we have had no tidings of them. The lady whose welfare is so important in your estimation was as usual very blooming and very happy during the whole of our residence at Bracknell—Ianthe grown surprisingly & Miss Westbrook ever smiling & serene. They have made an addition to their party in the person of Peacock a cold Scholar who I think has neither taste nor feeling. This Shelley will perceive sooner or later—for his warm nature craves sympathy, & I am convinced he will not meet it in Peacock. Mrs. Boinville who would be flattered by your inquiries if she knew of them was quite well a fortnight since. We all look with pleasure to your return not omitting Mr. Lawrence who always speaks of you as you deserve.

That the temper & habits of your associates do not meet all your wishes is far from surprising me. I never yet found in the country of this distinguished Isle—enlightened & agreeable persons of either sex. They are all too scattered for one to light upon them by accident. Even the capital is not too rich in unprejudiced thinkers & upon these Society with all its frauds lay so firm a claw that half their merit is of necessity cast into the shade.

I read the first part of your Leonora & see it as the production of a very young man many parts of which your mature judgment will not confirm. When we meet I will venture to discuss with you its beauties & defects. Mr. Newton has already acquitted himself of his agreeable debt to you & having of course talked of his health it only remains for me to speak of the other members of my family who would be pleased by your inquiries if they were old enough to estimate the value of them. Octavia & Camilla I think you will find improved, Augustus progressing toward scholarship—Chick traveling fast into breeches & Coraly light and nimble as a fairy. I hope you will eat your Christmas dinner with us whether you continue one of the Holy or not for no change Habits of such nature can alter the esteem with which I subscribe myself

Your very sincere friend
Cornelia Newton

Jefferson Hogg, Esqr
Norton
near Stockton upon Tees

Harriet Boinville to Frances Burney d'Arblay
March 7, 1814
Source: Original signed letter. The Henry W. and Albert A. Berg Collection of English and American Literature, The New York Public Library, Astor, Lenox and Tilden Foundations.

Dr. Charles Burney, Chelsea Cottage, near London
    Can it be that such feelings as you describe in your delightful letter have ever on any occasion reached your heart, my dearest Madam? And am I not a very Wretch to have found some thing like satisfaction in the thoughts that you too sometimes wish to do what you do not accomplish? I thought that of late ill concocted projects, fruitless efforts, baffled intentions with their offspring self-reproach had all taken up their abode with me, and least of all could I believe that you ever heard, or could know the feeling you have just painted in your peculiar lively manner. If I had thought so, long before this I would have sent you my whole heart in a letter, or have found you out and thrown myself into your arms to receive from your warm embrace the assurance that you had not driven me from the precious corner of your heart which once you gave me, and of which I have ever felt so proud.
    When I first heard you were in this country which was not very long after your arrival my heart sprang to meet you. I meant to write to you immediately but anxieties, cares & sorrows crowded fast upon me. My spirits sank. Day after day wore away while I talked of you to my children.
    While Cornelia reproached me for not writing, while she was in Paris she loved you and could not bear we should lose sight of you. It has been my pride & my pleasure to tell those of my family who only know & admire you through your works, how soothingly kind you were to me in my Illness in Paris. How condescendingly good to my children in my absence. In short though I have seemed to forget you I have thought of you and loved you and have dwelt

with affectionate boasting of every proof of regard you ever gave me and well I might for are not such proofs of regard from you badge of honour?

But while harassed by business in London I thought I would refresh myself with the sight of you my dear Madam. I walked a good way towards Mrs. Charles Burney's to find you out but before I could reach her home my spirits failed me. I felt unequal to the interview and turned back to throw myself into a chair and waste in unprofitable musing on things over which I have no power an hour I might perhaps have spent delightfully with you. And so our best pleasures often elude us while sorrow fastens upon us with a strong hold from which we can only free ourselves now & then with a struggle which exhausts our strength & lessens all our powers of enjoyment.

How much have we to ask this way of those to whom we belong? To me a part of this review is soul harrowing. I turn from it in pity to us both for I know that your powers of sympathy equal all your other moral powers and that you will grieve for me when I say that any certainty on the subject of my fears I think I could have as a comparative relief and I know that the worst would be less dreadful than to know nothing.

Your anxieties I feel tenderly—but they ought now I think to subside since it becomes evident that Paris has been saved. Monsieur d'Arblay is of course exempted from service & your maternal vigilance has saved the dear Alex! I know that he is at Cambridge where he is to distinguish himself by his degree as he has always distinguished himself. I cannot tell you with what pleasure we heard of his success at College from a friend of mine who though not of the same College could tell me that he's a marked man there. Of my own children it would be ungrateful affectation not to speak. I can only say that they are a never failing source of consolation & pleasure to me.

Cornelia is married to a man whose understanding and conduct satisfies entirely her mother. She's about to present us with a little one. This anxiety occupies me very much just now and will take us to Town next month for a few weeks. I trust you will then be in Town and that you will open your arms to receive us. My sister was delighted with her interview with you and hopes to be allowed to cultivate an intercourse with you. She told me you appeared in good health and your letter confirms the good news. Surely you could not so write if you were not well. I had a few lines from good Alex dated the 12th of Jan^{ry}. His silence respecting M^r d'Arblay proves to me that he was well. I have two channels through which I make efforts to write. Sometimes they succeed but half the letters ... and those that are sent us miscarry. Nevertheless it is worth while to try. I shall have the greatest pleasure in forwarding any letters for you my dear Madam.

Now the charm is broken I know not how to stop my pen. Prolix as I have been much more remains for me to say which my paper refuses to hold. Inquiries after every Member of your amiable family force themselves upon my pen and I do best respects to Dr. Burney and to everyone who will be kind enough to recollect me. Will you be vexed with me as an ... importunate creature if I say it would make me most happy to hear again from you—to be told what stay you are likely to make in this country and a thousand other things which interest you. To be assured that you can forgive me for I cannot forgive myself for not writing though it is my comfort to feel that in spite of appearances I deserve now as much as ever I did every kind feeling with which you have honoured me—and that if I could lay my heart naked in your hand not even your piercing anatomizing eye would find in its most secret fold anything to hate or despise though much to require indulgence and allowance. But I shall scarcely find room for that unfeigned appearance of affection & attachment such as you have a right my dear Madam to inspire.
[illegible address]
H. Boinville

Harriet Boinville to Thomas Jefferson Hogg
March 11, 1814
Source: The Carl H. Pforzheimer Collection of Shelley and His Circle: Manuscripts, 1772-1925. This letter is cited in *Shelley and His Circle, 1773-1822*, ed. Kenneth Neill Cameron (Cambridge, Mass.: Harvard University Press; London: Oxford University Press, 1970), SC 257, 3: 273-275. A few paragraph breaks and other editorial changes have been made to improve readability.

Bracknell, March 11th 1814.

Your most agreeable & welcome Letter is a bribe which will hardly let me tell you how much I was startled at the assertion to which I owe it. I cannot now I am sober confirm what you say I maintained the other night "that to follow our inclinations <u>on all occasions</u> is the first and great commandment. Look around and you will see that I would not mean this, at least as a general rule. And here is a new proof, which I wanted not, that from the wrath of argument never springs or can spring any thing but misstatement and misconception. If I should grant any thing like what you say I must load it with such limitations, exceptions, and explanations as will amount to a Lawyer's interpretation and that you will not thank me for. Perhaps the following precept of Champfort taken in its best sense will satisfy you and certainly comes much nearer to my meaning: "Jouis et fais jouir sans faire de mal à personne voila toute la morale". This I have always maintained against a dear and ingenious Sophist who labors hard to persuade us that in concerns of the heart "s'abstenir c'est jouir" and that it is wisdom to shut it against every feeling that can possibly bring with it any pain; as if every thing worth having must not be purchased at this price, which (to use the words of an arch friend of mine) "God in his infinite mischief" has been pleased to set on every pleasure he grants us, his poor suffering Children whom in his love he chasteneth. When I have been delighted by the beauty and fragrance of the rose I have sometimes doubted whether we could strip it of its thorns without injuring its beauty, and certainly I have never doubted whether it would be wise to renounce such beauty and fragrance because of the thorns that guard it. Alas! Yes. Joys <u>can</u> and <u>do</u> pass away and we must lament over them for ever; but that which does <u>not</u> pass away is the susceptibility of pure joys which with a lavish hand Nature scatters every where around her favoured Children, to whom she gives, to make amends for all their sorrows, the power of going out of themselves for pleasure. A loving Soul bears about within itself a living spring of Affection which keeps it fresh in spite of blights from evil things & evil Men and suffers no good feeling to wither & to die.

I will not have you despise homespun pleasures. Shelley is making a trial of them with us and he likes them so well that he is resolved to leave off rambling and begin a course of them himself. Seriously I think his Mind & body want rest. His journies after what he has never found have wracked his Purse & his Tranquility. He is resolved to take a little care of the former in pity to the latter which I applaud and shall second with all my might. He has deeply interested us. In the course of your intimacy he must have made you feel what we now feel for him. He is seeking a house close to us and if he succeeds we shall have an additional motive to induce you to come among us in the Summer.

If old Salomon had not his bewitching musical talent his lively feelings, to which by the bye he owes it, would seize upon our affections & hold them fast. Certain strains sung by my Sister make me so melancholy I cannot bear them, and if any thing should could make me a convert to her iron Philosophy it would be to hear her sing & think that she has never been happy. I hear at this distance the heartrending complaint of Ariadne and feel that the world is a Desert. With such a feeling as this Mad^{lle} de L.Espinasse is closely connected. Her suffering, often so forcibly & naturally expressed, interests me deeply. Read the long letter to the contemptible object of her unhappy passion soon after his marriage containing her character of him, and pity the Woman whose understanding so plainly saw his unworthiness and yet was so impotent in the struggle with her passion.

This speedy answer to your Letter says plainly that whenever you feel inclined to favour me with a Letter it will be right for you to follow your Inclination which must be productive of great pleasure to me. My Sister never writes—scold her for me if you can. At all times I can ill bear her silence & less well now than ever when I suspect it proceeds from low spirits. Thirty miles cannot separate me from my Friends. That is not the worst evil of absence for those we love we bear about in our hearts but the groundless apprehensions which spring up to alarm us when we might be tranquil are very hard to bear. Next Month we shall come to Town to pass some Weeks when I hope we shall see you often. Shelley will write to you the first day he is in the humour for writing, in the mean time he unites with every Member of this family in kind regards, to which I can only add the assurance of my cordial & friendly attachment.
H. Boinville

Excuse a thousand blunders & much confusion of expression because for I write talking occasionally to Shelley of twenty different subjects.

T. Jefferson Hogg, Esqre
4. Newman's Row
Lincolns Inn Fields
London

Harriet Boinville to Thomas Jefferson Hogg
April 18, 1814
Source: This letter is cited in *The Life of Percy Bysshe Shelley by Thomas Jefferson Hogg: With an Introduction by Professor Edward Dowden and an Index* (London: George Routledge & Sons, Ltd. New York, E. P. Dutton & Co., 1906). See page 565 of the Hardpress Classic Series.

Bracknell, April 18, 1814
 Do you forgive my silence, for I cannot forgive myself, and yet it has been quite impossible to write. My mind has not been free one hour since you were here; and even now I only send a few words to say, that you must wait for an answer to your letter til I come to town, when I shall have the pleasure of telling you how entirely and unavoidably I have been engaged. Mrs. N. is wonderfully recovered. Air and exercise, and friendly conversation, are just restoring her good looks. Shelley is again a widower; his beauteous half went to town on Thursday with Miss Westbrook who is gone to live, I believe, at Southampton.
 All here unite in kind remembrance; and I entreat you to excuse this abrupt and hasty scrawl, which does not satisfy my conscience or inclination, but which is all I can command time for to-day. I will let you know when we arrive in town; in the meanwhile, I am, very sincerely yours, Harriet B.

Harriet de Boinville to Mary Shelley
October 16, 1829
Source: University of Oxford, Bodleian Libraries Abinger Collec-

tion, Abinger Dep c. 516/1, c. 48, folios 55-6. A few paragraph breaks have been added to improve readability.

Note: The letter mentions Jane Williams; Charles Lamb, the author of *The Essays of Elia* (1823), and his sister Mary Lamb; the linguist Claude Fauriel; the Douglas's (Isabel Douglas, formerly Isabel Robinson, and Walter Douglas, a Scottish woman who used the pseudonyms Mary Diana Dods and David Lindsay); and someone named Schlabendorff (unknown identity).

October 16th 1829
My dear Mrs. Shelley,

I will not begin an answer to such a letter as yours by apologies for not writing sooner. I received it three months ago with almost equal pleasure & surprise & in the best sense of the word I have answered it five hundred times, yet not one written line has reached you. The perfect command you have at all times of your rare intellectual faculties makes it difficult for you to understand this, and long may your own happy experience teach you to wonder at that torpor of the mind which makes all exertion impossible for weeks & months together. Where there is much to admire I naturally conclude there may be much to love & if you had been within my reach I should have sought you out at the instant I received your kind letter, seduced by it in an uncalculating readiness to put our compatibilities to the test, in spite of a strong humiliating consciousness that a very little intercourse with my ruined sorrow-stricken self would destroy the Being to whom your fancy has been so lavish.

I well know how the heart & the Fancy delight to play round distant objects endowing them with all we wish and want & suiting them to the varying moods of our own Souls. What has Reality that could ever replace one of these our own creations? What could my intercourse afford you that would not fall far short of the pleasure of your own conceits at the moment of writing me that letter? I know all this—but so little power has what we know over what we feel that I cannot help wishing that something may bring you to Paris before very long. In the meantime if you can forgive my apparent neglect do, & write to me again with a perfect persuasion that I shall feel really interested in all you tell me of yourself.

I am not surprised at the dissatisfaction you often feel in those around you. You are an exotic transplanted unhappily into an unsuitable soil & shrinking before rude & chilling blasts that have succeeded to sweet & gentle zephyrs. Your early and intimate intercourse with the most refined of human beings has left you a standard for comparison which few in the most polished circles could bear & from which springs (by necessity) your dissatisfaction with your present society.

Need I tell you with what deep regret my mind often returns to all the endearing circumstances of my intimacy with that ethereal Being who did not belong to the gross & palpable world over which we still wander bearing about vain longings & warm regrets. My intimacy with Shelley ought not to have ended as it did. I say this with self reproach & I still feel the sharpened pang which this thought added to all my other feelings on his life. Many times after you went to Italy I was strongly tempted to write to him. Some tender recollection—some Verse of his—some ghost of former pleasures flitting before me would bid me write—yet I did not & for the very reason perhaps why I should have written—because I felt though suddenly & rudely parted by accidental circumstances & some discordant views & feelings—there still remained for us some sympathies which nothing could kill & which would sooner or later bring us together again. I felt that he in some measure belonged to me & I did not write because I knew that a line springing warm from my heart would at any time bring that wayward Child of Fancy from the world's end with uncalculating haste to see me & I would not have had him risk the uncalculable ills of such a visit to a country where there was so much to annoy him.

So I try to excuse myself to myself—but I am not satisfied for he is gone—& I can never more [torn] his soul one of those pure pleasurable feelings after which it [torn] & some of which he found with me. He's gone and I think in vain of the warm greeting, the interchange of glowing thoughts--and affectionate looks on which I used to reckon with blind forgetfulness of the instability of all things.

You see my dear Mrs. Shelley that if I have not written sooner 'tis not that I could find nothing in my heart to say to you. I am almost blind & absorbed in a most melancholy way for weeks & months together so that I undergo the almost insufferable privation of reading & writing & my mind is forced to look inward inwards & feed upon itself. When you write tell me something of Mrs. Williams, Mrs. Hogg, W. Peacock—tell me much of W. Godwin to whom I beg to be remembered in the kindest manner. Speak to me of Mr. [Charles] Lamb & his Sister—with the former Elia I have been sometimes so delighted that it was with difficulty I could keep myself from writing to him to express my gratitude for the pleasure he gave me & my longing to shake hands with him but such follies they say are only tolerated in the young—as if the heart could grow old & the sympathies of mind wear out.

 I cannot write this long letter over again so you must receive it with all its blots & blunders. The date will show you how long ago it was begun imperious & painful calls perpetually crop my purposes so that I am never sure of half an hour. I hear you made acquaintance here last year with a very distinguished frenchman. Is his name Fauriel? I think you saw him at the Douglas's & he is indeed a superior Being. Schlabendorff brought him two or three times to my house many years ago & he is one not to be forgotten. Adieu my dear Mrs. Shelley. Cornelia sends you her love &

 I am faithfully and affectionately yours,
 H. de Boinville

I am glad to hear so grand an account of Percy. Cornelia's Oswald is to me a bosom friend. Wm. Godwin scarcely admits the possibility of this but I have found & think that custom not nature distances Parents from Children. I am now Nov. 22nd returned to Paris & mail to me rue de clichy [illegible] & send your letter to Dr. Lambe's Holly Terrace Highgate.

Envelope:
Mrs. Shelley
33 Somerset Street
Portman Square
London

Figure A-1. Harriet de Boinville to Mary Shelley, October 16, 1829, page 1.

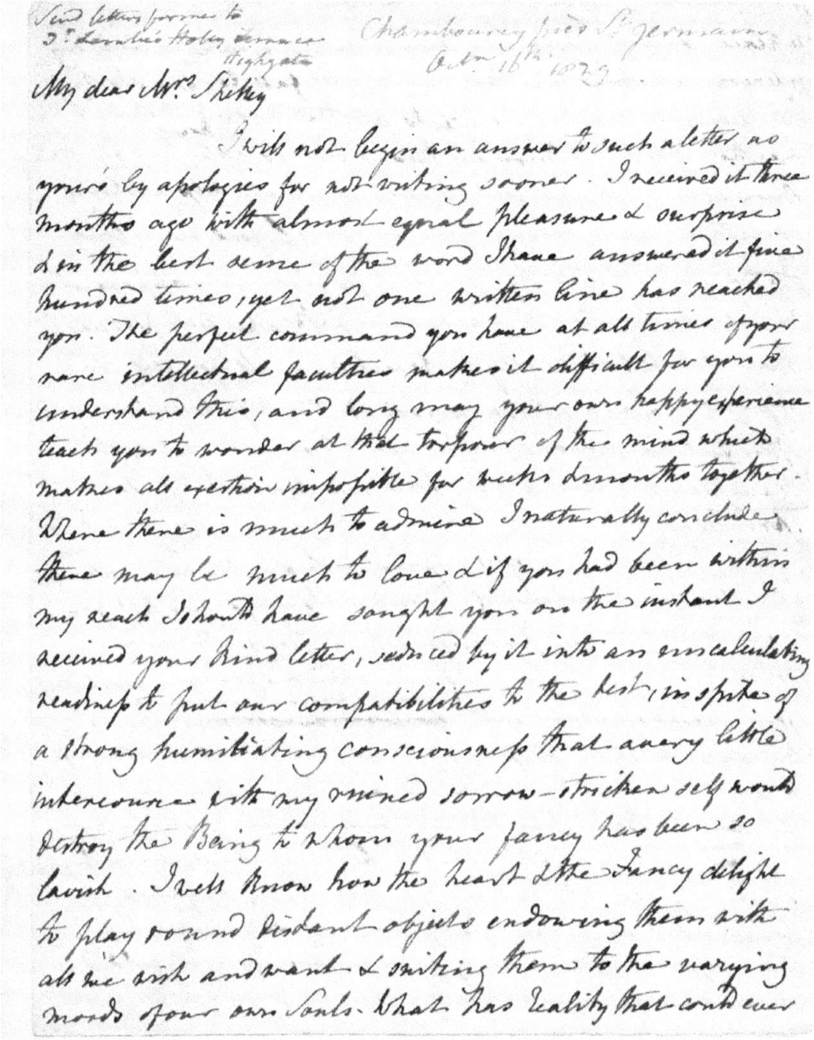

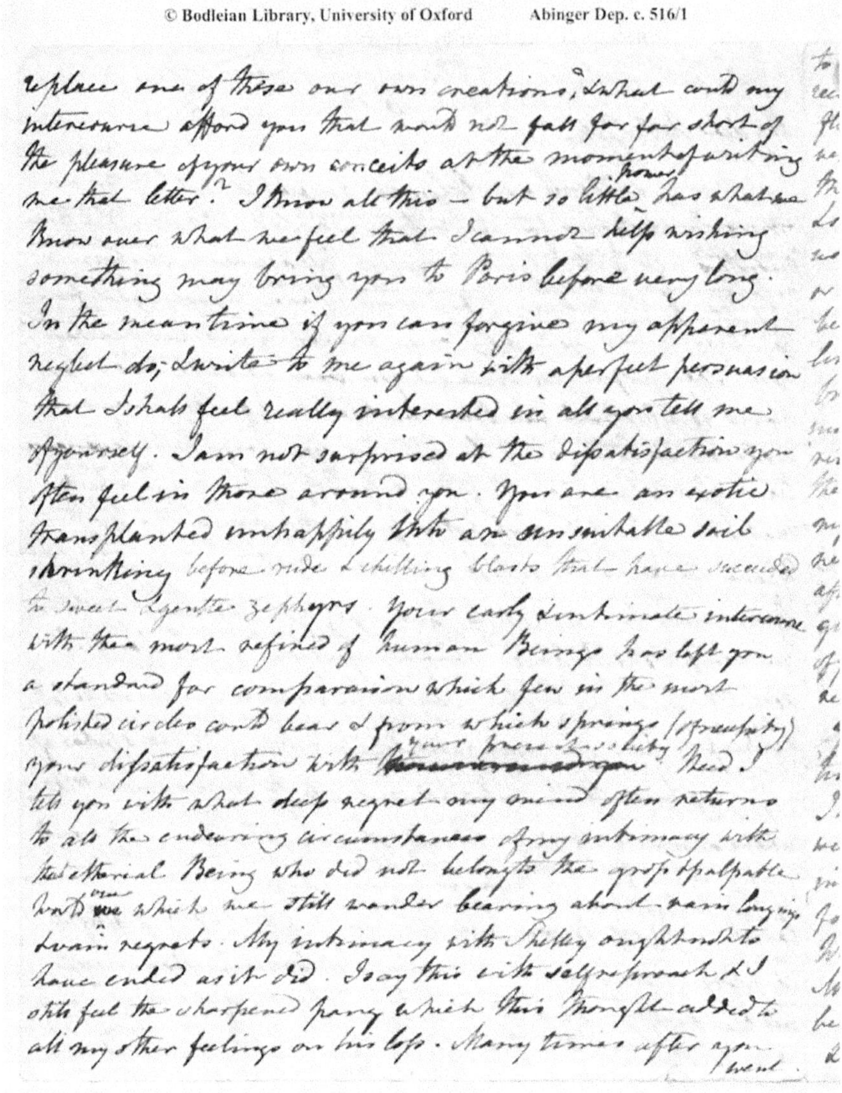

Figure A-1.2 Harriet de Boinville to Mary Shelley, October 16, 1829, page 2.

© Bodleian Library, University of Oxford   Abinger Dep. c. 516/1

to Italy, I was strongly tempted to write to him. Some tender recollection — some force of his — some ghost of former pleasures flitting before me would bid me write — yet I did not & for the very reason perhaps why I should have written — because I felt that though suddenly & rudely parted by accidental circumstances & some discordant views & feelings — there still remained for us sympathies which nothing could kill & which would sooner or later bring us together again. I felt that he in some measure belonged to me & I did not write because I knew that a line springing warm from my heart would at any time bring that wayward child of fancy from the world's end with incalculating haste to see me & I would not have had him risk the incalculable ills of such a visit to a country where there was so much to annoy him. So I try to excuse myself to myself — but I am not satisfied for he is gone — & I can never more say to his soul one of those pure pleasurable feelings after which it is said some of which he found with me. He is gone & I think in vain of the warm greeting, the interchange of glowing thoughts — & affectionate looks on which I need to reckon with blind forgetfulness of the instability of all things.

You see my dear M.rs Shelley that if I have not written sooner tis not that I could find nothing in my heart to say to you. I am almost blind & absorbed in a most melancholy way for weeks & months together so that I undergo the almost insufferable privation of reading & writing & my mind is forced to look inward & feed upon itself.

When you write tell me something of M.rs Williams, M.r Hogg, M.r Peacock — tell me much of M.r Godwin to whom I beg to be remembered in the kindest manner. Speak to me of M.r Lamb & his sister — with the former (Elia) I have been sometimes

Figure A-1.3 Harriet de Boinville to Mary Shelley, October 16, 1829, page 3.

Figure A-1.4 Harriet de Boinville to Mary Shelley, October 16, 1829, page 4.

Harriet de Boinville to Mary Shelley
June 11, 1836
Source: University of Oxford, Bodleian Libraries Abinger Collection, Abinger Dep C 516, c. 49, folios 40-1.

Rue de Clichy 74
June 11th 1836
My dear Mrs. Shelley,

I hope you will not measure my sorrow for your late loss by the tardiness of its expression; few believe me have felt it more sensibly. The extinction of a master mind gives a shock to the feelings for which mine were ill prepared, in this instance, having been lately assumed that we might hope to possess Mr Godwin many years as he was in good health and his mind in full vigor, tho his body began to bend under the weight of old age. In about a fortnight after came the sad news!

If I had never known Mr Godwin I should have felt the general loss, have been saddened by the gloom of another light put out, but accident had created for me a whole set of private feelings & associations connected with your father which have been revived by his loss & which drew me towards you at this moment with strong sympathy. I beg of you to write to me & to give me such details as you can bear to give of the melancholy event. I am anxious to hear he did not suffer much physically, whether he was aware of his approaching end, by what disease we have been robbed of him & where he is interred. Everything is interesting which relates to such a man, one of the gifted few under whose moral influences society is now vibrating. This & another loss which came still nearer to my heart and which we must unceasingly lament will never let us become Strangers to each other. Communication may be suspended but circumstances will be perpetually springing up to revive it, for it is the peculiar property of intellectual ties that they are not to be broken by the accidents which destroy more material ones.

It is so long since I heard from you that I do not even know where you live & must send you circuitously this letter which I hope you answer soon, for I want to know something of the present state of your mind. On certain points I know it can never change but an interval of several years with all its various incidents strangely modifies our thoughts & feelings, so that a letter addressed to the feelings which ruled you ten years ago may find little hold on those which possess you today.

When I last saw you you were looking with a tearful eye to Italy—as the land of your happiest recollections. Italian nature was to you beautiful nature and your regrets and longings were really touching; but the rust of absence has had time to form. Has it so eaten into your love that you take no great interest in the present affecting state of Italy? Even if it were so, which I should be sorry for, I think you will find in the little book of Poems which I send you enough of strength & originality & deep feeling to make them interesting to you. Accident has thrown me into contact with some Italian exiles, who to my interest in the struggles of Italy as part of a general struggle, add a peculiar interest in disasters which have presented to the world men so distinguished morally & intellectually as are very many amongst the exiles who have taken refuge here, where they live in honourable privation uncrushed morally by the numerous ills of exiles & devoted heart & soul to intellectual labours for the benefit of their country and of humanity. I say humanity for we are thro' miseries /inevitable I suppose/ arrived at the point where the true interests of particular nations merge in the true interests of all.

With the poems I send you the [illegible]th number of an Italian review just published. It is written by men of the first talent under restraints, which your piercing eye will discover, imposed by the desire of getting it admitted into Italy & circulated there, so as to produce good moral effects & to sow seed which may come up & in time produce a plentiful harvest. I wish you would give me your opinion of both, & tell me whether the two first articles of the review are likely to be accepted by any respectable English publications. If so, & you have still enough of Italian feeling about you to assist any efforts, I would send them you well translated into English. The first part of the [illegible number] article, especially adapted to Italian readers and the present state of Italy would probably be obscure & uninteresting to English readers, but has a great part of it that run great strength & beauty, is perhaps a necessary introduction to subsequent articles which might have a general interest, in as much as they will treat of a very extensive & important subject, the literary career & influence of great minds belonging not to one country but to Europe. In the number will be found many whom England makes a proud boast.

Moreover if you encourage me I will send you a short review of a late publication "Del Italia," a political & highly practical treatise on morals in the widest sense written by a powerful & original thinker. A true primitive Christian—a zealous republican [insertion: a roman catholic even in form and so man is made.] It is not necessary (as you will perceive by its effects on me) to be what is vulgarly called religious to admire the superiority of intellect which marks the work. The Poet is felt in every line, and it is curious to observe how he comes by, or rather with, religion even subjected to certain forms exactly to the point where he is met by the few real republicans & excellent free thinkers whose zeal for the general good has not been able to redeem the mistakes & crimes of pretenders. But I forget that the work is not before you. If you have a mind I will find you a few chapters that you may judge. At all events I will tell you that I do not know the author personally so that I am not bribed in my judgments by friendship.

I know that mind under any form has a strong hold on you so I will not say excuse my troubling you on this subject. I wish to know what you /a critic in the good sense of the word/ think of what I now send you—and I shall judge by your readiness or tardiness in answering this frightfully long letter whether you have found it intolerably tedious.

In writing pray tell me a great deal of yourself and your son now a young man with a claim to a rich inheritance of mind which I hope he will use as his fathers have done. Thrice I have heard you were going to be married. Do write to me about yourself & tell me if you enjoy a large share of happiness.

Since I last wrote to you Fanny Wright now Mme Darusmont & I have become acquainted—and immediately intimate & true friends. She is as you know a delightful creature—not only endowed with a strong intellect & great reasoning powers but with a quick sensibility & capability of loving which make her quite irresistible. She is most happily married to a man quite worthy of her morally—partaking her own enthusiastic views & hopes for improvements—with a very active mind well stored with scientific acquirements. They are a rare couple, tenderly united & enjoying a degree of happiness which is awful—for the Gods you know are jealous of such happiness. They are at present in America on private business.

What is your pen doing just now? I suppose you will give us the Memoirs of Mr Godwin—if so & you have no translator whom you favour, think of me & let me have the pleasure & benefit for a friend of whose capability I am quite sure.

Adieu my dear Mrs. Shelley the lengths & subjects of this letter will prove to you how much pleasure I should have in meeting you again. Are you never tempted to pass a short time in Paris? Accept from Cornelia the love of an old companion & friend
& believe me very affectionately yours
H. de Boinville

Tell me what is become of M Hogg & W. Peacock & if Mrs. Peacock's little girl has grown up all that his fondness could hope—remember me kindly to him & pray say to Mrs Godwin all that her melancholy loss can dictate.

Harriet de Boinville to Mary Shelley
December 18, 1837
Source: A copy of this letter in the hand of Richard Garnett is in the University of Oxford, Bodleian Libraries Abinger Collection, MS Abinger c. 77.

Rue de Clichy
18 Dec 1837
My dear Mrs. Shelley,

My friend Dr. Constancio is about to furnish a short memoir of Mr Godwin to a reputable biographical publication. Having a due appreciation of your distinguished father he has agreed & is well pleased to write this article & he wishes to address the best materials for it—for these we naturally apply to you and entreat you to send me some of the most striking circumstances of his life—with a correct list of his works—and the exact place & time of his birth with other such particulars as you may think best calculated for a limited Memoir. Some one will certainly write this article & we desire it should come from the pen of a lover of his fame & just appreciator of his doctrines. Whatever materials you may furnish will be valuable & we hope you will be disposed to aid this tribute to the memory of a great name; for the trouble it may give you I will make no apology, but entreat you to send me a speedy answer. Your pen I know flies like the wind so this will cost you less than it would any other person. We are looking with impatience for your own important memoirs of Mr. Godwin. Science has realized some of the dreams of political justice & many of the seeds scattered thro' his works are springing up here & there & making promise of future harvest.

I wrote to you not long ago & I hope that my letter has reached you. When you write pray tell me all you can of yourself. It would give me pleasure to hear that you are as happy as a thinking Being can be & that you have the society of a few friends that suit you; many you cannot expect to have for you naturally require more than is easily found. Percy you tell me contributes largely to your satisfaction. I rejoice at that & hope one day to know him. I shall be glad of the first opportunity of introducing Oswald to you. He is not an ordinary young man. Mr. Godwin & Shelley I am sure would have valued him—this is high praise but I feel that he deserves it. Do you see Mrs. [Norton?] now? How is she & what is she doing? and what are you doing? I am having a very retired life in this gay capital. With whom do you live in London? Cornelia desires to be very kindly remembered to you. Is Ianthe happy in her marriage? Does she inherit any of her father's moral & intellectual nature? I wish that instead of sending you this letter I could throw on my cloak & have an hour's chat with you. Speak of your health when you write & think of me sometimes as of an old friend who is affectionately yours
H. de Boinville

Pray present my comp^{ts} to Mr Hookham. I hope he & his family are well.
Envelope:
Mrs. Shelley
at Thomas Hookham Esq.

[illegible] Bond Street
London
to be forwarded immediately

Harriet de Boinville to Mary Shelley
January 26, 1839
Source: Original signed letter. University of Oxford, Bodleian Libraries Abinger Collection, MS Abinger c. 49, folios 128-9.

Paris, Jan ry 26th 1839
My dear Mrs. Shelley,
I seize an opportunity offered by a very obliging friend on whom I can depend to lend you my copy of Queen Mab. I confess that I lend it with reluctance & to no one but yourself would I confide it. I commit it to your care, and rest confidently on your promise to return it to me as soon as you have made the use you wish of it. Will you have the goodness to send it when you have Done with it in a sealed packet directed to me to the Chambers of John Flather Esq Lincoln's Inn. They used to be in Old Square No. 5 and his direction be had there but I believe he has changed Chambers. The first Inn porter who presents himself will point them out. I value highly this copy of Queen Mab for many reasons which you need not be told. It is a relic of genius, of friendship—of past happy days which it would really grieve me to lose. I hope to see you one of these days in Paris. It is a point from which one may reasonably and almost confidently look out for one's friends. It would give me great pleasure to see you & Percy & to introduce Oswald to you. Cornelia desires to be affectionately remembered to you—with love and my good wishes.

I am sincerely and aff ly yours,
H. de Boinville

Harriet de Boinville to her grandson, Charles de Boinville
January 6, 1842
Source: The following passage from this letter is quoted in Thomas

Constable, *Memoir of the Reverend Charles A. Chastel de Boinville Compiled from his Journals and His Letters* (London: James Nesbitt & Co., 1880), chapter 2, 36-38.

...How different the opening of this year from last, when we had you just arrived amongst us, with your troubles that were soon assuaged—or rather transmuted into others of a higher order and more obstinate—with your pleasant humour, which we all enjoyed and shall ever miss. And now you are away, not comfortable in any way, so that you are a subject of varied anxiety and regret for me. Our poor little girl gone for ever and some little circumstance perpetually starting up to bring her suddenly and painfully before us. These days have been hard to get over; and now, what will '42 bring? Let us not *think* of that but hide our faces thankfully in the obscurity of the future.... . Some of Emily's kindest thoughts flew off to Lille to visit her absent friend, and mine were fixed on him all day, and sad I was to think of him, without any circumstance to cheer. A dear friend of mine used to say that a loving unsullied soul carried everywhere a paradise within itself. *Is* that true? *You*, dear fellow, can tell. And now you are away, not comfortable in any way, so that you are a subject of varied anxiety and regret to me....

The cold has set in with a vengeance. *Do* tell me if you have plenty of firing, a warm room, and all-sufficient covering at night; these little things are most important to your old anxious granny, so—mind you answer categorically, or I shall conclude, that all is going wrong. Tell me too about your money; a great part of it, I dare say, has found its way into pockets more empty than your own. I wish you had some watchful loving sister to examine your hoard, and make a calculation for you as Mr. Venn has. ... Yesterday's post brought a few lines from R—, despairing over the want of money to go to the end of the month. I fear by this time you repent of having gone to live with them, for I suspect their roof affords no quiet of any kind. ...God bless you, dear boy, and preserve you from the dangers of your best qualities, but, "Nul ne peut sortir de la région intellectuelle qui lui est assigné, et les *qualités* sont encore plus indomptables que les *défauts*." [No one can leave the intellectual region assigned to him, and innate good qualities are even less easily changed, than defects.] Write, write, write—tutto, *tutto*, TUTTO!

Cornelia Turner to Claire Clairmont
October 3, 1852
Source: Carl H. Pforzheimer Collection of Shelley and His Circle, The New York Public Library. S'ANA 0124 call number.
Note: Ellipses indicate an illegible word and brackets what the word might be. The Mrs. de Boinville mentioned at the end of the letter is Harriet Lambe de Boinville.

My dear Mlle. Clairmont,

I answer, as you request, by return of post your letter of the ...nd instant which I have just received.

I can clearly state that I was acquainted with you when we were both girls, and that you were always ... ed to be three years younger than myself, who was born in 1795. I distinctly remember your being present at a dance on the day I completed my fifteenth year in 1810, and you were then to the best of my knowledge twelve years of age. I ... [realize] therefore that you are now fifty-four years of age.

I shall be glad if this statement can be of any service to you, and I am happy to gather from your letter that you are ... [well] in health, although saddened by the loss of your ... friends and relations. I had already heard with regret of the death of Mrs. Shelley, but I was not aware that you had also lost your dear Brother & her daughter. Octavia & Major Frye are well. Of my family have nothing more to tell.
I remain, yours truly
Cornelia Turner

I do not know Mrs.... . address
Mrs. de Boinville is at the Vicarage [illegible]. Therefore she lives with her son who is curate there.

Notes

Abbreviations

CCC *The Clairmont Correspondence: Letters of Claire Clairmont, Charles Clairmont, and Fanny Imlay Godwin,* ed. Marion Kingston Stocking. Vol. 1, 1808-1834. Vol. 2, 1835-1879. Baltimore: Johns Hopkins University Press, 1995.
FB *Fanny Burney: Selected Letters and Journals,* ed. Joyce Hemlow. Oxford University Press, 1987.
MWS *The Letters of Mary Wollstonecraft Shelley,* ed. Betty T. Bennett. Vols. 1-3. Baltimore & London: Johns Hopkins University Press, 1980.
PBS *The Letters of Percy Bysshe Shelley,* ed. Frederick L. Jones. Vol. 1: *Shelley in England.* Vol. 2: *Shelley in Italy.* Oxford: At the Clarendon Press, 1964.
PR *Practical Rules for the Management and Medical Treatment of Negro Slaves in the Sugar Colonies by a Professional Planter,* written by John Collins and published anonymously in 1803.
TC Thomas Constable, *Memoir of the Reverend Charles A. Chastel de Boinville Compiled from his Journals and His Letters.* London: James Nesbitt & Co., 1880.
TJH Thomas Jefferson Hogg, *The Life of Percy Bysshe Shelley,* 2 vols. London: 1858; reprinted in the HardPress Classics Series.
TLP Thomas Love Peacock, *Peacock's Memoirs of Shelley, with Shelley's Letters to Peacock,* ed. H. F. B. Brett-Smith. London: Henry Frowde, 1909.
SC Kenneth Neill Cameron, Donald H. Reiman, and Doucet Devin Fischer, eds., *Shelley and His Circle, 1773-1822,* 10 vols. Cambridge: Harvard University Press, 1961-2002.

Chapter 1. Birth and Life in the Dangerous Tropics, 1773–1788

1. Rick Atkinson, *The British Are Coming: The War for America, Lexington to Princeton, 1775-1777*, vol. 1 of the Revolution Trilogy (Henry Holt, 2019), 6.
2. Richard Dunn, *Sugar and Slaves: The Rise of the Planter Class in the English West Indies, 1624-1713* (New York: Norton, 1972), xiv-xvi, 14, and 18.
3. TC. On the term "Creole," see William Lux, *Historical Dictionary of the British Caribbean* (Metuchen, N.J.: The Scarecrow Press, 1975), 19. See also Percy Hintzen, "Race and Creole Ethnicity in the Caribbean," in *Caribbean Cultural Thought: From Plantation to Diaspora*, ed. Yanique Hume and Aaron Kumugisha (Kingston and Miami: Ian Randle Publishers, 2013), 62-74. On the part-Creole ancestry in Harriet's family, see Miranda Seymour, *Mary Shelley* (New York: Grove Press, 2000), 59.
4. PR. See also William Wilberforce, Letter to Henry Manning, October 18, 1809; Robert Isaac Wilberforce and Samuel Wilberforce, *The Life of William Wilberforce* (London: 1839), 3: 481.
5. PR.
6. William Wilberforce, Letter to Henry Manning, October 18, 1809; and Robert Isaac Wilberforce and Samuel Wilberforce, *The Life of William Wilberforce* (London: 1839), vol. 3, 481.
7. Ibid. On Collins's well-respected medical views, see *Medical Communications*, vol. 2, printed in London, MDCCXC, as well as "Letters of John Collins, Esquire of St. Vincent, to Benjamin Vaughan, Esquire, of London, on "The Subject of a Species of Angina, Maligna, and the Use of Capsicum in that and Several Other Diseases." Communicated by Adair Crawford, January 19, 1790. See also Richard B. Sheridan, *Doctors and Slaves: A Medical and Demographic History of Slavery in the British West Indies, 1580-1834* (Cambridge: 1985), 32-35.
8. Ron Chernow, *Alexander Hamilton* (Penguin Books, 2004), 37.
9. *An Account of the Late Dreadful Hurricane, Which Happened on the 31rst of August, 1772. Also the Damage Done on that Day in the Islands of St. Christopher and Nevis*. Printed and Sold by Thomas Howe in Basseterre, John Anderson, junior, in Nevis, and David Crawford, in St. Eustacia, 1772.
10. Ibid., 10.
11. The deeds, preserved in the British Museum, were digitized by Brunel University as part of the British Library, Endangered Archives Program. Professor Kenneth Morgan, Brunel University, London. See

also Michael Craton, *Testing the Chains: Resistance to Slavery in the British West Indies* (London: Cornell University Press, 1982); and Dunn, *Sugar and Slaves*.
12. One slave in St. Vincent wrote an account of his experiences on the Cane Grove Estate. The slave's name was Ashton Warner. See Norman Eustace Cameron, *The Evolution of the Negro*. 2 vols. (Westport, Conn.: Negro Universities Press, 1970).
13. Robert A. McDonald, ed., *Between Slavery and Freedom: Special Magistrate John Anderson's Journal of St. Vincent during the Apprenticeship, with a Foreword by Richard S. Dunn* (University of Pennsylvania Press, 2001), 131-132.
14. CCC 1: 6, note 1.
15. A. C. Carmichael, *Domestic Manners and Social Condition of the White, Coloured, and Negro Population of the West Indies*, 2 vols. (London: Whittaker, Treacher and Co., 1833), 24.

Chapter 2. "Une Enfant de la Révolution," 1789-1792

1. TC, 10-11.
2. William Wordsworth "The French Revolution as It Appeared to Enthusiasts at Its Commencement," and "The Prelude," Book 6, Cambridge and the Alps. See also Percy Bysshe Shelley, *Queen Mab: A Philosophical Poem with Notes*, line 77.
3. John Slater, *A Short History of the Berners Estate* (London, 1918), 43-45.
4. TC, 3.
5. Ibid.
6. Ibid., 6.
7. "Il y a de grandes connaissances à tirer de ce côté, et comme M. de Boinville en fera son occupation unique, ne doute pas qu'il ne me donne des avis trés utiles. Mémoires de Général Lafayette Publiés par sa Famille (Paris and London, 1837), 2: 429-431.
8. Meredith Hindley, "Ungoverned Passion," *Humanities: The Magazine for the National Endowment for the Humanities* (March/April 2012), vol. 33, no. 2.
9. Theodore Roosevelt, *Gouverneur Morris* (Haskell House Publishers, 1968), 262-263, 269, 273, 274, 288. First published 1888.
10. *Dictionnaire de Biographie des Hommes Célèbres de L'Alsace*, vol. 1, 194. "Une famille les plus nobles, les plus riches, les plus ancien de Strasbourg."

11. TC, 2.
12. Edmund Blunden, *Shelley: A Life Story* (Oxford University Press, 1965), 95; and Kenneth Neill Cameron, *The Young Shelley: Genesis of a Radical* (New York: Collier Books, 1962), 244-245. See also TC, 7-8; Mémoires ... de Général Lafayette Publiés par sa Famille (Paris and London, 1837), vol. 2, 429-431; and *The Journals of Mary Shelley: 1814-1844*, edited by Paula R. Feldman and Diana Scott-Kilvert (Oxford: At the Clarendon Press, 1987), vol. 1, 1814-1822, 133, note 3.

Chapter 3. A Disobedient Daughter Marries for Love, 1793

1. TC, 11.
2. Ibid., 3.
3. Ibid, 11.
4. John Gregory, *A Father's Legacy to His Daughters* (London: Cadelle and Davies, Strand, 1797), the chapter on conduct and behavior, 24.
5. Lucy Worsley, *Jane Austin at Home* (St. Martin's Press, 2017), 31. See also Marian Veevers, *Jane and Dorothy: A True Tale of Sense and Sensibility: The Lives of Jane Austen and Dorothy Wordsworth* (New York: Pegasus Books, 2018).
6. TC, 11.
7. Worsley, *Jane Austen*, 29.
8. TC, 11-12.
9. Kate Chisholm, *Fanny Burney: Her Life*, 1752-1840 (Vintage, 1999), 42.
10. Ibid., 232.
11. Claire Harman, *Fanny Burney, A Biography* (New York: Knopf, 2001), 225.
12. *The Diary of Fanny Burney*, ed. Lewis Gibbs (Dent and Dutton, 1960), 316.
13. Kate Chisolm, "The Burney Family" in *The Cambridge Companion to Frances Burney*, ed. by Peter Sabor (Cambridge University Press, 2007), 8-9.
14. Frances Burney d'Arblay, letter to Mrs. Marianne Waddington, 2 August 1793. FB, 28.
15. The Henry W. and Albert A. Berg Collection of English and American Literature, The New York Public Library, Astor, Lenox and Tilden Foundations.

Chapter 4. From Domesticity to Dangers at Sea, 1793-1796

1. TC, 12.
2. Ibid.
3. William Cowper, "The Task: A Poem in Six Books," first published in 1785 by Joseph Johnson in London. This stanza is from the book entitled "The Winter Evening."
4. TC, 13.
5. Ibid.
6. Ibid.
7. Robert A. McDonald, ed., *Between Slavery and Freedom: Special Magistrate John Anderson's Journal of St. Vincent during the Apprenticeship*, with a Foreword by Richard S. Dunn (University of Pennsylvania Press, 2001), 56.
8. Ibid., 57.
9. TC, 14.
10. Ibid.
11. Barbara Ehrenreich and Deirdre English, *Complaints and Disorders: The Sexual Politics of Sickness* (Old Westbury: The Feminist Press, 1973), 19. Ehrenreich and English are quoted in Sandra M. Gilbert and Susan Gubar, *The Madwoman in the Attic: The Woman Writer and the Nineteenth-Century Literary Imagination*, 2d ed. (New Haven: Yale University Press, 2000), 54.
12. Mary Wollstonecraft, *A Vindication of the Rights of Woman: With Strictures on Political and Moral Subjects*. Dublin, 1793. Printed by J. Stockdale for James Moore.

Chapter 5. A Young Mother in a War-torn Colony, 1797

1. Julie Chun Kim, "The Caribs of St. Vincent and Indigenous Resistance during the Age of Revolutions," *Early American Studies*, vol. 11, no. 1, Special Issue: *Forming Nations, Reforming Empires: Atlantic Polities in the Long Eighteenth Century* (Winter 2013), 117-132. MacNeil Center for Early American Studies, University of Pennsylvania.
2. Virginia Heyer Young, *Becoming West Indian: Culture, Self, and Nation in St. Vincent,* Smithsonian Series in Ethnographic Inquiry (Smithsonian Institution Press, 1993), 32-36.
3. Robert A. McDonald, ed., *Between Slavery and Freedom: Special Magistrate John Anderson's Journal of St. Vincent during the Apprenticeship, with a Foreword by Richard S. Dunn* (University of Pennsylvania Press, 2001), 61.

4. A. C. Carmichael, *Domestic Manners and Social Condition of the White, Coloured, and Negro Population of the West Indies*, 2 vols. (London: Whittaker, Treacher and Co., 1833).
5. Young, *Becoming West Indian*, 18-19, 36-37.
6. See Ebenezer Duncan, *A Brief History of St. Vincent with Studies in Citizenship*. Kingstown, St. Vincent, 1955. See also Young, *Becoming West Indian*, 43.
7. TC, 14.
8. Richard S. Dunn, *Sugar and Slaves: The Rise of the Planter Class in the English West Indies, 1624-1713* (New York: Norton, 1972), 341.
9. In the offices held by John Collins, see britishstvincent.com and *The St. Vincent Almanack of 1779*, digitized.
10. TC, 14.
11. Charles Shephard, *An Historical Account of the Island of St Vincent*, London, 1831, 53. On the British viewpoint of the First Carib War, see *An Account of the Black Charaibs in the Island of St. Vincent's with the Charaib Treaty of 1773 and other original documents compiled from the papers of the late Sir William Young*, bart. London: 1795. Eighteenth Century Collections Online.

Chapter 6. A Bold Traveler between Nations at War, 1797-1800

1. TC, 14-15.
2. Raymond Horricks, *In Flight with the Eagle: A Guide to Napoleon's Elite* (Tunbridge Wells: D. J. Costello, 1988), 59-60.
3. TC, 15.
4. Ibid.
5. Ibid., 10.
6. Ibid., 12
7. Ibid., 15.
8. Kenneth Neill Cameron, *The Young Shelley: Genesis of a Radical* (New York: Collier Books, 1962), 45.
9. The letter written in August 1795 was sent to a Monsieur Hugar. See http://founders.archives.gov/documents/Washington/99-01-02-00774. See also Cameron, *The Young Shelley*, 404, note 137.
10. TC, 15.
11. Tom Pocock, *The Terror before Trafalgar: Nelson, Napoleon, and the Secret War* (New York: Norton, 2002), 24.
12. TC, 15-16.

Chapter 7. An Empathetic Friend to Frances Burney d'Arblay, 1800- 1808

1. The Henry W. and Albert A. Berg Collection of English and American Literature, The New York Public Library, Astor, Lenox, and Tilden Foundations.
2. FB, 77. Fanny Burney, Letter to Esther Burney, March 22, 1802.
3. PR, chapter 1.
4. Claudia L. Johnson, *Equivocal Beings: Politics, Gender, and Sentimentality in the 1790s* (The University of Chicago Press, 1995), 1.
5. Harriet de Boinville, letter to Frances Burney d'Arblay, February 19, 1802. The Henry W. and Albert A. Berg Collection of English and American Literature, The New York Public Library, Astor, Lenox, and Tilden Foundations.
6. Harriet de Boinville, letter to Frances Burney d'Arblay, March 7, 1814. The Henry W. and Albert A. Berg Collection of English and American Literature, The New York Public Library, Astor, Lenox, and Tilden Foundations.
7. FB, 72-73.
8. Jean Baptiste Boinville, letter to Alexandre d'Arblay, September 24, 1793, The Henry W. and Albert A. Berg Collection of English and American Literature, The New York Public Library, Astor, Lenox, and Tilden Foundations.
9. TC, 14-15.
10. Claire Harman, *Fanny Burney: A Biography* (New York: Knopf, 2001), 278.
11. Pocock, *The Terror Before Trafalgar* (Norton, 2002), 43.
12. Ibid., 42.
13. Robert and Isabelle Tombs, *That Sweet Enemy: Britain and France: The History of a Love-Hate Relationship* (First Vintage Books Edition, January 2008), 229.
14. William Windham, The Windham Papers, 2 vols. (London: 1913), vol. 2, 181, quoted in Pocock, *The Terror Before Trafalgar*, 34.
15. Kate Adams, *Ambition and Desire:The Dangerous Life of Josephine Bonaparte* (New York: Ballantine Books, 2014), 199.
16. TC, 16.

Chapter 8. With the Proponent of Political Justice, William Godwin, 1809-1811

1. William Hazlitt, *The Spirit of the Age, or Contemporary Portraits*. First published in 1825; republished by Anodus Books, 2019.

2. *The Diary of William Godwin*, ed. Victoria Myers, David O'Shaughnessy, and Mark Philip (Oxford: Oxford Digital Library, 2010). See Bodleian Library website.
3. The original title was *An Enquiry Concerning Political Justice and its Influence on General Virtue and Happiness* (1793, published by G.G. Robinson). In the second edition (1796) and third edition (1798), General Virtue was changed to Morals.
4. See London's Global University, UCL, Legacies of British Slave-ownership (LBS). www.ucl.ac.uk/lbs/person/view/2146644943. British probate records, PROB 11/1439/198, Profile & Legacies Summary of John Collins of Berners Street.
5. Robert Gittings and Jo Manton, *Dorothy Wordsworth* (Clarendon Press Oxford, 1985), 17.
6. Peter Marshall, *William Godwin: Philosopher, Novelist, Revolutionary*, with a Foreword by John P. Clark (PM Press, 2017), 406. On James Marshall's visit to St. Vincent, see 66.
7. Ibid., 176.
8. Mary Wollstonecraft, *A Short Residence in Sweden, Norway and Denmark*, and William Godwin, *Memoirs of the Author of the Rights of Woman*, edited with an Introduction and Notes by Richard Holmes (Penguin Classics, 1987), Introduction, 10, 12.
9. See Marshall, *William Godwin*, the chapter titled The Most Odious of Monopolies, 173-194. See also Janet Todd, *Mary Wollstonecraft: A Revolutionary Life* (Columbia University Press, 2000), 389.
10. William Godwin, *Memoirs of the Author of a Vindication of the Rights of Woman* (J.J. Johnson, G.G. & J. Robinson, 1798; 2nd ed., J. Johnson, 1798).
11. Wollstonecraft, *A Short Residence*, Introduction by Holmes, 13.
12. Ibid., 180.
13. Janet Todd, *Death & the Maidens: Fanny Wollstonecraft and the Shelley Circle* (Counterpoint, 2007), 40.
14. C. Kegan Paul, *William Godwin: His Friends and Contemporaries* (2 vols., 1876), 2: 58.
15. Todd, *Death & the Maidens*, 57.
16. On the creation of the Juvenile Library, see Marshall, *William Godwin*, 265.
17. Ibid., 55-56.
18. Miranda Seymour, *Mary Shelley* (Grove Press, 2000), 65.
19. Eric G. Wilson, *Dream-Child: A Life of Charles Lamb* (Yale University Press, 2022), 301.

20. Ibid., 266
21. TC, 125.

Chapter 9. Harriet's Husband Rescues Madam d'Arblay, 1810–1812

1. FB, 152.
2. Claire Harman, *Fanny Burney: A Biography* (New York: Knopf, 2001), "Preface," xx.
3. Jean Baptiste Boinville, Letter to Alexandre d'Arblay, September 24, 1793. The Henry W. and Albert A. Berg Collection of English and American Literature, The New York Public Library, Astor, Lenox and Tilden Foundations.
4. FB, 154.
5. TC, 17.
6. Caroline Moorehead, *Dancing to the Precipice: The Life of Lucie de la Tour du Pin, Eyewitness to an Era* (New York: HarperCollins, 2009), 335.
7. John Wiltshire, "Journals and Letters," *The Cambridge Companion to Frances Burney*, edited by Peter Sabor (Cambridge University Press, 2007), 86.
8. FB, 133, 136-137.
9. Ibid., 133.
10. Ibid., 155. See also Kate Chisholm, *Fanny Burney: Her Life* (Vintage Books, 1999), 218.
11. Ibid., 157, 161, 162.

Chapter 10. Aaron Burr and the London Wedding of Godwin's Protégé, 1812–1813

1. Turner's letter, written on July 4, 1803, is quoted in William St. Clair, *The Godwins and the Shelleys: A Biography of a Family* (New York: Norton, 1989), 300-301.
2. *The Diary of William Godwin*, ed. Victoria Myers, David O'Shaughnessy, and Mark Philp (Oxford: Oxford Digital Library, 2010). Available online at the website of the Bodleian Library. Cornelia met her future husband at Godwin's home often (March 20, 1810, August 9, 1810, March 4, 1811, May 15, 1811, July 13, 1811, July 17, 1811, July18, 1811, September 9, 1811, October 1, 1811, October 19, 1811).

3. William St. Clair, *The Godwins and The Shelleys* (New York: Norton, 1999), 300-301.
4. Ibid., 299.
5. H.W. Brands, *The Heartbreak of Aaron Burr* (New York: Anchor Books, 2012), 16.
6. Ibid., 6-7.
7. Ibid., 7, 15.
8. Ibid., 59.
9. Ibid.
10. On Burr's friendship with William and Mary Jane Godwin and their three daughters, see Miranda Seymour, *Mary Shelley* (New York: Grove Press, 2000), 47, 59-60, 80n. See also Janet Todd, *Death and the Maidens: Fanny Wollstonecraft and the Shelley Circle* (Counterpoint, 2007), 62-63, 71.
11. This quote from Burr's journal is from the second volume of *The Private Journal of Aaron Burr*, which is available and searchable online via Gutenberg.org.
12. Edmund Blunden, *Shelley: A Life Story* (London: Collins, 1946). See 95-96 of 1965 Oxford University edition.
13. See Burr's journal, the second volume, *The Private Journal of Aaron Burr*, available and searchable online via Gutenberg.org.
14. St. Clair, *The Godwins and The Shelleys*, 180, 300. This portrait is now on display in the Edna Barnes Salomon Room of the New York Public Library. Many of Wollstonecraft's papers can be found in that library's Pforzheimer Collection.
15. Nancy Isenberg, *Fallen Founder: The Life of Aaron Burr* (New York: Viking, 2007), ix.
16. Harriet Boinville, March 7, 1814, Bracknell, Berkshire, letter to Frances Burney d'Arblay; envelope addressed to Dr. Burney's, Chelsea College, near London. This letter is preserved in the Berg Collection of the New York Public Library.

Chapter 11. Percy Bysshe Shelley Meets "Miamuna," Spring, 1813

1. TLP, 33.
2. James Bieri, *Percy Bysshe Shelley: A Biography* (Baltimore: Johns Hopkins University Press, 2008), 259.
3. Kenneth Neill Cameron, *The Young Shelley: Genesis of a Radical* (New York: Collier Books, 1962), 244, 246.
4. SC 3: 276.

5. Percy Bysshe Shelley, letter to Thomas Jefferson Hogg, October 4, 1814. PBS 1: 401.
6. Robert Gittings and Jo Manton, *Claire Clairmont and the Shelleys* (Oxford University Press, 1992).
7. Edmund Blunden, *Shelley: A Life Story* (London: Oxford University Press, 1965), 97.
8. Percy Bysshe Shelley, letter to Thomas Jefferson Hogg, October 4, 1814. PBS 1: 401.
9. Richard Holmes, *Shelley: The Pursuit, with a New Introduction by the Author* (New York Review Books edition, 1994); first published in 1974.
10. SC 3: 70, 427.
11. J. L. Bradley, *A Shelley Chronology* (The Macmillan Press, 1993), 73.
12. Percy Bysshe Shelley, letter to Elizabeth Hitchener, December 9, 1811. PBS 1: 199.
13. Percy Bysshe Shelley, letter to Elizabeth Hitchener, December 26, 1811. PBS 1: 213.
14. Percy Bysshe Shelley, letters to Thomas Jefferson Hogg, April 24, 1811, and August 3, 1811. PBS 1: 66, 131.
15. Holmes, *Shelley,* 60.
16. Percy Bysshe Shelley, letter to Thomas Jefferson Hogg, August 15, 1811. PBS 1: 135.
17. Percy Bysshe Shelley, letter to Thomas Jefferson Hogg, August 3, 1811. PBS 1: 131.
18. Holmes, *Shelley,* 79.
19. Sir Timothy Shelley, letter to John Hogg, September 8, 1811. SC 3: 9.
20. Percy Bysshe Shelley, letter to Sir Timothy Shelley, October 12, 1811. SC 3: 12-13.
21. Holmes, *Shelley,* 96
22. Percy Bysshe Shelley, letter to Thomas Jefferson Hogg, November 7-8, 1811. SC 3: 41.
23. Holmes, *Shelley,* 113.
24. Harriet Shelley wrote comments on her husband's letter to Elizabeth Hitchener, January 26, 1812. PBS 1: 241-242.
25. Holmes, *Shelley,* 129.
26. Ibid., 201, 208.

Chapter 12. Vegetarians and Egalitarians "Return to Nature," Summer 1813

1. TLP, 29-30.
2. John Williams, "The Vegetable System," *New York Times*, Sunday Book Review, March 2, 2014, BR4.
3. "Reports on the Effects of a Peculiar Regimen in Scirrhous Tumers & Cancerous Ulcers, by William Lambe, M.D." Printed for J. Mawman in the Poultry, 153.
4. Howard Williams, "The Ethics of Diet: A Catena," 1883, quoted by The International Vegetarian Union, ivu.org.
5. TJH, 503.
6. Ibid., 503-504.
7. Edward Dowden, *The Life of Percy Bysshe Shelley* (New York: Barnes & Noble edition, 1966), 214-215; first published in 1866.
8. James Henry Lawrence, *The Empire of the Nairs, or The Rights of Women. An Utopian Romance in Twelve Books* (London, printed for T. Hookham et al., No. 15, Old Bond Street, 1811).
9. William St. Clair, *The Godwins and the Shelleys: A Biography of a Family* (Norton, 1989), 262-263.
10. Percy Bysshe Shelley, letter to James Henry Lawrence, August 17, 1812. PBS 1: 322.
11. Harriet Shelley, letter to Catherine Nugent, August 8, 1813. PBS 1: 376.
12. TLP, 30. "Cold scholar" appears in Cornelia Newton's letter to Hogg on October 21, 1813. TJH, 535.
13. Richard Holmes, *Shelley: The Pursuit, with a New Introduction by the Author* (New York Review Books edition, 1994), 217.
14. Thomas Jefferson Hogg, "The Life of Percy Bysshe Shelley," in Humbert Wolfe, ed., *The Life of Percy Bysshe Shelley* (London: Dent, 1933), 2: 107.
15. Harriet is referring to a biblical command, Matthew 22, verse 38: "Love the Lord your God with all your heart, and with all your soul, and with all your mind. This is the first and greatest commandment."
16. Harriet Boinville, Letter to Thomas Jefferson Hogg, March 11, 1814.
17. Ibid.

Chapter 13. Shelley Retreats to Harriet's Home at Bracknell, February and March 1814

1. PBS 2: 383. Frederick L. Jones, the editor of Shelley's letters, notes that this was the first letter in which Shelley revealed "any lack of harmony between himself and his wife."
2. SC 3: 274-275.
3. PBS 1: 383-385.
4. PBS 1: 384.
5. Harriet Boinville, letter to Frances Burney d'Arblay, March 7, 1814. The Henry W. and Albert A. Berg Collection of English and American Literature, The New York Public Library, Astor, Lenox, and Tilden Foundations.
6. Percy Bysshe Shelley, letter to Thomas Jefferson Hogg, March 16, 1814. PBS 1: 384.
7. Richard Holmes, *Shelley: The Pursuit, with a New Introduction by the Author* (New York Review Books edition, 1994), 227-228; first published in 1974.
8. Ibid.
9. James Bieri, *Percy Bysshe Shelley: A Biography* (Baltimore: The Johns Hopkins University Press, 2008), 272.
10. TJH, 561.
11. Percy Bysshe Shelley, letter to Thomas Jefferson Hogg, March 16, 1814, PBS, 1: 384. See also SC 3: 278.
12. Holmes, *Shelley*, 227.
13. Percy Bysshe Shelley, letter to Thomas Jefferson Hogg, March 16, 1814. PBS 1: 384. See also SC 3: 278.
14. Holmes, *Shelley*, 227.
15. Bieri, *Shelley*, 272. See also SC 6: 579; and Edward Dowden, *The Life of Percy Bysshe Shelley* (Barnes and Noble edition, 1966), 261; first published 1866.
16. David Perkins, *English Romantic Writers* (New York: Harcourt, Brace and World, 1967), 958.
17. Holmes, *Shelley*, 226. See also SC 4: 769.
18. Percy Bysshe Shelley, Letter to Thomas Jefferson Hogg, October 4, 2014. PBS 1: 401.
19. See also the family tree titled "The Boinville and Turner Families" in CCC 2: 668.
20. Holmes, *Shelley*, 228.

Chapter 14. Broken Hearts and a Mourning Widow, Spring and Summer, 1814

1. Peter Marshall, *William Godwin: Philosopher, Novelist, Revolutionary* (PM Press, 2017), 306. The verse is from "To Mary," stanza XII of the dedication to *The Revolt of Islam*, originally published in 1817 as *Laon and Cythna; or The Thoughts of the Golden City: A Vision of the Nineteenth Century*.
2. Harriet Shelley, letter to Percy Bysshe Shelley, July 7, 1814. PBS 1: 389.
3. Ibid., 389-390.
4. Ibid., 390.
5. James Bieri, *Percy Bysshe Shelley: A Biography* (Johns Hopkins University Press, 2008), 281, 282.
6. Janet Todd, *Death & the Maidens: Fanny Wollstonecraft and the Shelley Circle* (Counterpoint, 2007), 13.
7. As told by Fiona Sampson, *In Search of Mary Shelley: The Girl Who Wrote Frankenstein* (New York: Pegasus Books, 2018), 75.
8. Ibid., 76.
9. Richard Holmes: *Shelley: The Pursuit, with a New Introduction by the Author* (New York Review Books edition, 1994), 235; first published 1974.
10. Sampson, *In Search of Mary Shelley*, 80.
11. Holmes, *Shelley*, 236; Bieri, *Percy Bysshe Shelley*, 286.
12. Bieri, *Percy Bysshe Shelley*, 239, 242, 243.
13. Percy Bysshe Shelley, letter to Harriet Westbrook Shelley, August 13, 1814. PBS 1: 391-392.
14. William Godwin, letter to Taylor, August 27, 1814. PBS 1: 390-391.
15. Holmes, *Shelley*, 247.
16. Sampson, *In Search of Mary Shelley*, 92.
17. Holmes, *Shelley*, 249.
18. Ibid.
19. Ibid., 250.
20. Miranda Seymour, *Mary Shelley* (New York: Grove Press, 2000), 113. Godwin's diary shows that Harriet Boinville included a member of the Voisey family, possibly Henry Voisey, in a tea party on January 28, 1810, and a dinner party on September 16, 1810. She was at the Godwins on numerous occasions when the Voiseys were present.
21. Charlotte Gordon, *Romantic Outlaws: The Extraordinary Lives of Mary Wollstonecraft & Mary Shelley* (New York: Random House Trade Paperback Edition, 2016), 125.

22. Percy Bysshe Shelley, letter to Harriet Shelley, September 16, 1814. PBS 1: 395.
23. Sylvain Tesson, *Berezina: From Moscow to Paris, Napoleon's Epic Fail* (Europa Studies, 2015). See also the *Wall Street Journal*, November 8, 2019, and Benjamin Shull's excellent review of this book. For a thorough and fascinating treatment of the Russia campaign, see Dominic Lieven, *Russia Against Napoleon: The True Story of the Campaigns of War and Peace* (Penguin Books, 2009).
24. A. Pigeard, "Le service des vivres dans les armées du prémière empire (1804-1815)," in Historical Annals of the French Revolution, 1996.
25. Paul Johnson, *Napoleon* (New York: Viking, 2002), 131-132.
26. Lieven, *Russia Against Napoleon*, 281.

Chapter 15. More than a Beauty: Cornelia Collins Newton, 1815-1816

1. Harriet Boinville, letter to Thomas Jefferson Hogg, March 11, 1814. SC 3: 253.
2. TJH, 491.
3. Cornelia Newton, letter to Thomas Jefferson Hogg, October 21, 1813. SC 3: 252-253.
4. Ibid.
5. Ibid. SC 3: 253.
6. Ibid.
7. Ibid.
8. TJH, 495.
9. Ibid.
10. Sarah Jane Downing, *Fashion in the Time of Jane Austen* (Oxford, U.K.: Shire Publications, 2010), 55, 63.
11. SC 3: 256.
12. Harriet Boinville, letter of March 11, 1814, to Thomas Jefferson Hogg. TJH, 553.
13. Beatrice Corrigan, "Giovanni Ruffini's Letters to Vernon Lee, 1875-1879," *English Miscellany* (1962), 183.
14. Harriet Boinville, letter to Frances Burney d'Arblay, March 7, 1814.

Chapter 16. The Deaths of Fanny Godwin and Harriet Shelley, Fall and Winter, 1816

1. In her notebook, Mary Shelley wrote about this stanza of Percy Bysshe Shelley's: "I think about FG. Written before Italy."
2. The exact date of the suicide note is in question. See SC 4: 802.
3. Letter of Mary Wollstonecraft to her friend Ruth Barlow, May 20, 1794, quoted in Lyndall Gordon, *Mary Wollstonecraft: A New Genus* (Little Brown, 2005), 230.
4. Janet Todd, *Death & the Maidens: Fanny Wollstonecraft and the Shelley Circle* (Counterpoint, 2007), 7.
5. Mary Wollstonecraft, *A Short Residence in Sweden, Norway and Denmark* and William Godwin, *Memoirs of the Author of the Rights of Woman* (Penguin Books, 1987), 158.
6. Todd, *Death & the Maidens*, 75.
7. Ibid., 94.
8. Fanny wrote Mary on May 29, 1816. Miranda Seymour, *Mary Shelley* (New York: Grove Press, 2000), 160.
9. Quoted in Mary Wollstonecraft, *A Short Residence in Sweden, Norway and Denmark* and William Godwin, *Memoirs of the Author of the Rights of Woman* (Penguin Books edition, 1987), 248.
10. PBS 1: 510, note 3.
11. Todd, *Death & the Maidens*, 3-4. See also PBS 1: 510.
12. CCC 1: 86-87.
13. PBS 1: 424.
14. SC 3: 259.
15. Kenneth Neill Cameron suggested that Cornelia Newton died there. SC 3: 259. See also James Bieri, *Percy Bysshe Shelley: A Biography* (Baltimore: The Johns Hopkins University Press, 2008), 361.
16. Todd, *Death & The Maidens*, 244, 245.
17. Ibid. 244, 245.
18. SC 4: 769-802.
19. Ibid., 776.
20. Edmund, Blunden, *Shelley: A Life Story* (Oxford University Press, 1965), 132. See also SC: 4, 776.
21. Ibid.
22. Thomas Hookham, letter to Percy Bysshe Shelley, December 13, 1816. SC 4: 776.
23. Bieri, *Percy Bysshe Shelley*, 362.
24. PBS 1: 522-523.
25. SC: 4, 802-806.
26. PBS: 1, 524.

Chapter 17. Mary's *Frankenstein*, Byron's "Love" Child, and Harriet's Son, 1817-1818

1. Mary Shelley, *Frankenstein, or The Modern Prometheus*, edited with an Introduction and Notes by Maurice Hindle (Penguin Classics, 1992 edition), 9. See "The Author's Introduction to the Standard Novels Edition" published in 1831.
2. Childe Harold's Pilgrimage: A Romaunt, I, 9, published between 1812 and 1818.
3. SC 3: 277.
4. Fiona Sampson, *In Search of Mary Shelley: The Girl Who Wrote Frankenstein* (Pegasus Books, 2018), 40, 42.
5. Charles Abram Marc Gaulis could not have been Claire Clairmont's father because he died on August 25, 1796. CCC 2: 26, note 4.
6. CCC: 1: xix.
7. CCC 1: 24-40. Claire Clairmont's letters, numbered by editor Marion Kingston Stocking, are 9-11, 13, 14-16, 18-19, and 21.
8. CCC 1: 38.
9. CCC 1:26, note 3.
10. Miranda Seymour, *Mary Shelley* (New York: Grove Press, 2000), 156.
11. Claire Clairmont, letter to Lord Byron, January 12, 1818. CCC 1: 111.
12. Charlotte Gordon, *Mary Shelley: A Very Short Introduction* (Oxford University Press, 2022), 2.
13. Mary Shelley, *Frankenstein, or The Modern Prometheus*. See "The Author's Introduction to the Standard Novels Edition" (1831), xii-xiii.
14. Gordon, *Mary Shelley*, 2.
15. Ibid, Quoted in Shelley, *Frankenstein*, Penguin Classics edition, xix.
16. Claire Clairmont, letter to Lord Byron, May 6, 1816. CCC 1: 44.
17. Claire Clairmont, letter to Lord Byron, November 19, 1816. CCC: 1: 90.
18. CCC 1: 110.
19. Seymour, *Mary Shelley*, 199.
20. TC, 18.

Chapter 18. "Tell them, especially Mrs. Boinville, I have not forgotten them," 1819-1826

1. Miranda Seymour, *Mary Shelley* (New York: Grove Press, 2000), 214.
2. MWS 1: 101.
3. PBS 2: 114.

4. Leigh Hunt, letter to Mary Shelley, March 9, 1819. SC 6: 792.
5. Mary Shelley, letter to Leigh Hunt, April 6, 1819. MWS 1: 91.
6. PBS 2: 92.
7. Ibid.
8. Bradley, *A Shelley Chronology* (The Macmillan Press, 1993), 48.
9. Ibid., 206.
10. CCC 1: 166-165, note 1.
11. Percy Bysshe Shelley, letter to Thomas Jefferson Hogg, July 25, 1819. Jones 2: 105.
12. J. L. Bradley, *A Shelley Chronology* (The Macmillan Press, 1993), 71.
13. PBS 2: 998.
14. Bradley, *Shelley*, 63.
15. PBS 2: 187.

Chapter 19. Leaving London and Reconciling with Mary Shelley, 1827-1829

1. Bodleian Library, Oxford University, The Abinger Papers, original signed letter, MS Abinger c. 48, folios 55-56.
2. Lyndall Gordon, *Mary Wollstonecraft: A New Genus* (Little, Brown 2005), 33.
3. Oswald Turner lived from 1814 to 1876 and Alfred Turner from 1817 to 1893, according to the inscription on Harriet's grave in Paris. These years differ from those on the family tree of the Boinville and Turner families in CCC 2: 668.
4. Peter Marshall, *William Godwin: Philosopher, Novelist, Revolutionary* (Oakland, Calif.: PMP Press, 2017), 361.
5. William Godwin, letter to Mary Shelley, October 9, 1827. Quoted in Marshall, William Godwin, 361.
6. TC, chapter 2, 24
7. CCC 2: 475 and 477, note 13.
8. Mary Shelley, letter to Leigh Hunt. See *The Letters of Mary Wollstonecraft Shelley*, Vol. 1: "A Part of the Elect," edited by Betty T. Bennett (Baltimore and London: The Johns Hopkins University Press, 1980), 91.
9. SC 3.

Chapter 20. Godwin's Death and Significance, "The Extinction of a Mastermind," 1830–1836

1. Bodleian Library, Oxford University, The Abinger Papers, dep C, 516.
2. Matthew Josephson, *Stendahl or the Pursuit of Happiness* (New York: Doubleday, 1945), 352, 353.
3. Ibid., 387.
4. TC, 25-26.
5. Ibid., 26.
6. Ibid.
7. Miranda Seymour, *Mary Shelley* (New York: Grove Press, 2000), 425.
8. MWS 2: 187, note 2.
9. Peter Marshall, *William Godwin: Philosopher, Novelist, Revolutionary, with a Foreword by John C. Clark* (PM Press, 2017), 375.
10. Marshall, *William Godwin,* 380, 384.
11. Ibid., 385.
12. Fiona Sampson, *In Search of Mary Shelley: The Girl Who Wrote Frankenstein* (Pegasus Books, 2018), 232.
13. Marshall, *William Godwin,* 385.
14. MWS 2: 270.
15. Robert Owen is mentioned thirty-five times in Godwin's diary between 1813 and 1835. On November 1, 1827, Mary accompanied her father to tea with Frances Wright in London. Robert Owen and his son Dale were also present. Five years later, on December 27, 1832, Mary and her father again had tea with Dale Owen, when he returned from America.
16. Seymour, *Mary Shelley,* 383.

Chapter 21. Harriet Rescues Shelley's *Queen Mab* for Posterity, 1837-1841

1. Bodleian Library, Oxford University, The Abinger Collection, c. 49, folios 128-129.
2. Miranda Seymour, *Mary Shelley* (New York: Grove Press, 2000), 450.
3. Ibid., 454.
4. From Mary Wollstonecraft's *Thoughts on the Education of Daughters: With Reflections on Female Conduct in the More Important Duties of Life,* published in 1787.

5. TLP, 30.
6. Seymour, 455.
7. Charlotte Gordon, *Mary Shelley: A Very Short Introduction* (Oxford University Press, 2022), 1, 106. See also Charlotte Gordon, *Romantic Outlaws: The Extraordinary Lives of Mary Wollstonecraft & Mary Shelley* (New York: Random House, 2015), 507.
8. MWS 2: 301, note 2.
9. Donald H. Reiman, "Percy Bysshe Shelley," *Encyclopedia Britannica*, 31 July 2020, digitized.
10. Richard Holmes, *Shelley: The Pursuit* (New York Review of Books edition, 1994), 208.
11. Ibid., 660.
12. Bouthaina Shaaban, *Shelley's influence on the Chartist poets, with particular emphasis on Ernest Charles Jones and Thomas Cooper*. PhD thesis, University of Warwick, 1981.
13. Peter Marshall, *William Godwin: Philosopher, Novelist, Revolutionary* (PM Press, 2017), 400.
14. Mary Shelley, letter to Harriet de Boinville. MWS 2.

Chapter 22. "A Noble Nature and a Loyal, Loving Heart," 1842

All the quotes in this chapter are from Thomas Constable, *The Memoir of the Reverend Charles A. Chastel de Boinville Compiled from his Journals and His Letters* (London: James Nesbitt & Co., 1880). Digitized.

Chapter 23. Claire Clairmont Joins Harriet's Circle in Paris, 1842-1845

1. MWS 2: 90.
2. The title of a chapter by Mary Wollstonecraft in *Thoughts on the Education of Daughters*, published in 1787 and now digitized.
3. Janet Todd, *Mary Wollstonecraft: A Revolutionary Life* (Columbia University Press, 2000), 116.
4. Claire Clairmont, Letter to Mary Shelley, September 24, 1822. CCC 1: 199.
5. Claire Clairmont, Letter to Mary Shelley, April 29, 1825. CC: 1: 215.
6. Ibid.
7. Claire Clairmont, Letter to Mary Shelley, November 22, 1842.
8. CCC 2: 368-369.
9. Mary Shelley, letter to Claire Clairmont, September 20, 1843. MWS 3: 90.

10. Claire Clairmont, Letter to Mary Shelley, March 18, 1844. CCC 2: 389.
11. Claire Clairmont, Letter to Mary Shelley, December 23, 1844. CCC 2: 391, note 7.
12. Claire Clairmont, Letter to Mary Shelley, December 9, 1844. CCC 2: 418.
13. Claire Clairmont, Letter to Mary Shelley. CCC 2: 425.
14. Claire Clairmont to Mary Shelley, June 24, 1845. CCC 2.
15. See Roy Porter, *Mind Forg'd Manacles: A History of Madness in England from the Restoration to the Regency* (Harvard University Press, 1987), 32; and Andrew Scull, "A Convenient Place to Get Rid of Inconvenient People: The Victorian Lunatic Asylum," in A. D. King, ed., *Buildings and Society* (London: Routledge & Kegan, Paul, 1980), 37-60.
16. Claire Clairmont to Mary Shelley. CCC 2: 477, n.13.
17. Mary Shelley, Letter to Claire Clairmont, December 23, 1845. MWS 3: 169.
18. Claire Clairmont, Letter to Mary Shelley, June 2, 1843. CCC 2: 376.

Chapter 24. Welcoming Refugees in her Final Years, 1845-1846

1. CCC 2: 458.
2. Giovanni Ruffini, Letter to Violet Paget about Vera de Kologrivoff. Quoted in Beatrice Corrigan, ed., "Giovanni Ruffini's Letters to Vernon Lee, 1875-1879," *English Miscellany*, 13 (1962), 216.
3. Ibid.
4. Ibid.
5. CCC 2: 458.
6. Corrigan, ed., "Giovanni Ruffini's Letters to Vernon Lee, 1875-1879."
7. Allan Conrad Christensen, *A European Version of Victorian Fiction: The Novels of Giovanni Ruffini* (Amsterdam & Atlanta, Georgia, Rodopi, 1996), 10, 11, 28.
8. Ibid., 12.
9. Christensen, *A European Version of Victorian Fiction*, 13, 20.
10. Ibid., 28, 31. She spent the winter of 1864-1865 in Paris.
11. Ibid., 12.
12. Ibid., 12.

Chapter 25: Harriet Dies and Giovanni Ruffini Comforts Her Family, 1847–1848

1. TC 90-91. "Je viens remplir un douloureux devoir au nom et lieu de votre tante Cornélia, brisée par la douleur et la fatigue. Hélas! Mon pauvre Charles, notre douce et bien-aimée Bonnemaman-à-tous n'est plus. Ce matin à 6 heures elle rendait le dernier soupir."
2. Allan Conrad Christensen, *A European Version of Victorian Fiction: The Novels of Giovanni Ruffini* (Amsterdam and Atlanta, Ga. 1996), 30; and Beatrice Corrigan, "Giovanni Ruffini's Letters to Vernon Lee, 1875-1879," *English Miscellany* 13 (1962), 182.
3. TC, 90.
4. TC, 37
5. See Cemetery Montmartre, grave of Cornelia Pauline Eugenia Chastel de Boinville, on Wikipedia.
6. Erminio Robecchi-Brivio, Una familia italiana: I Robecchi (Milan, 1938), 144.
7. Kenneth Neill Cameron, *The Young Shelley: Genesis of a Radical* (New York: Collier Books, 1962), 244, 246.
8. Harriet Boinville, letter to Mary Shelley, October 16, 1829. The Abinger Papers, Bodleian Libraries, University of Oxford. Original signed letter, MS Abinger c. 48, folios 55-56.
9. G. Store, ed., *The Letters of Charles Dickens: Vol. 9, 1859-1861* (Oxford: Clarendon Press, 1997), 54-55.
10. Christensen, *A European Version of Victorian Fiction,* 31-32.
11. Ibid., 14, 17.
12. Robert Louis Stevenson, *Memoir of Fleeming Jenkin* (1888).
13. TC, 108.
14. Christensen, A European Version of Victorian Fiction, 31, quoting Itala Cremona Cozzolino, "La donna nella vitadi Giovanni Ruffini," in *Giovanni Ruffini e I suoi tempi: Studi e ricerche.*
15. Christensen quoting from The Autobiography and Letters of Mrs O. W. O. Oliphant, ed., Mrs. Harry Coghill (Edinburgh, 1899), 103.

Chapter 26. Cornelia Turner and Vernon Lee Continue the Literary Life, 1848-1875

1. Cornelia Turner's second novel, *Charity, A Tale* (published anonymously in London in 1862 by Thomas Cautley Newby). See page 114 of a paperback re-issue of the novel by the British Library for its Historical Collection.

2. Cornelia Turner's first novel, *Angelo Sanmartino: A Tale of Lombardy in 1859*, which was published anonymously in 1860 in Edinburgh by Edmonston and Douglad. To obtain the modern paperback, created using optical character recognition software, see the web site of RareBooksClub.com.
3. Ibid.
4. Turner, *Charity: A Tale*, 4, 117–118.
5. Allan Conrad Christensen, *A European Version of Victorian Fiction: The Novels of Giovanni Ruffini* (Amsterdam and Atlanta, Ga. 1996), 33.
6. Patricia Cove, "Italian Exiles from Young Italy to 1848: Risorgimento Refugees in Giovanni Ruffini's *Lorenzo Benoni* and *Doctor Antonio*," in *Italian Politics and Nineteenth-Century British Literature and Culture*, Edinburgh Critical Studies in Victorian Culture (Edinburgh University Press, 2020). See also Christensen, *A European Version of Victorian Fiction*, 19.
7. Christensen, *A European Version of Victorian Fiction*, 33.
8. Beatrice Corrigan, "Giovanni Ruffini's Letters to Vernon Lee, 1875-1879," *English Miscellany* 13 (1962): 183.
9. Ibid., 185. See also Vineta Colby, *Vernon Lee: A Literary Biography* (University of Virginia Press, 2003), 17.
10. Christensen, *A European Version of Victorian Fiction*, 36. See also Peter Gunn, *Vernon Lee: Violet Paget*, 1856-1935 (London: Oxford University Press, 1964), 59-60.
11. Colby, *Vernon Lee*, 19, quoting Gunn, *Vernon Lee*, 60.
12. Corrigan, "Giovanni Ruffini's Letters to Vernon Lee, 1875-1879," 185, and Colby, *Vernon Lee*, 17.
13. Colby, *Vernon Lee*, 2.
14. Ibid.
15. Corrigan, "Giovanni Ruffini's Letters to Vernon Lee, 1875-1879," 187.

Afterword: Mark Twain and the Boinville Circle

1. Mark Twain, "In Defense of Harriet Shelley," *The North American Review*, vol. 159, no. 452 (July 1894): 108-119.
2. Miranda Seymour, *Mary Shelley* (New York: Grove Press, 2000), 549.
3. Charlotte Gordon, *Romantic Outlaws: The Extraordinary Lives of Mary Wollstonecraft & Mary Shelley* (Random House Trade Paperback Edition, 2016), 543.

4. Letter written in 1827 to Frances Wright. Quoted in Gordon, *Romantic Outlaws*, 538.
5. Fiona Sampson, *In Search of Mary Shelley: The Girl Who Wrote Frankenstein* (First Pegasus Books, 2018), 248-249.
6. R. Glynn Grylls, *Claire Clairmont: Mother of Byron's Allegra* (London: John Murray, 1939), 215.

Bibliography

Chapter 1. Birth and Life in the Dangerous Tropics, 1773-1788

An Account of the Late Dreadful Hurricane, Which Happened on the 31rst of August, 1772. Also the Damage Done on that Day in the Islands of St. Christopher and Nevis. Printed and Sold by Thomas Howe in Basseterre, John Anderson, junior, in Nevis, and David Crawford in St. Eustatia, 1772.

Atkinson, Rick. *The British Are Coming: The War for America, Lexington to Princeton, 1775-1777*, vol. 1 of the Revolution Trilogy. Henry Holt, 2019.

Cameron, Norman Eustace. *The Evolution of the Negro.* 2 vols. Westport, Conn.: Negro Universities Press, 1970.

Carmichael, A. C. *Domestic Manners and Social Condition of the White, Coloured, and Negro Population of the West Indies*, 2 vols. London: Whittaker, Treacher and Co., 1833.

Chernow, Ron. *Alexander Hamilton.* Penguin Books, 2004.

Constable, Thomas. *Memoir of the Reverend Charles A. Chastel de Boinville: Compiled from His Journal and His Letters*. London: James Nisbet & Co., 1880.

Craton, Michael. *Testing the Chains: Resistance to Slavery in the British West Indies*. London: Cornell University Press, 1982.

Duffy, Michael. *Soldiers, Sugar, and Seapower: The British Expeditions to the West Indies and the War against Revolutionary France*. Oxford: Clarendon Press, 1987.

Dunn, Richard. *Sugar and Slaves: The Rise of the Planter Class in the English West Indies, 1624-1713*. New York: Norton, 1972.

Hamshere, Cyril. *The British in the Caribbean.* Cambridge, Mass.: Harvard University Press, 1972.

Hintzen, Percy. "Race and Creole Ethnicity in the Caribbean." *Caribbean Cultural Thought: From Plantation to Diaspora*. Edited by Yanique Hume and Aaron Kumugisha. Kingston and Miami: Ian Randle Publishers, 2013.

Kent, Susan Kingsley. *A New History of Britain since 1688: Four Nations and an Empire.* New York and Oxford: Oxford University Press, 2017.

Lux, William. *Historical Dictionary of the British Caribbean.* Metuchen, N.J.: The Scarecrow Press, 1975.
McDonald, Robert A., ed. *Between Slavery and Freedom: Special Magistrate John Anderson's Journal of St. Vincent during the Apprenticeship.* With a Foreword by Richard S. Dunn. University of Pennsylvania Press, 2001.
Naidis, Mark. *The Second British Empire, 1783-1965: A Short History.* Addison-Wesley Publishing Co., 1970.
Nanton, Philip. *Frontiers of the Caribbean.* Manchester University Press, 2017.
Practical Rules for the Management and Medical Treatment of Negro Slaves in the Sugar Colonies by a Professional Planter, published anonymously in 1803 and written by John Collins, Harriet de Boinville's father. Forgotten Books edition, 2017.
Sheridan, Richard B. *Doctors and Slaves: A Medical and Demographic History of Slavery in the British West Indies, 1580-1834.* Cambridge: 1985.

Chapter 2. "Une Enfant de la Révolution," 1789-1792

Andress, David. *The Terror: The Merciless War for Freedom in Revolutionary France.* New York: Farrar, Straus, and Giroux, 2005.
Constable, Thomas. *Memoir of the Reverend Charles A. Chastel de Boinville: Compiled from His Journal and His Letters.* London: James Nisbet & Co., 1880.
Dictionnaire de Biographie des Hommes Célebres de L'Alsace, vol. 1.
Gottschalk, Louis, and Margaret Maddox, *Lafayette in the French Revolution: From the October Days through the Federation.* The University of Chicago Press, 1973.
Hindley, Meredith. "Ungoverned Passion," *Humanities: The Magazine for the National Endowment for the Humanities* (March/April 2012), vol. 33, no 2.
Johnston, Kenneth R. *Unusual Suspects: Pitt's Reign of Alarm and the Lost Generation of the 1790s.* Oxford University Press, 2013.
Mémoires de Général Lafayette Publiés par sa Famille. Volume 2. Paris and London, 1837.
Moorehead, Caroline. *Dancing to the Precipice: The Life of Lucie de la Tour du Pin, Eyewitness to an Era.* New York: HarperCollins, 2009.
Roosevelt, Theodore. *Gouverneur Morris*, first published 1888, republished 1968, Haskell House Publishers.
Slater, John. *A Short History of the Berners Estate.* London, 1918.

Chapter 3. A Disobedient Daughter Marries for Love, 1793

Bodek, Evelyn Gordon. "Salonieres and Bluestockings: Educated Obsolescence and Germinating Feminism." *Feminist Studies* 3.3/4 (1976): 185-199.

Burney, Fanny. *Fanny Burney: Selected Letters and Journals*, edited by Joyce Hemlow. Oxford University Press, 1987.

———. *The Diary of Fanny Burney*, edited with an introduction by Lewis Gibbs, an Everyman paperback. London: J. M Dent & Sons, 1940, last reprinted 1971.

Byrne, Paula. *The Real Jane Austen: A Life in Small Things*. New York: HarperCollins, 2013.

Chisholm, Kate. *Fanny Burney: Her Life, 1752-1840*. Vintage, 1999.

———. "The Burney Family." *The Cambridge Companion to Frances Burney*, ed. Peter Sabor. Cambridge University Press, 2007.

Constable, Thomas. *Memoir of the Reverend Charles A. Chastel de Boinville: Compiled from His Journal and His Letters*. London: James Nisbet & Co., 1880.

Copeland, Edward, and Juliet McMaster. *The Cambridge Companion to Jane Austen*, 2d ed. Cambridge University Press, 2011.

Eger, Elizabeth, ed. *Bluestockings Displayed: Portraiture, Performance and Patronage, 1730-1830*. Cambridge: Cambridge University Press, 2013.

Gregory, John. *A Father's Legacy to His Daughters*. London: Cadelle and Davies, Strand 1797.

Harman, Claire. *Fanny Burney: A Biography*. New York: Knopf, 2001.

Kaplan, Deborah. *Jane Austen Among Women*. Baltimore: Johns Hopkins University Press, 1992).

Kelly, Helena. *Jane Austin, the Secret Radical*. New York: Alfred A. Knopf, 2017.

Sabor, Peter, ed. *The Cambridge Companion to Frances Burney*. New York: Cambridge, University Press, 2007.

Todd, Janet. *Jane Austen and Shelley in the Garden*. Fentum Press, 2021.

Veevers, Marian. *Jane and Dorothy: A True Tale of Sense and Sensibility: The Lives of Jane Austen and Dorothy Wordsworth*. New York: Pegasus Books, 2018.

Worsley, Lucy. *Jane Austin at Home*. New York: St. Martin's Press, 2017.

Chapter 4. From Domesticity to Dangers at Sea, 1793-1796

Constable, Thomas. *Memoir of the Reverend Charles A. Chastel de Boinville: Compiled from His Journal and His Letters*. London: James Nisbet & Co., 1880.

Ehrenreich, Barbara, and Deirdre English. *Complaints and Disorders: The Sexual Politics of Sickness*. Old Westbury: The Feminist Press, 1973.

Gilbert, Sandra M., and Susan Gubar. *The Madwoman in the Attic: The Woman Writer and the Nineteenth-Century Literary Imagination*, 2d ed. New Haven: Yale University Press, 2000.

McDonald, Robert A., ed. *Between Slavery and Freedom: Special Magistrate John Anderson's Journal of St. Vincent during the Apprenticeship*. With a Foreword by Richard S. Dunn. University of Pennsylvania Press, 2001.

Wollstonecraft, Mary. *A Vindication of the Rights of Woman: With Strictures on Political and Moral Subjects*. Dublin, 1793. Printed by J. Stockdale for James Moore.

Chapter 5. A Young Mother in a War-torn Colony, 1797

Carmichael, A. C. *Domestic Manners and Social Condition of the White, Coloured, and Negro Population of the West Indies*, 2 vols. London: Whittaker, Treacher and Co., 1833.

DuBois, Laurent, and John. D. Garrigus. *Slave Revolution in the Caribbean, 1789-1804: A Brief History with Documents*. New York: Bedford/St. Martin's Press, 2006.

Duncan, Ebenezer. *A Brief History of St. Vincent with Studies in Citizenship*. Kingstown, St. Vincent, 1955.

Dunn, Richard. *Sugar and Slaves: The Rise of the Planter Class in the English West Indies, 1624-1713*. New York: Norton, 1972.

Hamshere, Cyril. *The British in the Caribbean*. Cambridge, Mass.: Harvard University Press, 1972).

Hintzen, Percy. "Race and Creole Ethnicity in the Caribbean." *Caribbean Cultural Thought: From Plantation to Diaspora*, edited by Yanique Hume and Aaron Kamugisha. Kingston and Miami: Ian Randle Publishers, 2013.

Jackson, Ashley. *The British Empire: A Very Short Introduction*. New York and Oxford: Oxford University Press, 2013.

Kim, Julie Chun. "The Caribs of St. Vincent and Indigenous Resistance during the Age of Revolutions." *Early American Studies*, vol. 11, no. 1, Special Issue: *Forming Nations, Reforming Empires: Atlantic Polities in the Long Eighteenth Century* (Winter 2013): 117-132. MacNeil Center for Early American Studies, University of Pennsylvania.

McDonald, Robert A. *Between Slavery and Freedom: Special Magistrate John Anderson's Journal of St. Vincent during the Apprenticeship*, with a

Foreword by Richard S. Dunn. University of Pennsylvania Press, 2001.
Naidis, Mark. *The Second British Empire, 1783-1965: A Short History*. Addison-Wesley Publishing Co., 1970.
Nanton, Philip. *Frontiers of the Caribbean*. Manchester University Press, 2017.
Shephard, Charles. *An Historical Account of the Island of St Vincent*. London, 1831.
St. Vincent Almanack of 1779, digitized. See website of British St. Vincent.
Young, Virginia Heyer. *Becoming West Indian: Culture, Self, and Nation in St. Vincent,* Smithsonian Series in Ethnographic Inquiry. Smithsonian Institution Press, 1993.

Chapter 6. A Bold Traveler between Nations at War, 1797-1800

Cameron, Kenneth Neill. *The Young Shelley: Genesis of a Radical*. New York: Collier Books, 1962,
Constable, Thomas. *Memoir of the Reverend Charles A. Chastel de Boinville: Compiled from His Journal and His Letters*. London: James Nisbet & Co., 1880.
Darwin, Erasmus. *A Plan for the Conduct of Female Education*. London: Printed by J. Drewry for J. Johnson, 1797.
Horricks, Raymond. *In Flight with the Eagle: A Guide to Napoleon's Elite*. Tunbridge Wells: D. J. Costello, 1988.
Pocock, Tom. *The Terror before Trafalgar: Nelson, Napoleon, and the Secret War*. New York: Norton, 2002.
Taylor, Christopher. *The Black Carib Wars: Freedom, Survival, and the Making of the Garifuna*. Jackson: The University Press of Mississippi, 2012.

Chapter 7. An Empathetic Friend to Frances Burney d'Arblay, 1800-1808

Adams, Kate. *Ambition and Desire: The Dangerous Life of Josephine Bonaparte*. New York: Ballantine Books, 2014.
Burney, Fanny. *Fanny Burney: Selected Letters and Journals,* edited by Joyce Hemlow. Oxford University Press, 1987.
———. *The Diary of Fanny Burney*. Edited with an Introduction by Lewis Gibbs. Everyman Library London: Dent, 1960.
Constable, Thomas. *Memoir of the Reverend Charles A. Chastel de Boinville*. London: James Nisbet & Co., 1880.
Harman, Claire. *Fanny Burney: A Biography*. New York: Knopf, 2001.

Johnson, Claudia L. *Equivocal Beings: Politics, Gender, and Sentimentality in the 1790s*. The University of Chicago Press, 1995.
Pocock, Tom. *The Terror before Trafalgar: Nelson, Napoleon, and the Secret War*. New York: Norton, 2002.
Practical Rules for the Management and Medical Treatment of Negro Slaves in the Sugar Colonies by a Professional Planter, published anonymously in 1803 and written by John Collins. Forgotten Books edition, 2017.
Tombs, Robert and Isabelle. *That Sweet Enemy, Britain and France: The History of a Love-Hate Relationship*, Vintage Books Edition, 2008.

Chapter 8. With the Proponent of Political Justice, William Godwin, 1809-1811

Constable, Thomas. *Memoir of the Reverend Charles A. Chastel de Boinville: Compiled from his Journal and His Letters*. London: James Nisbet & Co., 1880.
The Diary of William Godwin, ed. Victoria Myers, David O'Shaughnessy, and Mark Philip. Oxford: Oxford Digital Library, 2010.
German, Lindsey, and Rees, John. *A People's History of London*. London and New York: Verso, 2012.
Gittings, Robert, and Jo Manton. *Dorothy Wordsworth*. Clarendon Press Oxford, 1985.
Godwin, William. *An Enquiry Concerning Political Justice and its Influence on General Virtue and Happiness*. London: G.G. Robinson, 1793. In the second edition (1796) and third edition (1798) "General Virtue" was changed to "Morals."
_____. *Memoirs of the Author of the Rights of Woman*. J.J. Johnson, G.G. & J. Robinson, 1798; 2nd ed., J. Johnson, 1798.
Hazlitt, William. *The Spirit of the Age, Or Contemporary Portraits*, 1825. Republished by Anodus Books, 2019.
Johnson, Claudia L., ed. *The Cambridge Companion to Mary Wollstonecraft*. Cambridge University Press, 2002.
Jones, Vivien. "Wollstonecraft and the Literature of Advice and Instruction." *The Cambridge Companion to Mary Wollstonecraft*, ed. Claudia L. Johnson. Cambridge University Press, 2002, 119-140.
Lynch, Deidre Shanau, ed. *Mary Wollstonecraft, A Vindication of the Rights of Woman, An Authoritative Text, Backgrounds and Contexts Criticism*, 3d ed. Norton & Co., 2009.
Marshall, Peter. *William Godwin: Philosopher, Novelist, Revolutionary*. PM Press, 2017.

Obrien, Eliza, Helen Stark, and Beatrice Turner, eds. *New Approaches to William Godwin: Forms, Fears, and Futures* (Palgrave 2021). Palgrave Studies in the Enlightenment, Romanticism, and Cultures of Print.

Panton, Kenneth J. *Historical Dictionary of London*, Historical Dictionaries of the World, No. 11. Lanham, MD, and London: The Scarecrow Press, 2001.

Seymour, Miranda. *Mary Shelley*. Grove Press, 2000.

Todd, Janet. *Death and the Maidens: Fanny Wollstonecraft and the Shelley Circle*. Berkeley: Counterpoint, 2007.

Wilson, Eric G. *Dream-Child: A Life of Charles Lamb*. New Haven: Yale University Press, 2022.

UCL—London's Global University. Legacies of British Slave-ownership (LBS).

Wollstonecraft, Mary, *A Short Residence in Sweden, Norway and Denmark*, and William Godwin, *Memoirs of the Author of the Rights of Woman*, edited with an Introduction and Notes by Richard Holmes (Penguin Classics, 1987).

Chapter 9. Harriet's Husband Rescues Madam d'Arblay, 1810-1812

Burney, Fanny. *Fanny Burney: Selected Letters and Journals*, edited by Joyce Hemlow. Oxford University Press, 1987.

Chisholm, Kate. *Fanny Burney: Her Life*. Vintage Books, 1999.

Constable, Thomas. *Memoir of the Reverend Charles A. Chastel de Boinville: Compiled from his Journal and His Letters*. London: James Nisbet & Co., 1880.

Harman, Claire. *Fanny Burney: A Biography*. New York: Knopf, 2001.

Moorehead, Caroline. *Dancing to the Precipice: The Life of Lucie de la Tour du Pin, Eyewitness to an Era*. New York: HarperCollins, 2009.

Wiltshire, John. "Journals and Letters," Chapter 5 in *The Cambridge Companion to Frances Burney*, edited by Peter Sabor. Cambridge University Press, 2007.

Chapter 10. Aaron Burr and the London Wedding of Godwin's Protégé, 1812-1813

Brands, H. W. *The Heartbreak of Aaron Burr*. New York: Anchor Books, 2012.

Burr, Aaron. *The Private Journal of Aaron Burr*, Reprinted in Full from the Original Manuscript. W. H. Sampson Rochester, N.Y. 1903.

———. *The Private Journal of Aaron Burr*. Volume Two. Gutenberg.org.

Cameron, Kenneth Neill, ed. *Shelley and His Circle, 1773-1822*. The Carl H.

Pforzheimer Library, vol. 3 of 10 vols. Harvard University Press and Oxford University Press, 1970.
The Diary of William Godwin, ed. Victoria Myers, David O'Shaughnessy, and Mark Philip. Oxford: Oxford Digital Library, 2010.
Isenberg, Nancy. *Fallen Founder: The Life of Aaron Burr*. New York: Viking, 2007.
Melton, Buckner F., Jr. The Library of American Lives and Times, *Aaron Burr: The Rise and Fall of an American Politician*. New York: The Rosen Publishing Group, 2004.
Merrill, Jane, and John Endicott. *Aaron Burr in Exile: A Pariah in Paris, 1810-1811*. Jefferson North Carolina: McFarland and Company, 2016.
Seymour, Miranda. *Mary Shelley*. New York: Grove Press, 2000.
St. Clair, William. *The Godwins and the Shelleys: A Biography of a Family*. New York and London: W.W. Norton & Co., 1989.
Todd, Janet. *Death and the Maidens: Fanny Wollstonecraft and the Shelley Circle*. Berkeley: Counterpoint, 2007.
Van Doren, Mark, ed. *Correspondence of Aaron Burr and His Daughter Theodosia*. New York: Covici-Friede, 1929.

Chapter 11. Percy Bysshe Shelley Meets "Miamuna," Spring 1813

Bieri, James. *Percy Bysshe Shelley: A Biography*. Baltimore: Johns Hopkins University Press, 2008.
Blunden, Edmund. Shelley: *A Life Story*. London: Collins, 1946; Oxford University Press, 1965.
Bradley, J. L. *A Shelley Chronology*. The Macmillan Press, 1993.
Cameron, Kenneth Neill, ed. *Shelley and His Circle, 1773-1822*. The Carl H. Pforzheimer Library. Vol. 3 of 10 vols. Harvard University Press and Oxford University Press, 1970.
———. *The Young Shelley: Genesis of a Radical*. New York: Collier Books, 1962.
Gittings, Robert, and Jo Manton. *Claire Clairmont and the Shelleys: 1798-1879*. Oxford University Press, 1992.
Holmes, Richard. *Shelley: The Pursuit, with a New Introduction by the Author*. New York Review Books edition, 1994; first published in 1974.
Jones, Frederick L., ed. *The Letters of Percy Bysshe Shelley: Volume I: Shelley in England*. Oxford University Press, 1964.
Peacock's Memoirs of Shelley with Shelley's Letters to Peacock, ed., H. F. B. Brett-Smith London: Henry Frowde, 1909. Nabu Public Domain Reprint.
Schmid, Susanne. *British Literary Salons of the Late Eighteenth and Early Nineteenth Centuries*. Palgrave Macmillan, 2013.

Chapter 12. Vegetarians and Egalitarians Return to Nature, Summer 1813

Dowden, Edward. *The Life of Percy Bysshe Shelley*, originally published in 1866; Barnes and Noble edition, 1966.
Hogg, Thomas Jefferson. "The Life of Percy Bysshe Shelley," in Humbert Wolfe, ed., *The Life of Percy Bysshe Shelley*. Vol. 2. London: Dent, 1933.
Holmes, Richard. *Shelley: The Pursuit, with a New Introduction by the Author*. New York Review Books edition, 1994; first published in 1974.
Lambe, William, M.D., "Reports on the Effects of a Peculiar Regimen in Scirrhous Tumers & Cancerous Ulcers," Printed for J. Mawman in the Poultry.
Lawrence, James Henry. *The Empire of the Nairs, or The Rights of Women. An Utopian Romance in Twelve Books*. London, printed for T. Hookham et al., No. 15, Old Bond Street, 1811.
Peacock's Memoirs of Shelley with Shelley's Letters to Peacock, ed., H. F. B. Brett-Smith London: Henry Frowde, 1909. Nabu Public Domain Reprint.
St. Clair, William. *The Godwins and the Shelleys: A Biography of a Family*. New York: Norton, 1989.
Todd, Janet. *Jane Austen and Shelley in the Garden*. Fentum Press, 2021.
Williams, Howard. "The Ethics of Diet: A Catena," 1883, quoted on the web site of the International Vegetarian Union.
Williams, John. "The Vegetable System," *New York Times*, Sunday Book Review, March 2, 2014, BR4.

Chapter 13. Shelley Retreats to Harriet's Home at Bracknell, February and March 1814

Bieri, James. *Percy Bysshe Shelley: A Biography*. Baltimore: Johns Hopkins University Press, 2008.
Cameron, Kenneth Neill, ed. *Shelley and His Circle, 1773-1822*. The Carl H. Pforzheimer Library. volumes 3, 4, and 6 of 10 volumes. Harvard University Press and Oxford University Press, 1970.
The Clairmont Correspondence: Letters of Claire Clairmont, Charles Clairmont, and Fanny Imlay Godwin. Volume 2: 1835-1879. Edited by Marion Kingston Stocking. Baltimore and London: The Johns Hopkins University Press, 1995.
de Boinville, Harriet. Letter to Thomas Jefferson Hogg. March 11, 1814. The Carl H. Pforzheimer Library. *Shelley and His Circle, 1773-1822*.

Volume 3: 273-275. Edited by Kenneth Neill Cameron. Harvard University Press and Oxford University Press, 1970.
Dowden, Edward. *The Life of Percy Bysshe Shelley*, originally published in 1866; Barnes and Noble edition, 1966.
Hogg, Thomas Jefferson. *The Life of Percy Bysshe Shelley*. London: George Routledge & Sons, 1906; available in Hardpress Classics Edition.
Holmes, Richard. *Shelley: The Pursuit, with a New Introduction by the Author*. New York Review Books edition, 1994; first published in 1974.
Jones, Frederick L., ed. The Letters of Percy Bysshe Shelley: Volume I: Shelley in England. Oxford University Press, 1964.
Perkins, David. *English Romantic Writers*. New York: Harcourt, Brace and World, 1967.
Schmid, Susanne. *British Literary Salons of the Late Eighteenth and Early Nineteenth Centuries*. Palgrave Macmillan, 2013.
Shelley, Percy Bysshe. Letter to Thomas Jefferson Hogg. March 16, 1814. In Frederick L. Jones, ed. *The Letters of Percy Bysshe Shelley: Volume I Shelley in England*. Oxford University Press, 1964.

Chapter 14. Broken Hearts and a Mourning Widow, Spring and Summer, 1814

Bieri, James. *Percy Bysshe Shelley: A Biography*. Baltimore: Johns Hopkins University Press, 2008.
Constable, Thomas. Memoir of the Reverend Charles A. Chastel de Boinville: Compiled from his Journal and His Letters. London: James Nisbet & Co., 1880.
Gordon, Charlotte. *Romantic Outlaws: The Extraordinary Lives of Mary Wollstonecraft & Mary Shelley*. New York: Random House Trade Paperback Edition, 2016.
Holmes, Richard. *Shelley: The Pursuit, with a New Introduction by the Author*. New York Review Booksse edition, 1994; first published in 1974.
Johnson, Paul. *Napoleon*. New York: Viking, 2002.
Lieven, Dominic. *Russia Against Napoleon: The True Story of the Campaigns of War and Peace*. Penguin Books, 2009.
Marshall, Peter. *William Godwin: Philosopher, Novelist, Revolutionary*. PM Press, 2017.
Pigeard, A. "Le service des vivres dans les armées du prémière empire (1804-1815)." *Historical Annals of the French Revolution*, 1996.
Sampson, Fiona. *In Search of Mary Shelley: The Girl Who Wrote Frankenstein*. New York and London: Pegasus Books, 2018.
Seymour, Miranda. *Mary Shelley*. New York: Grove Press, 2000.
Tesson, Sylvain. Berezina: From Moscow to Paris, Napoleon's Epic Fail. Europa Studies, 2015

Todd, Janet. *Death and the Maidens: Fanny Wollstonecraft and the Shelley Circle.* Berkeley: Counterpoint, 2007.

Chapter 15. More than a Beauty: Cornelia Collins Newton, 1815-1816

Cameron, Kenneth Neill, ed. *Shelley and His Circle, 1773-1822.* The Carl H. Pforzheimer Library. Volume 3. Harvard University Press and Oxford University Press, 1970.
Corrigan, Beatrice. "Giovanni Ruffini's Letters to Vernon Lee, 1875-1879." *English Miscellany* vol. 13 (1962).
de Boinville, Harriet. Letter to Thomas Jefferson Hogg. March 11, 1814. Quoted in The Carl H. Pforzheimer Library. *Shelley and His Circle, 1773-1822.* Volume 3: 273-275. Edited by Kenneth Neill Cameron. Harvard University Press and Oxford University Press, 1970.
Downing, Sarah Jane. *Fashion in the Time of Jane Austen.* Oxford, U.K.: Shire Publications, 2010.
Hogg, Thomas Jefferson. *The Life of Percy Bysshe Shelley.* London: George Routledge & Sons, 1906; Hardpress Classics Edition.
Newton, Cornelia. Letter to Thomas Jefferson Hogg. October 21, 1813. Quoted in The Carl H. Pforzheimer Library. *Shelley and His Circle, 1773-1822.* Edited by Kenneth Neill Cameron. Harvard University Press and Oxford University Press, 1970. Volume 3: 252-254.

Chapter 16. The Deaths of Fanny Godwin and Harriet Shelley, Fall and Winter 1816

Bieri, James. *Percy Bysshe Shelley: A Biography.* Baltimore: The Johns Hopkins University Press, 2008.
Blunden, Edmund. *Shelley: A Life Story.* Oxford University Press, 1965.
Cameron, Kenneth Neill, ed. *Shelley and His Circle, 1773-1822.* The Carl H. Pforzheimer Library. Volumes 3, 4, of 10 volumes. Harvard University Press and Oxford University Press, 1970.
The Clairmont Correspondence: Letters of Claire Clairmont, Charles Clairmont, and Fanny Imlay Godwin. Volume 1: 1808-1834. Edited by Marion Kingston Stocking. Baltimore and London: The Johns Hopkins University Press, 1995.
Gordon, Lyndall. *Mary Wollstonecraft: A New Genus.* Little Brown, 2005.
Jones, Frederick L., ed. *The Letters of Percy Bysshe Shelley: Volume I Shelley in England.* Oxford University Press, 1964.
Seymour, Miranda. *Mary Shelley.* New York: Grove Press, 2000.
Todd, Janet. *Death and the Maidens: Fanny Wollstonecraft and the Shelley Circle.* Berkeley: Counterpoint, 2007.

Wollstonecraft, Mary, *A Short Residence in Sweden, Norway and Denmark,* and William Godwin, *Memoirs of the Author of the Rights of Woman,* edited with an Introduction and Notes by Richard Holmes. Penguin Classics, 1987.

Chapter 17. Mary's *Frankenstein,* Byron's Love Child, and Harriet's Son, 1817-1818

The Clairmont Correspondence: Letters of Claire Clairmont, Charles Clairmont, and Fanny Imlay Godwin. Volume 1: 1808-1834. Volume 2: 1835-1879. Edited by Marion Kingston Stocking. Baltimore and London: The Johns Hopkins University Press, 1995.

Constable, Thomas. *Memoir of the Reverend Charles A. Chastel de Boinville: Compiled from his Journal and His Letters.* London: James Nisbet & Co., 1880.

Porter, Roy. *Mind Forg'd Manacles: A History of Madness in England from the Restoration to the Regency.* Harvard University Press, 1987.

Sampson, Fiona. *In Search of Mary Shelley: The Girl Who Wrote Frankenstein.* New York and London: Pegasus Books, 2018.

Seymour, Miranda. *Mary Shelley.* New York: Grove Press, 2000.

Shelley, Mary. *Frankenstein, or The Modern Prometheus,* edited with an Introduction and Notes by Maurice Hindle. Penguin Classics edition, 1992; "The Author's Introduction to the Standard Novels Edition (1831)."

Chapter 18. "Tell them, especially Mrs. Boinville, I have not forgotten them," 1819-1826

Bradley, J. L. *A Shelley Chronology.* The Macmillan Press, 1993.

Cameron, Kenneth Neill, ed. *Shelley and His Circle, 1773-1822.* The Carl H. Pforzheimer Library. Vol. 6 of 10 volumes. Harvard University Press and Oxford University Press, 1970.

Jones, Frederick L., ed. *The Letters of Percy Bysshe Shelley: Volume II: Shelley in Italy.* Oxford University Press, 1964.

Seymour, Miranda. *Mary Shelley.* New York: Grove Press, 2000.

Shelley, Mary. *The Letters of Mary Wollstonecraft Shelley.* Volume 1: "A Part of the Elect." Edited by Betty T. Bennett. Baltimore and London: The Johns Hopkins University Press, 1983.

Chapter 19. Leaving London and Reconciling with Mary Shelley, 1827-1829

Cameron, Kenneth Neill, ed. *Shelley and His Circle, 1773-1822.* The Carl H. Pforzheimer Library. Vol. 3 of 10 volumes. Harvard University Press and Oxford University Press, 1970.

The Clairmont Correspondence: Letters of Claire Clairmont, Charles Clairmont, and Fanny Imlay Godwin. Volume 2: 1835-1879. Edited by Marion Kingston Stocking. Baltimore and London: The Johns Hopkins University Press, 1995.

Constable, Thomas. *Memoir of the Reverend Charles A. Chastel de Boinville: Compiled from his Journal and His Letters.* London: James Nisbet & Co., 1880.

de Boinville, Harriet. Letter to Mary Shelley. October 16, 1829. University of Oxford, Bodleian Libraries Abinger Collection, Abinger Dep c. 516/1, MS. Abinger, c. 48, fols. 55-6.

Gordon, Lyndall. *Mary Wollstonecraft: A New Genus.* Little Brown, 2005.

Marshall, Peter. *William Godwin: Philosopher, Novelist, Revolutionary.* PM Press, 2017.

Sampson, Fiona. In Search of Mary Shelley The Girl Who Wrote Frankenstein. Pegasus Books, New York and London, 2018.

Shelley, Mary. *The Letters of Mary Wollstonecraft Shelley.* Vol. I. "A Part of the Elect." edited by Betty T. Bennett. Baltimore and London: The Johns Hopkins University Press, 1983.

Chapter 20. Godwin's Death and Significance, "The Extinction of a Mastermind," 1830-1836

Constable, Thomas. *Memoir of the Reverend Charles A. Chastel de Boinville: Compiled from his Journal and His Letters.* London: James Nisbet & Co., 1880.

The Diary of William Godwin, ed. Victoria Myers, David O'Shaughnessy, and Mark Philip. Oxford: Oxford Digital Library, 2010.

de Boinville, Harriet. Letter to Mary Shelley. June 11, 1836. University of Oxford, Bodleian Libraries Abinger Collection, MS Abinger C 49, fols. 40-1, dep C, 516.

Josephson, Matthew. *Stendahl or the Pursuit of Happiness.* New York: Doubleday, 1945.

Marshall, Peter. *William Godwin: Philosopher, Novelist, Revolutionary.* PM Press, 2017.

Sampson, Fiona. *In Search of Mary Shelley: The Girl Who Wrote Frankenstein.* New York and London: Pegasus Books, 2018.

Seymour, Miranda. *Mary Shelley*. New York: Grove Press, 2000.
Shelley, Mary. *The Letters of Mary Wollstonecraft Shelley*. Vol. II. "Treading in Unknown Paths." edited by Betty T. Bennett. Baltimore and London: The Johns Hopkins University Press, 1983.

Chapter 21. Harriet Rescues Shelley's *Queen Mab* for Posterity, 1837-1841

de Boinville, Harriet. Letter to Mary Shelley. December 8, 1837, University of Oxford, Bodleian Libraries Abinger Collection. Abinger Dep c. 516/1, MS. Abinger, c. 48, folios 55-56.
_____. Letter to Mary Shelley, January 26, 1839. University of Oxford, Bodleian Libraries Abinger Collection, MS. Abinger c. 49, folios 128-129.
Gordon, Charlotte. *Mary Shelley: A Very Short Introduction*. Oxford University Press, 2022.
_____. *Romantic Outlaws: The Extraordinary Lives of Mary Wollstonecreaft & Mary Shelley*. New York: Random House Trade Paperback Edition, 2016.
Holmes, Richard. *Shelley: The Pursuit, with a New Introduction by the Author*. New York Review Books edition, 1994; first published in 1974.
Peacock's Memoirs of Shelley with Shelley's Letters to Peacock, ed., H. F. B. Brett-Smith. London: Henry Frowde, 1909. Nabu Public Domain Reprint. First published in two installments in 1858 and 1860.
Marshall, Peter. *William Godwin: Philosopher, Novelist, Revolutionary*. PM Press, 2017.
Reiman, Donald H. "Percy Bysshe Shelley." *Encyclopedia Britannica*, July 31, 2020.
Seymour, Miranda. *Mary Shelley*. New York: Grove Press, 2000.
Shaaban, Bouthaina. *Shelley's influence on the Chartist poets, with particular emphasis on Ernest Charles Jones and Thomas Cooper*. PhD thesis, University of Warwick, 1981.
Shelley, Mary. Letter to Thomas Jefferson Hogg. December 11, 1838. *The Letters of Mary Wollstonecraft Shelley*. Vol. II. "Treading in Unknown Paths." Edited by Betty T. Bennett. Baltimore and London: The Johns Hopkins University Press, 1983.
Wollstonecraft, Mary. *Thoughts on the Education of Daughters: With Reflections on Female Conduct in the More Important Duties of Life*, 1787.

Chapter 22. "A Noble Nature and a Loyal, Loving Heart," 1842-1843

Constable, Thomas. *Memoir of the Reverend Charles A. Chastel de Boinville Compiled from his Journals and His Letters.* London: James Nesbitt & Co., 1880.
de Boinville, Harriet. Letter to Charles A. Chastel de Boinville. January 6, 1842. Thomas Constable, *Memoir of the Reverend Charles A. Chastel de Boinville.*

Chapter 23. Claire Clairmont Joins Harriet's Circle in Paris, 1842-1845

Clairmont, Claire. Letters to Mary Shelley. September 24, 1822; April 29, 1825. *The Clairmont Correspondence: Letters of Claire Clairmont, Charles Clairmont, and Fanny Imlay Godwin.* Volume 1: 1808-1834. Edited by Marion Kingston Stocking. Baltimore and London: The Johns Hopkins University Press, 1995.
———. Letters to Mary Shelley. July 12, 1842; November 22, 1842; June 2, 1843; March 18, 1844; December 9 and 23, 1844; *The Clairmont Correspondence: Letters of Claire Clairmont, Charles Clairmont, and Fanny Imlay Godwin.* Volume 2: 1835-1879. Edited by Marion Kingston Stocking. Baltimore and London: The Johns Hopkins University Press, 1995.
de Boinville, Harriet. Letter to Charles A. Chastel de Boinville. January 6, 1842. Constable, Thomas. *Memoir of the Reverend Charles A. Chastel de Boinville Compiled from his Journals and His Letters.* London: James Nesbitt & Co., 1880.
Shelley, Mary. Letters to Claire Clairmont. September 20, 1843; December 23, 1845. *The Letters of Mary Wollstonecraft Shelley.* Volume 3: "What Years I Have Spent!" Edited by Betty T. Bennett. Baltimore and London: The Johns Hopkins University Press, 1988.
Porter, Roy. *Mind Forg'd Manacles: A History of Madness in England from the Restoration to the Regency.* Harvard University Press, 1987.
Todd, Janet. *Mary Wollstonecraft: A Revolutionary Life.* Columbia University Press, 2000.
Wollstonecraft, Mary. "The Unfortunate Situation of Females Fashionably Educated and Left Without a Fortune." *Thoughts on the Education of Daughters: With Reflections on Female Conduct in the More Important Duties of Life,* 1787.

Chapter 24. Welcoming Refugees in Her Final Years, 1845-1846

The Clairmont Correspondence: Letters of Claire Clairmont, Charles Clairmont, and Fanny Imlay Godwin. Volume 2: 1835-1879. Edited by Marion Kingston Stocking. Baltimore and London: The Johns Hopkins University Press, 1995.

Christensen, Allan Conrad. *A European Version of Victorian Fiction*. Amsterdam- Atlanta, Georgia: Rodopi, 1996.

Corrigan, Beatrice. "Giovanni Ruffini's Letters to Vernon Lee, 1875-1879." *English Miscellany* vol. 13 (1962).

Vescovi, Alessandro, Luisa Villa, and Paul Vita, eds. *The Victorians and Italy*. Monza: Polimetrica, 2009. "Genova La Superba in Novels by Giovanni Ruffini and Henrietta Jenkin," 135-148.

Chapter 25. Harriet Dies and Giovanni Ruffini Comforts Her Family, 1847-1848

Antinucci, Raffaella. "'An Italy Independent and One': Giovanni (John), Britain and the Italian Risorgimento." In *Britain, Ireland and the Italian Risorgimento*. Edited by Nick Carter, pp. 104-121. Palgrave Macmillan, 2015.

The Autobiography and Letters of Mrs. O. W. O. Oliphant. Edited by Mrs. Harry Coghill. Edinburgh, 1899.

Cameron, Kenneth Neill. *The Young Shelley: Genesis of a Radical*. New York: Collier Books, 1962.

Christensen, Allan Conrad. *A European Version of Victorian Fiction*. Amsterdam- Atlanta, Georgia, Rodopi, 1996.

Constable, Thomas. Memoir of the Reverend Charles A. Chastel de Boinville Compiled from his Journals and His Letters. London: James Nesbitt & Co., 1880.

Corrigan, Beatrice. "Giovanni Ruffini's Letters to Vernon Lee, 1875-1879." *English Miscellany* vol. 13 (1962).

Cove, Patricia. "Italian Exiles from Young Italy to 1848: Risorgimento Refugees in Giovanni Ruffini's *Lorenzo Benoni* and *Doctor Antonio*." In *Italian Politics and Nineteenth-Century British Literature and Culture*, Edinburgh Critical Studies in Victorian Culture. Edinburgh University Press, 2019.

Ruffini, Giovanni. Letter to Charles de Boinville. March 1, 1847. Quoted in Constable, Thomas. *Memoir of the Reverend Charles A. Chastel de Boinville Compiled from his Journals and His Letters*. London: James Nesbitt & Co., 1880.

Stevenson, Robert Louis. *Memoir of Fleeming Jenkin*. 1888.

Store, G. ed. *The Letters of Charles Dickens: Vol. 9, 1859-1861.* Oxford: Clarendon Press, 1997.

Vescovi, Alessandro, Luisa Villa, and Paul Vita, eds. *The Victorians and Italy.* Monza: Polimetrica, 2009. "Genova La Superba in Novels by Giovanni Ruffini and Henrietta Jenkin," 135-148.

Chapter 26. Cornelia Turner and Vernon Lee Continue the Literary Life, 1848-1875

Christensen, Allan Conrad. *A European Version of Victorian Fiction.* Amsterdam- Atlanta, Georgia: Rodopi, 1996.

Colby, Vineta. *Vernon Lee: A Literary Biography.* University of Virginia Press, 2003.

Constable, Thomas. *Memoir of the Reverend Charles A. Chastel de Boinville Compiled from his Journals and His Letters.* London: James Nesbitt & Co., 1880.

Corrigan, Beatrice. "Giovanni Ruffini's Letters to Vernon Lee, 1875-1879." *English Miscellany* vol. 13 (1962)

Cove, Patricia. "Italian Exiles from Young Italy to 1848: Risorgimento Refugees in Giovanni Ruffini's *Lorenzo Benoni* and *Doctor Antonio*." In *Italian Politics and Nineteenth-Century British Literature and Culture,* Edinburgh Critical Studies in Victorian Culture. Edinburgh University Press, 2019.

Turner, Cornelia. *Angelo Sanmartino: A Tale of Lombardy in 1859.* Edinburgh: Edmonston and Douglad, 1860. Published anonymously. Available from the web site of RareBooksClub.com.

———. *Charity, A Tale.* London: Thomas Cautley Newby, 1862. Published anonymously; reissued by the British Library for its Historical Collection.

Zorn, Christa. *Vernon Lee: Aesthetics, History, and the Victorian Female Intellectual.* Athens: Ohio University Press, 2003.

AFTERWORD: Mark Twain and the Boinville Circle

Dowden, Edward. *The Life of Percy Bysshe Shelley,* originally published in 1866; Barnes and Noble edition, 1966.

Twain, Mark. "In Defense of Harriet Shelley." *The North American Review,* vol. 159, no. 452 (July 1894): 108-119. Available as a *Project Gutenberg Ebook.*

Closing the Circle:
On the lives of Harriet de Boinville's Friends after her death

Christensen, Allan Conrad. "The Novels of Cornelia Turner: A Joint Venture with Giovanni Ruffini and Henrietta Jenkin," *Rivista Di Studi Vittoriani*, Anno XXIII, Gennaio 2018, Fasciola 45.
Grylls, R. Glynn. *Claire Clairmont: Mother of Byron's Allegra*. London: John Murray, 1939.
Sampson, Fiona. *In Search of Mary Shelley: The Girl Who Wrote Frankenstein*. New York and London: Pegasus Books, 2018.
Seymour, Miranda. *Mary Shelley*. New York: Grove Press, 2000.

Index

A
Abolition of Slavery Act of 1833, 52
Africans enslaved on Caribbean plantations, 3-5, 9, 31-33, 42; John Collins book about, 5-6, 7, 9, 10, 42; branding and naming of, 9; high death rate of, 4
Austen, Jane, 18, 19, 59

B
Berners Street, London, 25, 52
Bieri, James, 79, 100, 107
Blunden, Edmund, 74, 131, 132
Boinville, Harriet de. *See* de Boinville, Harriet Collins
Bonaparte, Napoleon. *See* Napoleon I
Bracknell, 93, 95, 99, 100, 103, 104, 116, 119, 221; geographic location of Harriet's home, 77
Bradley, J. L., 151
Burke, Edmund, 11
Burney, Dr. Charles, 20, 41, 61, 65, 212; criticism of Peace of Amiens, 46; disapproval of Fanny's marriage, 22-23; *Evelina*, dedication to, 139; Hogg's criticism of, 118, 119; musicianship of, 118; watch given to Violet Paget, 215
Burney, Esther, 64
Burney, Frances. *See also* d'Arblay, Frances Burney; courtship, 21; *Evelina*, xiv, 20, 66; Harriet de Boinville on her powers of observation, 43; Hogg's critique of, 118; Queen Charlotte, 22, 43; literary fame, 20; marriage, 21, 22, 23; royalist views of, 22; watch of father, 215
Burr, Aaron, 7, 67, 69, 71-73; admiration for Mary Wollstonecraft, 69; Cornelia de Boinville's London ball, 74; direction of daughter's education, 72; duel with Alexander Hamilton, 69, 73; exile in London, 71; flight to Louisiana territory, 73; friendship with the Godwins, 74-76; London diary, 69, 74; outing with Fanny Godwin, 76; treason trial of, 73; on *Vindication of the Rights of Woman*, 71-72
Burr, Theodosia, education of, 72-73
Byron, George Gordon; Lord; character of, 138; *Child Harold's Pilgrimage*, 138; Claire Clairmont pursues, 137-138; disinterest in infant daughter, 135; ghost stories at Villa Diodati, 138; Fanny Godwin's interest in, 127, 128; letters from Claire Clairmont, 137, 140; on "natural children," 151; refusal to

294 Index

write to Claire, 140-141; sailing with P.B. Shelley, 152; sends Allegra to convent, 150

C

Cameron, Kenneth Neill; on Harriet de Boinville and her circle, 79-80, 203; on Hogg's view of Cornelia Newton, 116

Caribbean; British and French colonists in, 3-4, 31; British–French sea battles in, 26-27; civil war in St. Vincent, 26; indigenous Caribs, 29-31; sugar plantations, 4, 5, 9, 42; travel to by sea, 3, 26-28; Scottish magistrate, views of, 9, 27

Caribs, indigenous, on St. Vincent, 29-31; Africans' views of Caribs, 9, 31-33; Chief Chatoyer and his son, 29-31; culture and traditions, 29-31; rhetoric of French Revolution, 29-31; Second Carib War (1795–1796), 29-31

Carmichael, Mrs. A.C., on St. Vincent, 10, 31

Chamfort, Sebastien-Roche Nicolas, 96

Chastel de Boinville, Charles. *See* de Boinville, Charles

Chastel de Boinville, Harriet. *See* de Boinville, Harriet Collins

Chastel de Boinville, Jean Baptiste. *See* de Boinville, Jean Baptiste

Chatoyer, Chief Joseph, 29

Chisholm, Kate, 22

Christensen, Allan Conrad, 199, 201, 206, 209-210

Church of England, 82, 184

Clairmont, Charles, 125

Clairmont, Claire; attends de Boinville ball, 69, 74; bravery and resilience of, 189, 136; called Jane in Godwin family, 58; childhood on Skinner Street, 58-59; Cornelia Turner, 1850 letter to, 224, 250; daughter Allegra, 140-141, 150-151, 190-192; death of, 224; earns living as governess, 189-192; on Italians in de Boinville circle, 197, 198; liberalism of, 191, 192; and Lord Byron, 136, 137-138, 140-141; Paris correspondence with Mary Shelley, 189, 192-196; view of gender disparities in education, 191; view of conversations at Madame de Boinville's, 91-92

Clairmont, Mary Jane. *See* Godwin, Mary Jane

Clint, Alfred, portrait of Shelley by, *146*

Coleridge, Samuel Taylor, 60, 143

Collins, Anna (Harriet's grandmother), 39, 53

Collins, Cornelia (Harriet's sister). *See* Newton, Cornelia Collins

Collins, Harriet. *See also* de Boinville, Harriet; birth in St. Christopher and early life, 3-12; birth name Henriette, 4; courtship, 11-12; disobeys father to elope, 17, 18; dons red sash; 11, 13; falls in love, 12; interest in French Revolution, 13; mother's unknown identity, 5

Collins, John (Harriet's father), 4-6, 9, 11; book to influence British planters in Caribbean, 5-7; friendship with French exiles in London, 17; fundraising for

Lafayette in prison, 38; James Marshall, visit to, 51, 169; opposition to daughter's marriage and reconciliation, 19, 25; *Practical Rules* (1803), 5-6, 7; St. Vincent property damage, 26; sale of slaves, 187; views on management and medical treatment of slaves, 5-6, 9, 10, 42, 187; will of, 52; William Wilberforce endorses book, 5
Collins, John Alfred (Harriet's brother); helps Harriet elope, 19; inheritance of, 53; mental illness of, 60, 189, 213; place in family, xi
Constable, Thomas, 157, 210, 248-249
Constancio, Francisco Solano, 176, 177, 178
Corrigan, Beatrice 201, 212
Cove, Patricia, 210
Cowper, William, 25
Creole, definitions of, 4, 5

D
d'Arblay, Alexander Charles Louis Piochard, 66, 231, 232
d'Arblay, Alexandre Jean Baptiste Piochard, 227, 232; friend of Harriet's husband, 20; letter from Jean Baptiste de Boinville, 23-24, 225-227; marriage to Frances Burney, 21-22; planned expedition to Santo Domingo, 43; post in French government, 45; return to military service, 41-43
d'Arblay, Frances Burney. *See also* Burney, Frances; aided by Jean Baptiste de Boinville, 61-67; Cornelia Newton, interview with, 118; letters from Harriet de Boinville, 227, 230-232; marriage of, 20, 21-23, 45; mastectomy of, 64-65; portraits of, *21, 64;* son Alex, 41, 61, 66
Darwin, Erasmus, 35
de Boinville, Charles Alfred (Harriet's grandson); birth of, 143; charitable acts of, 185-186; farming in Dilwyn, 167-168; on grandmother's character and philosophy, 60, 187, 201-202; on grandfather's life, 63, 113; letters from grandmother, 166-167, 248-249; memoir about family members, 157-158, 215; ministry in France, 183; siblings, 184; mental illness of father, 155; on Peace of Amiens, 44; place in family, xi; schooling, 183-184, 186; sightseeing in Paris, 166, 184; witness to Paris fighting (1848), 205
de Boinville, Cornelia (Harriet's granddaughter), 187-188
de Boinville, Cornelia (Harriet's daughter). *See also* Turner, Cornelia; birth in Willesden, 25; Bantry Bay medical crisis, 27; childhood playmate of Godwin sisters, 59; meeting of future husband, 69, 259; reunion in Nantes with father, 47; nuptial ball in London, 69;
de Boinville, Frank (Harriet's grandson); mental illness of, 157, 158, 196, 213
de Boinville, Harriet Collins. *See also* Collins, Harriet; appearance, 59, 79, 170, 187, *203,* 218, 219; at Bracknell, 89, 91, 92-96, 177, 217-219; bravery,

296   Index

36, 37, 39-40, 41, 46-47, 58, 62; death and burial, 201-202, 220; deaths of loved ones, 112, 119, 185, 121, 213, 237, 243, 249; depression of, 160-161, 164, 165, 237; Dunkirk rescue of, 37; failing eyesight, 164, 203, 237; family of, xi; financial dependence on father, 35, 38; fluency in French and Italian, 59, 86, 187; and Frances Wright, 245-246; on Godwin's death, 165, 169, 243; on Godwin's morality and intellect, 247; Harriet Shelley, friends with, 131, 134, 161-162; Hogg caricature of, 218-219; illness in Paris, 42, 47, 184, 194; imprisonment at The Hague, 39-40; inheritance of, 39, 52-53; interest in Mary Shelley's writing, 246; kind nature of, 171, 183, 186, 236, 241; and Lafayette, 37-38, 167: last name, changes in, x, 164; letters to Francis Burney d'Arblay, 227, 230-232; letters to Hogg, 230-235; letters to Mary Shelley, 152, 155, 158-161, 173, 182, 203, 235-248; Madam d'Arblay, friends with, 41-43, 99, 227, 230-232; meets Louisa Mercier Holcroft, 60; and Mary Shelley, 134, 170, 193; mediator in P.B. Shelley custody battle, 132, 148; meets mother-in-law in Paris, 37, 38; meets Samuel Taylor Coleridge at Godwin's, 60; negative criticism of, 92-93; 217-225; P.B. Shelley writes about, 105, 149, 150, 151; portrait of in old age, 203; *Queen Mab* loan to Mary Shelley, 175, 178-179, 248; refugees welcomed by, 197-200, 201; regrets about her own behavior, 237; resemblance to "Miamuna," 79; and suicide of Harriet Shelley, 129-131, 145, 148; Twain on, 217, 218; vegetable diet of, 89, 91; view of by Mary Shelley, 148, 159, 193-194; views on happiness, 96; views on marriage equality, 172; wearing of red sash, 11, 59, 79, 187

de Boinville, Harriet Lambe (Harriet's daughter-in-law); children of, 167-168; Church of England, member of, 184; education of children and Bible reading, 183-184; husband's mental illness, 155, 157-158; marriage of, 135, 142-143, 157; mother-in-law's admiration for, 167; son Charles, 183-184

de Boinville, Jean Baptiste (Harriet's husband); appearance and temperament, 12; assists Madam d'Arblay, 62-63, 65-67; bravery aboard British ship, 27, 28; children, 25, 33; courtship, 11-12, 17, 24; death as POW, 112-114; discontent in England and in St. Vincent, 29, 31, 33, 34, 36, 45; elopement and marriage, 18, 19, 25; first marriage, wife's death and firstborn son Eugene, 17, 36; friend of Alexandre d'Arblay, 23-24, 62; fundraising for Lafayette's release, 38; Gouverneur Morris connection, 14; letter to General d'Arblay, 62, 225-227; London mission from Lafayette, 12, 14; mother of, 37-38; with Napoleon, 70, 77, 79, 112-114; place in family, xi; portrait of, *12;* property confiscated, 36, 45; relatives killed, 16; rescue of wife at Dunkirk, 37; responsibilities in Napoleon's army, 63; return to France, emigrant status, 35-36; role under Lafayette, 13-14, 17, 215; son Eugene, 17, 36; title as second son, 15; at Versailles, 13

de Boinville, John Alfred (Harriet's son); birth in St. Vincent, 33, 35; early life, 142; Harriet's heartbreak, 157; marries well, 135, 142, 143; fathers five children, 142; place in family, xi; son Charles Alfred, 143; tragic incapacity and institutionalization in Ivry, France, 155, 158

In Defense of Harriet Shelley (1894) by Mark Twain, 217, 218

Dissenting tradition, 184, 186. *See also* Religion

Dowden, Edward; on Cornelia Turner, 220; on Hogg as unreliable biographer, 221; Twain's satire of Dowden's PBS biography, 217-220

Duc d'Orleans, Louis-Philippe Joseph, 14

Durasmont, Madame, 172-173. *See also* Frances Wright.

Dussek, Ladislav, 120

E

The Empire of the Nairs, or The Rights of Women; An Utopian Romance in Twelve Books (1811), 92, 93

A European Version of Victorian Fiction: The Novels of Giovanni Ruffini (1996), 199,

F

Female conduct, John Gregory on, 18. *See also* Women in Britain

France; Austrian and Hessian allies, 27; declaration of war on Britain, 15; emigrants' status, 35, 41; sea battles with Britain, 26-27; peace treaty with Britain (1802), 45-46; resumption of war (1803), 46

Franco-Prussian War, 213

Frankenstein, or The Modern Prometheus (1818); authorship by Mary Shelley, 135; conception of in Byron's villa, 138; Mark Twain satirizes, 219; source of name Frankenstein, 108, 111; success of, 138-139

French Constitutionalists, 12, 22, 45

French Enlightenment, 60, 92-93

French Revolution, 11; Edmund Burke on, 11; effects in Caribbean, 26-27; events at Versailles, 13; Paris National Guard, 13; The Terror, 16

G

Garibaldi, Giuseppe, 205

George III, 59

George IV, 59

Gisborne, Maria (earlier Reveley); comparison to Harriet de Boinville, 151; infancy of Mary Godwin, 146

Godwin, Fanny; biological father of, 123, 124; birth in France, 123, 128; childhood, 55, 57, 58; friendship with Aaron Burr, 126; mother writes about, 123; Percy Bysshe Shelley grieves for, 123; last days, 128, suicide note, 128

Godwin, Jane. *See* Claire Clairmont
Godwin, Mary. *See also* Shelley, Mary; birth of and mother's death, 56; childhood playmate of Cornelia de Boinville, 135; dawn flight from home and travels with P.B. Shelley 108-112; disapproval of Harriet de Boinville, 110; dislike of stepmother, 58; marriage to Shelley, 134; Shelley's attraction to, 105, 106-107; son William, 132, 168
Godwin, Mary Jane; approach to Godwin, 57-58; burial place of, 222-223; children of, 57, 58, 136; death of Godwin, 168; erudition and industriousness, 58; friend to Burr, 74; Harriet de Boinville, sympathy for 168, 246; mercurial personality, 58; merging of Godwin family, 125; Juvenile Library, 58; visit to Bracknell, 130; urging Jane (Claire) to return home, 108-109
Godwin, Mary Wollstonecraft. *See* Wollstonecraft, Mary
Godwin, William; bankruptcy of, 156; biographer of, suggested by Harriet, 176-177, 178; children of, 56-58; concern about Mary Shelley, 156; correspondence with P.B. Shelley, 85; diary of, 55, 59, 60, 62, 156; James Marshall, Caribbean trip for, 9, 51, 169; death of, 165, 168-169; death of Fanny Godwin, 129; death of William Jr., 168; defense of William Holcroft, 156; financial problems, 110, 111, 156, 168; friendship with Harriet, xiii, 9-10, 47, 52, 80, 156, 176-178; 243; *An Inquiry Concerning Political Justice*, 51, 52, 93, 177; kindness and generosity of, 53, 69, 71; literary legacy of, 169, 173, 175-176, 203; memoir of Mary Wollstonecraft, 56-57, 176; PBS, betrayal of, 107,109; reburial of body, 222; views on property, 53; will of, 175
Godwin, William, Jr., 108, 168
Gordon, Charlotte, 111-112; on *Frankenstein*, 139; on *Falkner*, 178; on Mary Shelley, 223
Gouverneur Morris, 14, 15
Gretna Green, Scotland, 19-20, *20*, 81
Grove, Harriet, 81

H
Hamilton, Alexander, 7, 69, 73
Harman, Claire, 62
Hitchener, Elizabeth, 81, 85
Hogg, Thomas Jefferson, 163, 173, 246; advances on Harriet Shelley, 84, 94; on Bracknell experience, 91, 95-96, 100, 218-219; caricature of Harriet de Boinville, Cornelia Newton on, 116, 117; Dowden criticism of, 221; friendship with P.B. Shelley, 80, 82-84, 88, 147; guest of Thomas and Cornelia Turner, 147; Harriet de Boinville letters to, 96, 97, 115, 232-235; and Jane Williams, 221; Cornelia Newton, letter to, 228; *Leonora*, 117, posthumous memoir of P.B. Shelley, 115, 118-119, 218, 221; PBS letters from Bracknell, 97, 98, 99, 100, 103; at Vauxhall with PBS, 116; on vegetable diet of Harriet de Boinville, 91
Holcroft, Thomas, 60, 156

Holmes, Richard; on Bracknell gatherings, 95; on *Queen Mab*, 86; on P.B. Shelley's admissions about marriage, 104; on Shelley's financial issues, 111; on Shelley's "genius for disturbance," 84
Hookham, Thomas, 106, 109, 131
Hunt, Leigh, 59, 131, 152; London dinner with Turners, 147-148; Mary Shelley letter to on Harriet de Boinville, 149-150, 159
Hunt, Marianne; Mary Shelley, letter to, 146; London dinner with Turners, 147-148

I
Imlay, Fanny. *See* Fanny Godwin
Imlay, Gilbert; affair with Mary Wollstonecraft, 123; deceitfulness and infidelity of, 124, 125;
An Inquiry Concerning Political Justice, and Its Influence on Morals and Happiness (1793), 51-52, 177
Institutionalization for madness in England, 195-196
Ireland; Bantry Bay skirmishes, 27; Catholic emancipation of, 85; Harriet Shelley writes to friend in Ireland, 85, 93, 129; P.B. Shelley's calls for reform of, 85
Isenberg, Nancy, 76
Italy, 171, 207, 208; *Studies of the Eighteenth Century in Italy*, 212; See also *Risorgimento*

J
Jenkin, Fleeming, memoir by Robert Louis Stevenson, 205
Jenkin, Henrietta Camilla, 205, 206, 209

Johnson, Samuel, on Dr. William Lambe, 143
Juvenile Library, 58, 60

K
Keats, John, 188
Kologrivoff, Vera de, 197-198, 199

L
Lafayette, Marquis de, 165, 167, 171, 215; and Jean Baptiste de Boinville, 12-14; Harriet de Boinville meets in Paris, 37-38; imprisonment in Austria, 38; letter thanking Jean Baptiste preserved in George Washington's papers, 38; London mission of Jean Baptiste for, 14; at Versailles, 13
Lamb, Charles, 59, 60, 143, 238
Lamb, Mary, 60, 238
Lambe, Harriet (Harriet's future daughter-in-law). *See* de Boinville, Harriet Lambe
Lambe, William; eldest daughter Harriet, 135, 157, 201-202; integrity and learning of, 143; marriage of daughter to John Alfred de Boinville, 135, 142-143, 157; physician renowned in London, 89; vegetarian diet advocacy, 89-90, 143
Larrey, Dr. Baron, 64
Lawrence, James Henry; author of *The Empire of the Nairs, or The Rights of Women: A Utopian Romance in Twelve Books* (1811), 92; friendship with Harriet de Boinville, 92; influence on de Boinville circle, 93; Mary Wollstonecraft, influence on, 92
Lee, Vernon. *See also* Paget, Violet;

300 Index

explanation of Violet Paget's choice of Vernon Lee pseudonym, 212; Giovanni Ruffini's influence on literary career, 211-212
Lee-Hamilton, Eugene; introduces Violet Paget to Cornelia Turner and Giovanni Ruffini, 210; literary ambitions, 213; visitor on Cornelia's behalf to French asylum, 213
Lethbridge, Sir John, 136
Lieven, Dominic, *Russia Against Napoleon*, 114, 265
Louis-Philippe Joseph, Duc d'Orleans, 14
Louis XVIII, Charter of 1814, 183
Louis Philippe, King, abdication of (1848), 205

M
Madness, 60, 158, 195
Marshall, James; mission for Godwin to St. Vincent, 9, 51; witness at Godwin's marriage, 55
Marshall, Peter, 156, 168. 181; on Godwin's politics, 181; on Mary Wollstonecraft, 54
Mazzini, Giuseppe, 199, 200, 204, 205
Medwin, Tom, 84
Memoir of the Reverend Charles A. Chastel de Boinville Compiled from His Journals and Letters (1880), *157*, 215, 249, 270
Memoirs of the Author of A Vindication of the Rights of Woman (1798), 56-57, 176
Morris, Gouverneur, with Jean Baptiste de Boinville, 14

N
Napoleon I; Austrian army defeat, 36; censorship under, 63; elected Consul for Life, 46; Josephine, marriage to, 36; Paris improvements, 62; Lafayette freed from prison, 38; rise to power, 35-36; Russian campaign, 70, 112-114; territorial conquests, 46, 62; veterans' payments in arrears, 63
Napoleon III (1848), 205
Nashoba Commune, Tennessee, 171-172
Nelson, Admiral Horatio, 39
New Harmony, Indiana, 172
Newton, Cornelia (Harriet's sister), 115-121; accomplished musician, 120-121; at Bracknell, 90, 119; critique of Hogg's novel *Leonora* and Richardson's novel, 117, 228; death of, 119, 130; health practices of, 90; illness of, 115, 119; inheritance of, 53; meets Frances Burney d'Arblay, 118; on mother's correspondence with Madam d'Arblay, 230; and Percy Bysshe Shelley, 80, 116; sister's concern for, 115-116, 120; text of letter to Hogg, 228-229; Twain ridicules, 220
Newton, John Frank; author of *The Return to Nature*, 89-90, 142; wife's illness and death, 115, 119, 129-130; meeting Shelley, 80; Shelley on Newton family, 116; William St. Clair on, 92-93
Newton, Octavia, 193, 194
Nugent, Catherine (friend of Harriet Shelley), 85, 93, 129

Index   301

O
Old Blacksmith's Shop, Gretna Green, 19, *20*
Oliphant, Margaret, on Cornelia Turner and Giovanni Ruffini, 206
Opie, John, portrait of Mary Wollstonecraft, 76, 169
Owen, Dale, 172
Owen, Robert, 172

P
Paget, Violet. *See also* Lee Vernon, 120, 198; mentored by Cornelia Turner, 211-212; encouraged by Cornelia Turner's remembrances of Shelley, received Dr. Charles Burney's watch from Cornelia Turner, 215
Paine, Thomas, 54, 85
Paris Revolution (1848); abdication of King Louis Phillipe, 205; described in Robert Louis Stevenson memoir, 205
Payne, Sir Ralph, 54, 85
Peace of Amiens (1802); British people rejoice, 44-45; British Tories complain about treaty terms, 45-46; duration of, 44; end of French Revolutionary Wars (1792–1802), 44-46; Jean Baptiste returns to work in Paris, 45; Watford postmaster announcement to de Boinvilles, 44
Peacock, Thomas Love, 163, 173, 246; at Bracknell, 89, 94-95, 177; dinner guest of Turners, 147; Harriet Shelley ally, 111; on Harriet de Boinville's appearance, 79; letter from P.B. Shelley in Italy, 145; memoir of P.B. Shelley, 221
Penn, Richard, 8
Pope Pius IX, fleeing Rome (1848), 205
Practical Rules for the Management and Medical Treatment of Negro Slaves in the Sugar Colonies by a Professional Planter (1803), 5-7 42, 187

Q
Queen Mab; A Philosophical Poem (1813); composition by P.B. Shelley, 86, 89; and Harriet de Boinville, 86, 175, 179; radical themes of, 86; 86, 87, 178, 179; dedication to Harriet Shelley, 88; text of letter by Harriet de Boinville to Mary Shelley about, 248; vegetable-fed children in, 88

R
Religion; Charles Wesley and Methodists, 186; Church of England, 184; dissenting religious tradition in Britain, 184, 186; ministry to French Protestants, 183
The Return to Nature, Or, a Defense of the Vegetable Regimen (1811), 89-90
Revolutions of 1848, 204-205
Risorgimento, in Italy, 171, 199-200, 204, 207
Robecchi, Giulio, 194, 213; burial in Harriet de Boinville's plot, 199, 202; Harriet de Boinville meeting of, 200
Robinson, Henry Crabb, 60
Rothwell, Richard, portrait of Mary Shelley, *181*

302   Index

Rousseau, Jean-Jacques, 60
Rubio, Luigi, 187, 198-199
Ruffini, Giovanni, Cornelia Turner's literary collaborator, 209-210; Cornelia Turner's partner, 197, 204, 209; death of, 213; librettist and student of British literature, 200; influence on writing of Violet Paget (Vernon Lee), 211-212; as rebel fighter in Genoa, 199-200; reports death of Harriet de Boinville, 201; seven novels of, 204

S
St. Augustine's *Confessions*, 100
St. Christopher, Caribbean; hurricane, 3-4, 7-8; stratified society, 3-6, 8-9
St. Clair, William, 71, 92-93, 259
St. Vincent. *See also* Caribs; *An Historical Account of the Island of St. Vincent*, 34; John Collins plantation on, 9, 31; map of, 32; positions in colonial government, 33; scenery, 31
Salomon, Johann Peter, 120
Sampson, Fiona; on Mrs. Godwin, 109; on *Frankenstein*, 111, 223-224, 264
Samuelian, Kristin, xiii
In Search of Mary Shelley: The Girl Who Wrote Frankenstein (2018), 111
Seymour, Miranda; on death of Mary Shelley, 222; on Frances Wright, 172; on Godwin family life, 58-59; on Godwin's will, 175, 178; on Voisey family, 111, 264
Shelley, Claire Everina, birth of, 138-139

Shelley, Harriet. *See also* Westbrook, Harriet; Edinburgh marriage and honeymoon, 83-84; English remarriage for legal reasons, 102; description of in *Queen Mab*, 88; disappearance of husband, 106; friendship of Harriet de Boinville, 130, 149, 161; PBS letters to, 106, 107, 109, 112; PBS financial provisions for, 130; John Frank Newton, sympathy for, 129; last days and Harriet de Boinville, 130-131; suicide of, 129-131, 145, 148; suicide note, 133
Shelley, Lady Jane, 222-223
Shelley, Mary. *See also* Godwin, Mary; death of, 222; deaths of children, 145-146, 150; death of father, 165, 168; death of husband and pyre on beach, 152; desecration of grave of, 222; father-in-law's constraints on, 175-176; depression of, 156, 168; editing of poetical works of PBS, 180; *Falkner*, 178; *Frankenstein*, 135, 138-140, 152, 219, 223-224; literary legacies of father and husband, 176-178, 246; Harriet de Boinville, criticism of and reconciliation with, 155; and Italian exiles in Paris, 165, 171, 173; letters from Harriet de Boinville, 160-164, 169, 236-249; literary career of, 158, 178; marriage to Shelley, 134; move to Italy and marital unhappiness, 141-142, 145-146, 170; portrait of by Richard Rothwell, *181;* son Percy Florence, 150, 161, 168,

182; visit to sister in Paris, 193; will of William Godwin and directives to, 158, 169, 175, 176; writing life, 168, 178, 180

Shelley, Percy Bysshe. *See also Queen Mab*; association with Harriet Grove and Elizabeth Hitchener, 81, 85; at Bracknell, 89, 91, 92, 97-103; and Cornelia Turner, 74-75, 98-101, 116-117, 147, 148; Cornelia Turner's memories of, 211-121; correspondence with William Godwin, 85, 86; custody of children, 131-134, 141, 148; daughter Clara, 141, 145-146; daughter Ianthe, 98, 106, 141; death of, 152 and pyre on beach; diet and vegetarianism of, 80, 88, 89; Harriet Westbrook, courtship and marriage to, 82, 83, 102; erotic notebook, 99; and Fanny Godwin, 128-129, 145; and Harriet de Boinville, xvii, 79-80, 86, 97, 98, 106, 107, 109-110, 149-150, 152, 168, 170, 175, 203, 220; and Harriet Shelley, 129, 131, 133, 145, 148; inheritance of, 80-81, 82, 93, 94, 102-103; letters to Harriet Shelley, 107, 109, 112; love for Mary Godwin, 105, 106-107, 134; marital problems in Italy, 145, 147-148; poems about Cornelia Turner, 101-102, 103; portrait of, *146;* post-obituary bonds, 102-103, 109; rupture with Harriet de Boinville, 134, 150, 152, 161-162; text of Harriet de Boinville's letter about Shelley after his death, 237; views on obedience and the institution of marriage, 81, 82, 84; *Vindication of a Natural Diet,* 89, writers' block of, 211-212

Shelley, Percy Florence, 150, 161, 168, 176, 182, 221, 248

Shelley, Sir Timothy, 80-81, 82, 83-84, 88, 158, 174, 175, 176

Slavery, abolition of in Britain and British colonies, 52

Southey, Robert, 79, 80, 85

Stendahl, on Lafayette, 165

Stevenson, Robert Louis; memoir of Fleeming Jenkin, 205; on 1848 revolution in Paris

Stocking, Marion Kingston, 136, 137, 283, 285

T

Tesson, Sylvain, on Napoleon's retreat from Russia, 113

Tighe, Margaret (Lady Cashell), 190, 192

Todd, Janet; on Fanny Godwin's suicide, 128; on Gilbert Imlay deceitfulness, 124; on Godwin sisters' dawn departure, 108; on Mary Jane Clairmont, 57-58; on Shelley's and Burr's influence on Fanny, 126-127

Toussaint L'Ouverture, leader of slave rebellion in Santo Domingo (Haiti), 42

Trelawney, Edward John, 152

Tuberculosis; deaths of Harriet de Boinville's granddaughters, 185, 187-188; death of Keats brother; 188

Turner, Alfred, 193, 199

Turner, Cornelia (Harriet's daughter). *See also* de Boinville, Cornelia; children of, 155, 157, 184, 185, 187-188, 268; "daughter worthy of her mother," 206, 207-208; death of, 213; death of mother, 201; on English country gentlemen, 208; friendship with Frances Burney d'Arblay, 248; marriage to Thomas Turner, 69, 74; Mary Shelley's view of, 148; mentor to Violet Paget, 210, 212, 215; move to Paris, 155; novels of, 207-209, 215, 272-273; literary muse of Giovanni Ruffini, 209-210; on musical talents of aunt Cornelia Newton, 119-121; partner of Giovanni Ruffini, 197, 204, 209; on religious tolerance in novels, 209; republican ideals of, 207; separation from husband, 155-156; Shelley's attentions to, 74-75, 98-101, 149, 150, 207; tombstone, 214; Twain depiction of, 218, 219

Turner, Oswald (Harriet's grandson), 164, 184, 248, 268; birth of, 77; burial in Harriet de Boinville's plot, 199; grandmother's devotion to, 247, 248; mental illness of, 164, 189, 193-196, 213

Turner, Pauline (Harriet's granddaughter); death of, 185, 187, 188; Harriet expresses her grief, 184-185

Turner, Thomas (Harriet's son-in-law); Godwin's help in sexual crisis of, 70-71; Harriet's praise of, 231; hosts dinner for Peacock and Hogg, 147; marriage and marital separation, 69, 75, 76, 101, 155-156; Mary Shelley's dislike for, 148; move to Italy, 156; P. B. Shelley and wife of, 99

Twain, Mark; *In Defense of Harriet Shelley* , 217; on Dowden's *Life of Percy* Shelley, 217-220; on egalitarian Harriet de Boinville, 219; on literary style of Dowden, 218; on Mary Shelley's *Frankenstein*, 219; satirical attack on "Boinville Hysterical Society," 220; on Shelley's Italian lessons at Bracknell, 219

V

Vegetarians in de Boinville Circle; Harriet's vegetable diet, 89; W. Lambe's research on natural diet, 89-90, 143; J.F. Newton's vegetable diet, 89-90; Shelley's *Vindication of Natural Diet*, 90

W

War of 1812, 65-66, 75
Washington, George, 38
Wesley, Charles, 186
Westbrook, Harriet, 81, 82, 83, 103, 108, 142. *See also* Shelley, Harriet
Westbrook, Eliza, 84, 98, 130, 133
Westbrook, John, 82, 84, 148; agrees to pay Shelley's debt, 112; agrees to witness daughter's remarriage, 102; helps daughter move away from home, 131
Whitton, William, 82, 84
Wilberforce, William, 5
Williams, Edward, 151, 152, 179
Williams, Jane, 151, 152, 221
Wiltshire, John, 65
Windham, William, 46
Wollstonecraft, Mary, 10, 47; abandons anti-matrimonial principles, 54, 55; birth of daughter Mary, 56, 125; Burr's admira-

tion for, 69, 71-72; death of after childbirth, 56, 125; daughter Fanny, 55, 123, 124, 125; depression of, 125, 128, 156; Godwin's *Memoir of the Author of Vindication...*, 56-57, 176; *Letters Written During a Short Residence*, 109; novel *Mary*, 109; reburial of, 222, 223; *Thoughts on the Education of Daughters*, 10; *A Vindication of the Rights of Woman*, 17, 56; on women as rational creatures, 36; on women's need for strength, 25, 28; on women's minds, 177

Women in Britain; laws concerning, 92-93; education of, 10, 72, 190; married women's legal rights, 38-39, 92, 155; norms of behavior, 18; occupations open to, 190, 191

Wordsworth, Dorothy, 18, 53

Worsley, Lucy, 18, 36, 272, 295

Wright, Frances, 171-172, 181

Writers in Britain, summary of Harriet de Boinville's influence on, 203